HONEY AND DUST

HONEY AND DUST

TRAVELS IN SEARCH
OF SWEETNESS

PIERS MOORE EDE

BLOOMSBURY

Grateful acknowledgement to New Directions for permission
to quote lines from *Residence on Earth* by Pablo Neruda,
translated by Donald D. Walsh, 1973

*Ahead of All Parting: Selected Poetry and Prose of
Rainer Maria Rilke*, copyright © 1995 by Stephen
Mitchell. Used by permission of Modern Library,
a division of Random House, Inc.

Bloomsbury Publishing Plc, 38 Soho Square,
London WID 3HB

A CIP catalogue record for this book
is available from the British Library

ISBN 07475 7492 8
ISBN-13 9780747574927

Typeset by Palimpsest Book Production Limited,
Polmont, Stirlingshire
Printed by Clays Ltd, St Ives plc

Drawings by
Robin Moore Ede

All papers used by Bloomsbury Publishing are natural, recyclable
products made from wood grown in well-manged forests. The manufacturing
processes conform to the environmental regulations of the country of origin.

A bee settling on a flower has stung a child. And the child is afraid of bees and declares that bees exist to sting people. A poet admires the bee sucking from the chalice of a flower and says it exists to suck the fragrance of flowers. A beekeeper, seeing the bee collect pollen from flowers and carry it to the hive, says that it exists to gather honey. Another beekeeper who has studied the life of the hive more closely says that the bee gathers pollen dust to feed the young bees and rear a queen, and that it exists to perpetuate its race. A botanist notices that the bee flying with the pollen of a male flower to a pistil fertilises the latter, and sees in this the purpose of the bee's existence. Another, observing the migration of plants, notices that the bee helps in this work, and may say that in this lies the purpose of the bee. But the ultimate purpose of the bee is not exhausted by the first, the second, or any of the processes the human mind can discern. The higher the human intellect rises in the discovery of these purposes, the more obvious it becomes, that the ultimate purpose is beyond our comprehension.

Leo Tolstoy
War and Peace

For Joan, of course

CONTENTS

PROLOGUE

I WAS LIVING during that curious pre-millennium summer in San Francisco. It was the year of the dot-com boom and the city reeked of money earned too quickly, of the recklessness that had burgeoned in a generation. The café where I worked was in the Mission district, a formerly run-down neighbourhood of Mexican immigrants. Full of taco joints, bakeries selling traditional pastries called *cuernitos* and *campechanas*, the neighbourhood had once boasted some of the cheapest rents in the city.

All of that had changed in the last months. Websites seemed to pop up overnight like mushrooms, each of them wanting loft space big enough for their hip basketball-hooped offices. Artists talked of leaving for Marin Country or Portland before the gentrification set in like a rash. And though no one knew for sure what the future might hold, there was a general intimation that things could only go downhill from here.

None the less, I was a young man discovering life that summer. From 7 a.m., I brewed espressos for the dot-com crowd and a residual collection of hippies and graffiti artists who would not relinquish their neighbourhood coffee house to the newcomers. At nights I explored the city, listening to would-be Jack Kerouacs in beatnik dives and sometimes not making it home until dawn's grey light. I had never felt so carefree.

Occasionally, at the end of the day, I'd walk through the eucalyptus groves of Golden Gate Park and down towards Ocean Beach. Thick waves pound the shore there, providing a playground for surfers, and it was peaceful to watch them carve their great arcs of spray and vanish into the liquid barrels.

I met a girl, too. She was called Joan, and when I first saw her she was wearing a torn suede jacket and was speaking eloquently about an ongoing battle to save a stand of old-growth redwoods up in Humboldt County. She seemed the feminine incarnation of San Francisco to me right then, and on that first night I realised this might be someone I could love. Six hours after our first words to each other we were already hopelessly involved. Hand in hand, we strode the empty midnight streets, wisps of summer fog floating in under the trolley wires, and felt like the only people in the world.

At weekends we'd take trips to Point Reyes National Park and listen to the seal pups, abandoned by their mothers, barking on the shoreline. Soon, when hunger grew too much for them, they'd pluck up the courage to launch into the sea for the first time, out into the wintry Pacific where the great white sharks waited.

One morning I left for work at 5.30 a.m. It was a Monday, which meant there'd be long queues at the café, one weary face after another demanding their respective fix. It had been a hell of a weekend. Beck had played a concert in the park and we'd danced among ten thousand people and got too much sun and felt madly alive. There are maybe one or two weekends in a lifetime like that.

I mounted my bike at the top of Haight Street and felt the raw air of morning bringing me awake. It was utterly quiet; there wasn't a soul about. On the horizon I could see the tepid glow of the sun, like a filament charging with heat, and I knew that in about ten minutes the shadows would shorten under the eaves and the first warm strands of daylight would brush the windows.

Haight Ashbury is a long steep hill, a ripple on the twisted spine of the San Andreas Fault. Cycling down it one has nothing to do but brake, and then only when the speed becomes too much to handle. The tarmac drops away like a roller-coaster track and the pull of gravity does the rest. Day after day I would hurtle down that stretch, helmet on, priding myself on keeping absolute focus. I'd even scan the wing mirrors of the parked cars in case someone was going to open their door without looking behind them. A lot of cyclists got hit like that.

That morning, I wasn't wearing a helmet. I'd forgotten it, the day before, in my haste to make it to the concert on time. Nor, perhaps, was I as focused as usual. The course of my life seemed to have reached a peak and the altitude was making me dizzy. I thought only of the day ahead and the slight blurring tears brought about by the crisp air. The bicycle wheels were singing.

When the white truck jumped the light in front of me, I must have been doing well over forty miles an hour. One minute I was a twenty-five-year-old on my way to work; the next I was meeting the chrome radiator grille of a light truck at speed and I was skimming across the tarmac on my face for about thirty yards. All I remember is the taste of metal on my tongue.

Looking back on it, I try to isolate the moment, the *exact* moment, when my field of vision met the fast-moving vehicle approaching from the left. It's a difficult thing to grasp, like tinkering with an ancient security camera to capture some significant clue. But sometimes I do remember. I see that moment, frozen in time; I rest in it and allow myself to breathe, as if it were a spinning coin in a beam of sunlight and this the most important call of my life.

Hollywood is right about that at least. Slow motion *exists* once we are helpless to change a course of events whose outcome we know will be dangerous to us, perhaps fatal. The reel reduces speed. The world proceeds in the manner of a stunted cartoon.

Nausea blooms in my stomach as the realisation sinks in and stays there, that it's too late to swerve away, that this time I'm not going to make it. Then, in the last fragment of time, I see everything condense. The world in a single atom of light.

A homeless man pulled me off the street – I recollect that much. 'That *mother*fucker,' I heard a distant voice scream. 'Jesus Christ, I saw him stop. Circled you, he did, drove away. That son of a *bitch*. Hey, don't move, man, I got you.'

Later, the dissonance of neon lights in the paramedics' van. Walkie-talkies; the squawking of machines. I knew neither night nor day, not my own name, only Joan's phone number, repeated mantra-like before I lapsed into coma.

Coming round for the first time, I saw myself as if from a bird's eye. I seemed more machine than man, threaded with tubes and blinking lights, kept alive by silent liquids swimming down needles into my arm. Joan sat beside the bed with red-ringed eyes and it was her gaze that, momentarily, told me things were far from good. And yet, though I sensed the situation to be grim, I felt no panic whatsoever. In truth, there *were* no thoughts in my head, no masks, screens or defences. I seemed to have passed beyond fear to a dynamic state of calm, an emptiness. It was strangely liberating.

If I knew pain in the days to come, it was primarily in the faces of those who visited me. Despite my condition, and the heady cloud of drugs upon which I floated, I knew what was going on. But what almost broke me, slicing through the pharmaceutical bolster like a guillotine, was the bizarre event that befell my parents when they disembarked from their plane at San Francisco airport. The experience would leave its own kind of scar upon their faces, as noticeable to me, perhaps, as mine were to them.

At the terminal, realising she didn't know what my parents looked like, Joan asked a flight attendant to deliver them a note, suggesting a meeting place. Yet when the woman finally found the right two English passengers, waiting anxiously to leave their aeroplane, she broke it to them that I had died in my hospital bed that morning. It had been peaceful, she explained. I had not suffered.

My parents endured a twenty-minute walk through the baggage hall firmly believing the worst.

How the mistake occurred was never discovered. Joan and I have only ever found the courage for a single conversation on the way that strange, unhappy rendezvous panned out. Of the first impression she gained of the two haggard parents appearing from the throng, staring into the distance with madness in their eyes.

Of course, Joan told my parents in a heartbeat that she'd seen me only a few hours before and that there must have been some kind of terrible mixup. And yet what a mixup! How was it possible for words to have such a life of their own?

For a time, the three of them stood there in horror, spectres amidst the frantic commotion of the arrivals lounge. And in the ensuing relief there was simply no *time* for anger. No time for reprisal or regret. So they turned and marched hurriedly away, desperately treading water against the current.

Recovery was a slow process. First there were weeks in San Francisco, pink morphine at three-minute intervals, familiar faces appearing and receding like tides. Later, an uncomfortable flight to England, months of physiotherapy, cosmetic surgery. I grew used to the sterile smell of doctors' clinics, the starch of the nurses' crisp uniforms, the gentle hum of the neon lighting. And through all of this, I kept asking myself, what would I do next? How could anything continue to have *meaning* against a backdrop like this? Could I just step back into my life as into a pair of cast-off shoes?

Looking in the mirror was, in itself, a kind of challenge. Back in San Francisco they'd covered the reflective surfaces in my hospital room with paper so that I wouldn't suffer the shock of seeing my own face. That brown paper filled my dreams.

I glimpsed my face, Narcissus-like, in a bowl of water before too long. What I saw appalled me but, in a curious way, I felt detachment from the wreck staring out at me. As if I were the victim of a witch's spell, I knew that the real me was lurking in there somewhere. My conception of the self was based more on some interior nucleus than on the way I looked, and that nucleus was unchanged, despite the fact that the tissue around it had suffered the ravages of a trench war.

Others, of course, did not share this interior knowledge. I watched friends enter the room all smiles, observed their sudden disbelief, watched their eyes betraying them with tears. Children were the worst. I'd see them staring at me, frowning or pointing, and, though it was a gesture wholly devoid of malice, it wounded me like a sashimi knife.

'I'd like to find that guy who hit you and put him where you are,' muttered more than one friend, as they stood glowering beside my bed. 'Wouldn't you like to beat the living *shit* out of him?'

It was an understandable question. Their rage was touching – if such a thing can be said of rage – but, to be honest, I didn't share it. Had the driver stayed to claim responsibility for what he'd done, it would have changed nothing. Except perhaps it would have broken a second life in two.

Prisoners, of war or circumstance, learn to dwell in dreams. The life of the imagination is of integral value to the captive, and is perhaps the main reason behind the enormous human capacity to endure. Studies of circus animals – who do not, as far as we know, share this human aptitude for dreaming – show that prolonged confinement leads to a number of unpleasant psychological reactions including hyper-aggression, apathy and self-mutilation. The nomadic creatures fare the worst: birds used to flying up to five hundred miles a day confined to a shit-strewn cage.

I felt a bit like a circus animal myself. People would make an afternoon of coming to visit, feed me treats, try to provoke reactions. I watched them leave, helplessly, as if I were a white panda marooned in a small concrete pen.

Paradoxically, one feeling readily assumed prominence as I came to terms with my situation. That was a feeling of enormous good fortune. How easily might things have turned out differently. I could have been killed outright, brain-damaged or paraplegic.

With that sense came a surge of feelings about my place in the world, an amplified resolution to suck the marrow out of life. Not for me the quotidian nine to five, a dour maisonette in the suburbs. It was nothing less than my duty to seek the very highest goals, to truly live a life of eventfulness.

Of course, I realised these were naive, somewhat conventional aspirations for someone in my position – but they filled the chasm at the time and I was glad of that. It had been a steep hill indeed down which I had fallen and I needed elaborate dreams if I was going to find the courage to climb it again.

Other thoughts followed. Friendships I had allowed to lapse, particular memories of elation. It was as if a huge boulder had splashed into my mind's centre, throwing everything into disarray. And it was only when the waters had begun to settle again that I examined what was in my grasp, which treasures I had wrestled instinctively from the deep.

I remember climbing the great falls at Yosemite with two old friends. A perfect, clean memory smelling of pine resin and smoke. We stood at the top and watched all the energy in the world rushing down and giving birth to rainbows.

I remember surfing at a reef called Hell's Gate in north-western Australia. There was a light offshore wind. Just two of us out and these great steep ramps rising up like gifts from some benevolent god.

Tastes, textures, poems. Lies told; promises too casually broken. The quality of light on Christmas morning that year it snowed and I was a week late for school.

Small shards to rake from the ashes. But they were invaluable to me during those exasperating months. Those relics seemed to be a yardstick by which I might come to some understanding of what in my life had true value.

I yearned to travel again. The broad expanses of the world loomed ever more alluringly to the castaway that I was, marooned in a small metropolitan island. Although I knew London to be a vast, stimulating city, it seemed intolerably stifling as I limped through its tired, polluted streets between home and the offices of whichever doctor that day's appointment was with.

In the end I tried to concentrate on the task in hand. I applied the salves and lotions with gritted teeth; I took faltering walks against the keen edge of the wind. I practised yoga to quieten my mind and build up my feeble strength. People complimented me on my fortitude and on the speed of my recovery. And while I thanked them as sincerely as I could, privately I was coming apart in brittle clumps.

I tried to conceal it for too long. A depression had fallen on me once my bones had begun to knit. It was not a run-of-the-mill kind of depression, a passing melancholy, or even post-traumatic stress — although that provided a convenient excuse for a time. It was a mass that eclipsed my every capacity to rest peacefully within my own skin. And when it came and I realised that it would not dissipate of its own accord, or move on like a cloud nudged by some novel draught of wind, I sank down to my knees one evening on the stairs to my parents' empty flat and wept as if I were the single human channel for suffering.

Who knows where it came from? I wondered, remorselessly, whether the sharp blow to the head had in some way altered the chemistry of my brain. I imagined a valve wrenched from its housing, leaking away in some inner neurological recess. It was an analogy born not so much out of logic as from a desire to translate this pain into some rational form. Rationale was one of the things I had lost.

As the weeks passed, I barely left the house. Joan and I were renting a flat off the Gloucester Road – a small but peaceful space on a leafy street, which soon became a haven I was afraid to leave. And yet there were times when I had no choice but to enter the world. I had to buy food, walk to the bank, post a letter. Those mundane jaunts felt like walking on broken glass to me, only that comparison fails where it begins because physical pain can be addressed as we know its source. This was a pain without foundation and, especially to strangers, without an exterior form.

People have told me that I looked normal during those bleak months. Yet I was a stranger to myself.

I marvel at how little we know of the people that pass us. That man there behind the newspaper, that woman stooped under her golf umbrella – what state of mind do they inhabit? Some days the possibility that they may feel anything within the same dimension as what I felt then clouds my every interaction.

I told no one of what was happening to me. Instead, I read fervently around the subject in the hope that by understanding it, I would know my enemy and therefore what weapons to apply.

But it soon became obvious that I was wasting my time. The truth of the matter is: we do not know what really causes depression any more than Hippocrates did in around 400 BC. He believed that mental disorders result from an imbalance of four body fluids: blood, phlegm, yellow and black bile. Depression supposedly resulted from an excess of black bile, or in Greek: *melan chole*.

Denied a scientific grasp of what my life had become, I fell back on instinct and impulse. I needed somewhere quiet to get my strength back. Somewhere without cars or credit cards and, preferably, without too much rain. Ideally there would be no computers there either, no microwaves, sports utility vehicles or mobile phones. I wanted a life of the senses, tradition and the work of the hand. I craved the true experience of silence, to fall asleep where there was no background hum: the distant roar of a 747 consuming aviation fuel within a night sky.

If I could find these things, lose myself in physical work, I hoped that I might relearn how to live in the world.

ITALY

CHAPTER ONE

IN EARLY APRIL 2001, I found myself aboard a rickety *treno regionale* speeding south along the Tuscan coast. I was cadaverously thin and my stomach bore a long purple cicatrisation. Nor had the reconstructive surgery on my right eye been wholly successful; I looked like an out-of-work prize-fighter, a fragment of the man I'd once been.

Joan had watched my deterioration as a fisherman's wife might see her husband's trawler dashed on to an offshore reef: with every desire to help, but without the power to oppose the laws of nature. One morning in London, where she was temping to pay for our food and rent, I announced that I had to get out of the city at all costs. She was at the door when I said it, late for work and fumbling with keys. She looked up – a slant of winter sun catching the plane of her face – and stared into my eyes. 'You make a plan,' she said gently, 'and when I get back from work you can tell me what we're going to do.'

I sat listlessly for several hours that morning, frozen into a state of lassitude. A meaningless chat show flickered on the television. Outside the window, I could see a bird struggling to fly against the easterly wind. I tried to read but soon tossed the book to the ground. I made coffee but found I couldn't stomach it. Finally, I put on my jacket and went for a walk down the Gloucester Road.

I walked for an hour, no destination in mind. Wet leaves scudded in the autumn wind. Eventually I found a cyber café and went in to check my email. It was then that I found a website coordinating volunteers for organic farms. I hadn't been looking for it – it was an anomaly, a gift from the internet gods. And yet the moment I saw it I knew that it was exactly what I needed. In exchange for a day's work, workers are given three meals and a place to sleep. More importantly, the experience promised immersion in deepest countryside, wholesome food, and work that would tire out the body but allow the mind to rest.

I told Joan that evening, the first animation in months colouring my voice. With characteristic enthusiasm and loyalty, she loved the idea. We booked our tickets the following day.

It was early evening when Joan and I disembarked at the rural station of Castagneto Carducci. The train journey had been full of unexpected halts and delays; we had dozed intermittently then sprung awake, afraid of missing our stop. We sat on the station bench, fending off stares, sharing an ice-cream cone. After a while, we noticed the approach of a battered Fiat estate, dirty white, driven by an unshaven man of about sixty-five. His skin was chestnut-brown, his hair was drawn into a silver ponytail and he was heavily built, with a boxer's breadth of shoulder. We felt like children before him as he leapt, cumbersomely, from the car. '*Ciao, ciao. Guten Tag.* You are the ones that called me, *ya*? I'm Gunter.' He proffered a hand, which I gripped forcefully, perhaps to assure him that my frail appearance did not belie a willingness to work hard.

He drew air through his teeth. '*Madonna mia!* You Inglesi and your handshakes. But mine is a little fragile just now.'

Looking down, I noticed that his hand was severely blistered. I apologised profusely.

He shrugged. 'It's my fault. A burn. I should have gone to the *ospedale* at the time but I was too busy. One of the chickens had escaped and there was a fuel line to mend and so on.'

We crammed into the back of the car, which was a minefield of mysterious-looking objects. Grimy balls of wax, rectangular wooden frames, matchboxes, sticky jars.

'Forgive all this. But I never seem to find the time to clean.'

'Are you German?' I asked, detecting an accent.

'*Ya*, Swiss-German, once upon a time. But I have been here now for forty years.' He gave a strange bird-like whistle. 'Now I am everything. Ha! Or perhaps I am nothing?'

'Why did you come to Italy then?'

He rolled down the window to light an unfiltered cigarette. 'Well, you waste no time in formalities, Inglesi. I like that. That's *part* of why I came here – to get out of all that bullshit. I was tired of my life, you see. Tired and pissed off. As a young man, I was an *architetto* in Zurich. A partner in a small firm. And we were building new things, shiny, glass things, and I got sick of it. I'd just got married at that time – my wife wanted an adventure too

– and so we decided to buy some land in the country and try and live more naturally. Get back to the root of things. My brother already owned the farm where we now live and he was thinking of getting rid of it so I said I'd buy it.'

'That was brave,' said Joan.

'*Ya*. Well we didn't realise how brave at the time. In fact, perhaps it would have been braver to stay. Braver to put up with all the shit until we got a little money. And then distract ourselves with the money for the rest of our lives like everyone else. Ha! Yes, that would have taken courage.

'But I know what you mean. New country, new language. When we got here there was no electricity, no running water, barely even a road. We got here in the dead of winter, snow on the ground, and the place had holes in the roof as big as soup plates. Like living in a goddamn Swiss cheese. First thing I did when it grew light on the first morning was to go into town and buy tarpaulin for the roof. Had to keep that rain out! But no matter how hard I tried, it didn't work properly. Drips here, drips there. A man could go *pazzo* with so many drips. Eventually we spent some of our savings on a caravan which we lived in until we could afford to have the roof redone.' He whistled again at the recollection. '*Sì*. I remember now. That roofer. He had some fancy name. Fiorovante, I think. *Ya*, what a *bastardo*! Overcharged me two times over. Thought we were rich foreigners here to play at being gardeners. What I wouldn't give to run into him some dark night . . .'

Through the smeared window we saw cobbled lanes and paths, a twisted fig tree, acacia and elders. It was getting dark now and there were lights coming on behind the flaking wooden shutters.

The road narrowed and steepened as we drove on, up towards the quietness of the hills.

'You live up there?' said Joan, pointing.

'*Ya, ya*. Not down *here*.' His tone suggested that to have been a most absurd suggestion. 'When we came here the village was OK but now, this . . . *principessa* is coming here for her summer holidays and the place is not what it was.' Gunter shook his head. 'Too much people and noise.'

'Princess? Which one?' I asked.

Gunter waved his cigarette around indifferently. 'Principessa Fergus, I think.'

'Ah, Fergie!'

'*Ya*, that's her. She has the red hair, no? *Come un porco*.'

We veered off the main road on to a track, and instantly it was as if we had crossed a border into a different realm. A fast-flowing stream rushed down, parallel to the road, over smooth stones. Above us the tips of the trees bowed like supplicating monks, so low that their foreheads brushed each other. It felt as though we were travelling through a green tunnel.

'Our place is some way down this track,' said Gunter. 'Be careful of the dog if you walk down here on your own. A white beast with a very bad temper. Always carry a stick.'

At last we arrived. The air felt suddenly chill as we stepped out into the night; the sky was rich with stars. Both of us were shattered.

'You will be tired,' said Gunter. 'You want pasta or something? I will have pasta.'

'Just a little sleep,' said Joan. 'We'll be fine tomorrow.'

A small-framed, nervous-looking woman came out to meet us. Her dress was bright even under cover of this gloaming, a pattern of psychedelic flowers that would have fitted in perfectly at Woodstock. 'I'm Sabina.' She proffered a tiny hand that had the consistency of sandpaper.

'They are tired,' said Gunter. 'I'll take them down to the van.'

'*Buona notte, ragazzi,*' said Sabina. 'Breakfast is at seven.'

I remember little else of that night. There was a sheer, slippery hill. Gunter led the way by the light of a kerosene lantern. Finally, Joan and I were left alone inside a tiny caravan, perfectly secluded at the base of the valley. We lit candles so that we could unpack our sleeping bags, our breath forming frost clouds in the yellow light.

Gunter was a beekeeper. The first one I'd ever met. Of course, he had to do other things – making olive oil and chestnut flour, for example – but none of those had any real bearing on who he was as a man. In the same way that a man who builds dry walls for a living, returning home at night to sculpt, will consider himself a sculptor: anything else is circumstantial.

Gunter and Sabina's house was a ramshackle dwelling on the crest of a hill, heated by a wood-burning stove and with a kind of improvised loft substituting for a first floor. The kitchen was always full of bustle and steam; different animal carcasses hung from its oak beams: pheasants, pigeon, rabbits or hares, a bloody haunch of lamb. A large earthenware pot full of stock simmered gently on the stove – a convenient resting place for all manner of vegetable and animal left-overs. Nothing was ever wasted in that house.

The house smelt of drying sage and burnt wheat dough and of

the two ancient mutts who whiled away their lives snoozing by the fire. Gunter and his wife were never inside much anyway. He was off at first light, tearing around the narrow lanes on his antiquarian John Deere; Sabina might be found in the vegetable patch, tying beanstalks to a cane with the finesse of a seamstress.

We had been there a week before I got close to the bees. Left alone much of the time, we felt as if we were the gardeners of some forgotten province, hacking at briars, clearing land unkempt as jungle. One afternoon, while Joan was off picking medicinal herbs with Sabina, Gunter gave me my first glimpse into his private universe. He ambled up as I was taking a quick breather from splitting logs.

'This will make you strong, *ya*,' he said, giving me a friendly slap on the back that would have felled an ox.

'I hope so.'

'What happened to you then?' He gestured to my face.

'Truck.'

'*Dio*,' he muttered. 'You look pretty bad.'

'To be honest,' I said, 'I feel it.'

'But in your eyes. You look . . . *molto nervoso* . . . frightened all the time.'

I was startled by his directness. 'I am,' I said eventually. 'Things haven't been too good since that day.'

He took the axe from me and thunked it firmly into a tree stump. 'Leave this for now.'

I followed without comment through a copse of trees, our feet crunching on dry twigs, the afternoon breeze reminding us of winter's lingering grasp. I watched Gunter's long, certain gait, the deep thrust of his hands into pockets, the weathered folds

of skin on the back of his neck. He seemed completely at home here, which made me think there was still hope for someone like myself, not born in the country, to make the same adjustment. Already, I could feel the peace of this place working on me, as if the current that had been permanently jangling my nerves had begun to abate.

'Do you ever regret coming out here?' I asked, breaking the silence.

'Me . . . no. Never. This is my place, this countryside is in my blood. But I think perhaps my wife does sometimes miss Zurich. It's lonely out here. I mean, we have friends, but to the Italians we will always be foreigners. There is a grudging acceptance – more so for me because I work with them so much – but they are . . . *insulare*.'

'But it's a hard life,' I said. 'I mean, you work bloody hard. Long hours.'

He gave one of his inimitable shrugs. 'Hard work is good. I like hard work. I find a great value in it. But it would be nice to have a little more money, fix the place up a bit. And I don't like working for other people so much, pruning their trees, building their fences. I would like to stay with my bees. Get more hives. Really get them strong.'

'Can I see your bees at some point?'

'*Ya*, of course. That's what we're doing now. You like bees?'

'I like honey.'

'But you're not frightened of them?'

'Not unduly. I've been stung a couple of times. Hurt for a while, then it stopped.'

'*Ya*,' said Gunter. 'They will come at you, of course, when I open the hive. But just let them have a look at you and they'll move on.'

The hives — resembling crude wooden boxes — were versions of what I would later learn to be the standard Langstroth design used by the majority of the world's beekeepers. About ten of them formed a crescent shape around a thicket of rosemary. We could smell the oil in the needles as we drew near; small pink buds were beginning to form on the bushes. Bees, like tiny full stops in the air, streamed in all directions. Each bloom was a beacon for them, each bee like a grateful ship sheltering from the storm.

'*Rosmarino*. Strong honey,' growled Gunter approvingly. 'Good for the circulation.' He gestured to me to stay back, then he moved forward towards the bees. There was a slight stirring of activity as they recognised his approach. And yet, without gloves or veil, Gunter was able to lift the roof of one of the hives, withdraw one of the pale yellow frames, and hold it up to the light for examination. He swept a legion of bees away with his hand and then, once satisfied, he walked towards me.

'*Perfetto*, Piers,' he said with a smile. 'Feel the weight of this.'

Rather nervously, since there were more than a few bees still clinging to it, I took the frame from him. It was startlingly heavy, several inches thick with honey. About fifteen bees immediately leapt on to my hand.

'*Calma*,' whispered Gunter. 'They are friendly bees — just keep still.'

I exhaled slowly, getting used to the sensation. I could feel their tiny fur coats against my hand.

'You can see that is ready,' explained Gunter, 'because of this

layer of wax on the outside. Once each cell is full, they seal it with
a plug of wax.' He took a pocket knife from his jacket and opened
the blade. 'We try, eh?' he said. Taking back the frame, he cut a
wedge of comb from the middle. 'Don't worry, in a few hours
they will have repaired that.' He gestured to the damage. 'You won't
even know it was there.'

That was my first taste of honey straight from a hive. We stood
there in the clearing, with the afternoon sun warm upon our faces,
honey running down our fingers, and let the sweetness wash over
our tongues. The honey, indeed, had a strong taste of rosemary,
and to see the spiny green bushes right beside us, and then to taste
the result here and now, was by no means any great scientific
discovery, but it felt strangely wonderful – like an insight into the
order of things.

That afternoon I watched Gunter at work among the hives. The
nature of the relationship between a beekeeper and his bees is a
subject over which there are wide differences of opinion. I'd like
to believe, as Gunter does, that one can build up a particular relationship with bees, that certain people have a natural affinity and ease
with them. Eva Crane, perhaps the world's leading authority on
apiculture, would later tell me that such notions are romantic
nonsense. 'A good beekeeper is one who has achieved a sound
scientific knowledge,' she said brusquely. 'Plain and simple.'

Well, she might be right. Beekeeping, after all, has always been
known as the most intellectual of the country pursuits. But, to my
mind, a world viewed through the lens of science is a very dull
one indeed. How bland is an outlook that relegates all human
creativity to mere electrical current passing through a neural web!

Can this be said of Eliot, Dante, Basho? I won't believe it. So I choose the quixotic over the technical, the poetic over the prosaic, and I flick through the *New Scientist* as quickly as possible.

The reason I'm writing about all this is because Gunter was no scientist. And his knowledge of apiculture was learnt not from books or academic study, but by word of mouth, trial and error, one sting after another. Yet when he drew close to those bees, I saw a change come over him that affected me very deeply. His movements became soft and economical. His stance widened, his shoulders lowered, the creases in his brow relaxed and disappeared. It was something that is very difficult to explain in plain terms. Perhaps he simply stopped thinking about anything extraneous at all – what a Zen Roshi might call a state of 'no mind'. And this state brought him a great deal of peace, as much as it allowed him to work within the tiny universe of his bees with great facility.

I remember that day very clearly indeed. Since that fateful September dawn, very little had made me glad to be alive. I had stopped reading novels or listening to music. I took no pleasure in friendship or the natural world. But in that moment, some mechanism started up in me again. I became aware of every moisture-clad blade of grass around me, of bees catching the afternoon light like sparks rising from a fire. There was a harmony to the series of events that I was observing; a perfect symbiosis. I burned with the wonder of it all.

We spent three months in Tuscany. The cold tang in the air gave way to a burning heat. Flowers revealed petals of such brilliance it was as if they were cut-outs of stained glass. Joan and I began to feel at home in our caravan, our own Thoreauvian retreat from the world. Our front door looked on to a sloping pasture of wild flowers: violets, cyclamens, orchids. Every night we were serenaded by nightingales.

And during the long summer days I learnt more about bees. I learnt how to nail together the simple wooden frames, then fit the wax foundations upon which the bees would work their magic. I learnt how to load and spark the smoker which Gunter used to puff smoke into the hive. It was in effect a simple metal lung that could pacify the hive with its breath. I learnt how to slot the heavy combs into the centrifuge, a merry-go-round for honey, whose rotations would spin the honey from its wax housing. It was nothing, barely a beginning, by the standards of real beekeepers, but it was enough to fascinate me; it was the germ, in effect, of a much longer journey.

I came to respect Gunter as I have respected few men. He had changed the course of his life by the sheer sweat of his brow. He had a restless streak, a refusal to compromise, which I identified with. But he was no saint. He had his flaws, not least of which was an abruptness with his wife which I found difficult to listen to. I sensed that their marriage was failing; perhaps it had been from the start?

But in matters of the natural world he possessed real wisdom, a wisdom lived. A Luddite; an ardent sceptic of 'progress'; a solitary fatalist who scorned the heavy industrialisation of our time. In temperament he was irascible, domineering, he smoked more Merits than was good for any man. But when I was alone with him, quaffing local Chianti after a hearty dinner, he would say things that suggested the soul of a poet.

One night I recall in particular. Supper had been a fairly silent affair, with things obviously at a low ebb between Gunter and his wife. Joan and I couldn't wait to be alone in the caravan, away from all the bickering, the sullen looks, the emotional currents that were so wearisome to be around. But Gunter seemed determined to salvage something from the evening. While we were washing up, he announced his intention to build a fire outside. It looked as if we weren't going to escape just yet.

Some time later, before a fierce blaze of olive logs and dry vine cuttings, we sat drinking wine and warming our hands. From our vantage point outside their house, we could see the whole valley laid out below us. A granite moon sat heavily in the sky.

'What bad times we're going through!' said Gunter, almost to himself.

'I'm sorry,' said Joan.

He sighed and all the muscles in his great burly torso went slack. 'When we were first married I would have gone with her *all'inferno* if she'd asked. And now, I suppose that we have fallen . . . out of love.' He took a long, keen drag of his cigarette. 'She was too young, I think, to realise the sacrifices this life would entail. Perhaps she resents me?'

Looking up, he found me watching him and our eyes locked. 'I'm not saying don't do it, if it's a life like this you want. Just be sure. There is a price.'

'But you were happy when you first got here?' I said.

He nodded. '*Ya*. We were. I mean, it was difficult but that was part of it.' He smiled wistfully. 'After the first winter we were so grateful for the warmth of the sun. But within a matter of weeks it became like a goddamn *furnace* on the top of this hill. That was

a bad summer – even the locals couldn't remember anything like
it. At that time there were very few trees up here even – we had
no shade!'

'How do you mean there were no trees?' asked Joan, pointing
to the towering trunks that surrounded the house.

'I planted those,' said Gunter. 'All of them. That first summer
I got up at five every morning, and planted trees for three or four
hours. I did that for five months straight. I planted oak, chestnut,
beech, cypress. Also eucalyptus because they grow so fast. Later
I planted the orchard down at the bottom. Apples, kiwi, peach,
nut trees. I ordered rare species from Roma. I couldn't stop.'

He fell silent. All around us the leaves of Gunter's trees shivered in the breeze, their trunks creaking like galleons at sea. A fox
gave a dry bark some distance to the east.

'That's unbelievable!' I said. 'You planted an entire wood!'

He shrugged. 'Well, it's still young. But I like to think I've
done something which will outlive me. Something bigger than
myself. Well, it's nothing really. Now, if I could have been a
dottore!'

'And your bees?' asked Joan, steering the topic to something
she knew to be dear to his heart.

His eyes brightened. 'I got them maybe two or three years after
we came here. We were so poor we were looking for ways to cut
down on expenses. Sabina suggested that if we got some bees
then we wouldn't have to buy sugar. I liked the idea – especially
because I had recently read an article about the dangerous chemicals they spray on sugar cane – so I got a book on *apicultura* and
a couple of hives.' He tutted, as if to remonstrate with his former
self. '*Ya*, I was young and I thought I could do anything.' He refilled

his glass to the brim and handed me the bottle. 'I was working late one night that first year with the bees. You can only move the hives at night – I knew that much. And, Christ, I suppose I was moving too fast or something because I tripped and dropped it! *MINCHIA!* I was stung maybe sixty or seventy times. Bees were in my hair, my beard, under my shirt. After that I lay in bed for three days, delirious. The bee venom can make you *pazzesco* like that.'

'You could have been killed,' I said.

He nodded. 'You have to be stung something like seven hundred times for that. But, *ya*, it could have been very bad.' He chuckled. 'Believe me, it *was* bad!'

And so the conversation continued into the night. As the flames dwindled, Gunter talked on and on about the bees. It was as if he couldn't stop. Sometimes, he explained, he just liked to watch the goings-on within the hive, as a way of gaining perspective on the events of his own life.

'Sometimes I like to watch the bees being born,' he whispered, hunching himself into a foetal position in mimicry of an infant bee. 'You can see them pushing themselves from their larvae. They come out, and then . . .' Gunter shook himself vigorously, like a dog coming out of a river. 'They shake themselves and, within five seconds, they start carrying food to the queen.' A smile lit up his face. '*Un miracolo!* And at the same time other bees are dying, falling to the bottom of the hive. The whole cycle is there. *La vita e la morte.*'

'Do you think beekeepers feel like . . . God?' said Joan.

Taking the question in his stride, Gunter shook his head, then looked away across the valley. 'No,' he murmured. 'Simpler than that. We feel as if there *is* a God.'

We fell quiet. It is a powerful thing to hear a man declare his faith. And, if the truth be known, I could see that Gunter *had* found a kind of confirmation of his philosophies in the process of managing honeybees. Some basic tenet of his worldview was ratified every time he donned his bee veil, every time he removed a full comb of honey. It was an appealing metaphor, the beekeeper as mediator between man and nature, a priest of trees and flowers.

'You know man was eating honey *thirty* thousand years before he was cooking his food,' Gunter said. '*Dio!* Imagine that! And think about all those countries in the world, all the different plants that grow there, and the taste of some of that honey. *Merda,*' he said, in awe. 'I would like to taste them all.'

CHAPTER TWO

THAT WAS THE start of it all – the seed of an idea that would take determined root in me. I grasped hold of it as if it were a magic beanstalk I might climb towards a new life.

Of course, tasting every honey on the planet was a little ambitious. But I would do what I could. I envisaged a series of journeys in search of the most esoteric varieties. I wished to discover their source, observe their creation and extraction. I had in mind a quest that would lead me to the very nucleus of the honey world: its beginnings, its eccentricities, its marvels.

For as long as I can remember, honey has been my favourite food. As a child I avoided all jams, conserves and marmalades in favour of it. Honey was an integral part of my breakfast, melted on to hot toast with yellow farmhouse butter, or drizzled on to steaming porridge. And for tea, returning from a bike ride or a freezing voyage in our family sailing dinghy, honey lathered on to crusty bread. Best of all was to eat the comb itself, straight from the jar, a feast of textures, scents and chewy wax.

But this wasn't just a child's hankering after sugar, for I quickly learnt that honey, like wine or coffee, is capable of immense subtleties. The worst kind of honey, the nadir of discerning beekeepers the world over, is the pale watery substance which one usually finds encased within a plastic bear. At the other end of the spectrum, one finds a honey so delicate in its flavours, so redolent of the landscape that has helped fashion it, that one's tongue simply cannot believe its good fortune.

As my taste for honey developed, I began to ask people to keep an eye out for interesting varieties on their travels. My mother was travelling a lot in France and Italy at the time and would always remember my request, so that as a small boy returning from boarding school for the odd exeat, I'd find a jar waiting for me on my bed, its foreign label bearing words like *Miele d'Arancia,* or *Miel de Garrigue.*

To the small boy that I was, enamoured with Marco Polo, Rider Haggard, Dumas, each one of these jars seemed to contain a story. They told of the landscape over which the bees had flown: the hot, dry dusty *garrigue,* thick with wild thyme and sage brush, or the orange groves just south of Palermo, where if the wind is right one can smell the blossom for twenty miles.

My father also welcomed my interest in honey. He, too, had grown up in its thrall. During World War II, his grandmother had learnt to keep bees so as to provide the family with sugar during the lean times of rationing. I often heard him reminisce about that spry battleaxe who would take him with her to watch the bees fly, or to move the hives from Worcester up into the Malvern Hills when the heather was in flower. Later, she became something of an expert and even invented an early version of a queen bee carrier, so that queens could be safely posted through the mail.

Gunter's idea, therefore, had a particular resonance for me. As well as being intrinsically linked with my childhood, it invariably conjured up for me the concept of travel itself. Although I'd never broken it down to such minutiae before, I realised that Gunter's notion of tasting all the honeys of the world was, in fact, the closest a person *could* get to absorbing the complexities of a foreign landscape – each jar is literally *made up* of the thousands, if not millions, of flowers, bushes and shrubs which grow there.

Up until now, though, my knowledge had been amateur. If I was really to go through with this, there was much to be learnt. Just as vintners school themselves in grape varieties, soil conditions and viticultural lore, so I would try to understand the honey world. I ordered a number of impressive-sounding books from the International Bee Research Association: *The World History of Beekeeping and Honey Hunting, The Sacred Bee, The Golden Throng*. I immersed myself in bee lore, apicultural terminology, the Latin names of flowers that provide the best nectar for bees. I leafed through ancient tomes in the British Library, written by archaeologists who had unearthed primitive clay cylinders in the Middle East, believed to be the earliest beehives of man's design.

This was back in February, a bleak, overcast month in which it seemed that London was under the influence of a Narnian

spell. I pored over maps, analysed temperature charts and rain-
fall averages, and began to envisage the journeys I might make
over the year ahead. The honey I ate for my breakfast took on
even greater significance. I sat with my coffee and toast
surrounded by books and dreamt of the bees at work in some
far-off pasture.

I sent hundreds of emails: to the Arab Beekeeping Federation,
to a Nepalese NGO called ICIMOD working with indigenous
honey-hunters, to a fantastic organisation called Bees for
Development whose aim it is to empower local people by teaching them how to keep bees and make a living by them. I spoke
to an interesting man, David Wainwright, whose exotic honeys,
largely harvested from jungles and impenetrable forests, had
caught my eye in a London health-food store. He was fascinated
by my idea and spoke dramatically about the wild landscapes
from which he sourced his honeys and their powerful healing
properties.

Part of the idea's appeal was that, within certain parameters,
there was almost nowhere in the world I *couldn't* go in search of
honey. Regions habitable for honeybees only really exclude deserts,
due to a lack of water, and areas of high latitude where the cold
seasons are too long for them to over-winter.

An initial week of research nearly overwhelmed me with possibilities. I read about the Hazda of Tanzania and the Mbuti pygmies
of the Congo, for whom honey plays an essential role in nutrition.
The Veddhas, or Wild Men, of Sri Lanka esteem honey so highly
that they regularly risk their lives to obtain it. And in the New
World, the Guayaki Indians of Paraguay have honey as the very
basis of their diet and culture.

Or what about the Rajis, who live in the Napalese Terai, in the northern part of the Ganges plain? A nomadic forest-dwelling tribe, they are known as 'the Bee People' by the Nepalese, living and moving in strict accordance with the bees. Yet deforestation is dwindling their homeland by thousands of acres a year. When the forest vanishes, the Rajis, like the trees themselves, will disappear.

Further possibilities leapt out at me. Could I find the cave at Mount Dikta in Greece where the infant Zeus was reared by sacred bees? Or the Lapos valley in Transylvania where a sunflower is used as a bee bait in summer? Then there was the unique manuka honey collected by the beekeepers of New Zealand, reputedly possessed of near-magical healing properties. Or the wild honey gathered by the Bassari tribes of Senegal who practise sexual abstinence for three days before the hunt.

During that first morning of research, I perceived a clear link between the hunting of honey and the earliest origins of man. There seems something so elemental about the concept of taking honey from wild nests, the sating of some primordial urge for sweetness on the tongue. How must it have felt to those Neanderthal hunters who, half-crazed with stings, first dipped their fingers into that golden nectar?

But it was the metaphorical level that really appealed to my imagination, the notion that *Homo sapiens*, a creature with a primary instinct, like all species, to find sustenance, had stumbled across something so *perfect* in the forest, so dazzling to the senses, that it would not simply assuage his hunger but capture his imagination, enter his rituals and his worship of unknown gods.

Finally, as an environmentalist, I could see a contemporary

relevance to the journey. Gone are the days when the Pharaohs elected valued court officials to the position of royal honey-hunter. Long gone. Now is the age of saccharin and Nutrasweet; our Pharaohs are men in Armani suits, and the most esteemed of the court officials hold their fingers over buttons which may, one day not too far from now, bring an end to the last bee's drone.

Bees are a species very much under threat, like the fragile ecosystems in which they play such an integral part. And though the green-washers and the corporate-funded think-tanks are becoming dazzlingly skilful at painting ecologists as jeremiahs, as panic merchants and enemies of the notion of progress, there *is* no debate about this any more, not among the realists and the well-informed. The hourglass is running out for the natural world: for biodiversity and tribal peoples and clean water. And that there are still small coteries of men hunting sweetness from trees and cliffs in far-off places, as there have been for many thousands of years, is an utterly remarkable fact. In a generation's time, I very much doubt there will be still.

Was it too much of a leap to suppose that this journey might fulfil a double objective? I needed to regain my own equilibrium; that was foremost. But in the process I would see those landscapes I'd always dreamed of, those wild, uncorrupted backdrops to the relentless human world in which I'd lost my faith.

Chinese poetry speaks of something called 'the dust world'. The term occurs often, especially in the work of the Taoist poets of the T'ang dynasty, who were also concerned about the plight of nature. 'The dust world' was what they called that mundane arena of human affairs – unimportant, to their mind, beside the vastness and profundity of the wild. For some reason this term stayed very much in my mind during the period of the accident and the adventures which came after. It seemed so fitting as a motif of what I was running away from.

Honey, on the other hand, with all its myriad connotations, seemed exactly what I should be running towards.

CHAPTER THREE

BEFORE DECIDING UPON my first destination, I went to see Eva Crane, an old lady who is something of a legend in beekeeping circles. Given a swarm of bees for a wedding present in 1942, she found the whole process so absorbing that her interest soon evolved. More than sixty years later, she is one of the world's most respected apiculturists, a scientist, author of many books, and was director of the International Bee Research Association for some thirty-five years. Her name had come up so many times in my research that it seemed a necessary step to go and ask her advice. After all, she had spent her life working with bees and had travelled to a great many countries in their pursuit – more than sixty, I had read. Now in her eighties, she no longer keeps bees, but maintains a lively interest in current apicultural developments. I contacted her through her publisher and set out, one chill spring afternoon, to meet her.

Admittedly, when I'd woken up that morning, I hadn't planned as much. The meeting had been set for the following day and I'd intended to spend the day in the British Library preparing some questions. At about lunchtime, however, as I was taking some fresh air in the library courtyard, my telephone began to vibrate.

'Are you coming then?' said a rather brisk voice.

'Is that Mrs Crane?' I said, surmising that there was only one old lady likely to be calling me.

'That's right. What time shall I expect you?'

'Ah, I thought I was coming tomorrow.'

'Oh . . . I see . . . Oh dear, I *am* getting forgetful. Well, what about today – that's *much* more convenient.'

'Oh, all right then.' I was momentarily lost for words. 'Yes, I can manage that. I'll leave now then – I've got the directions you gave me in my notebook.'

'Fine. Thank you, Mr Moore Ede, see you at three p.m. sharp.'

I was left standing, rather bemusedly, on the flagstones. Nevertheless, though slightly unprepared, I saw no reason why I shouldn't make the most of the opportunity. I boarded an east-bound train and set off.

I walked the mile from the station. A thin rain was falling; red lorries rumbled past me towards the motorway. Eva Crane's house turned out to be a classic suburban piece of England, ivy-clad and surrounded by a privet hedge. A rose bush at the front of the house had new shoots again after the long winter. Outside the door, I brushed off my clothes and rapped loudly. No answer. I rapped again. At length, I heard a distant shuffling and the sound of approaching footsteps.

When the door opened I saw a stooped figure, elderly but with eyes still flashing with vigour. Her skin was pale and mottled, her white hair drawn severely into a bun.

'Hello, Mr Ede. Do come in. Let's go into my study, shall we?' she said. 'Don't mind the cat. He won't eat you.'

We sat down in the study: a sombre room stacked with highly esoteric apicultural texts, several archaic filing cabinets and a modest teak writing desk. It took me back to my housemaster's study at school.

'Jog my memory, Mr Ede. You're writing a book on bees.'

'I hope to.'

'Tell me again how long you've been keeping bees. '

I reminded her of our telephone conversation when I'd explained that I was not, in fact, a beekeeper at all. She looked troubled.

'So you're writing a book on bees but you're not a beekeeper. I'm afraid you've lost me.'

'Well, I'd like to *become* a beekeeper. But really, this is to be more of a literary adventure. I'd like to meet beekeepers, honey-hunters and so on and also to taste some of the world's most unusual honeys. And to merge all that into some kind of travelogue.'

Her eyes narrowed. 'Well, you see, I've done a *lot* of travelling to meet beekeepers. And they were all very happy to talk to *me* because it was an exchange of information – they told me their techniques, I told them mine. But they won't talk to someone who isn't a beekeeper. Why *should* they?'

My face fell. This was not the encouraging pep talk I'd envisaged. 'I'm intrigued by the old traditions,' I began, struggling to find something that would pique her interest. 'The clay cylinders in the Middle East, the honey-hunters in Nepal. There's an environmental theme. I'd like to document some of these things before they vanish.'

She peered at me steadily. 'I see . . . Do you speak Arabic?'

'No.'

'French?'

'Passable.'

'Nepalese? Tamil? Hindi?'

'No.'

'Spanish?'

'No.'

She blinked at me. 'Well, it's not going to be easy is it, dear? But I suppose if your French is passable you must go to France then. No point going anywhere else.'

'Look, if I *must* get a translator, then I shall. I was just hoping for you to give me, say, three places which are *particularly* exciting. I understand you've travelled a lot in search of honey.'

She pursed her lips. 'Well, I daresay I've got the odd contact or two. Slightly out of date, perhaps, but they may do. Let me have a look.' She glided to one of the filing cabinets and began rooting round in it.

'For example,' I said, 'where's been the most fascinating place you've travelled to for honey?'

She rustled some papers. 'Well, they've all been lovely, dear.'

I tried again. 'Well, what's been the most *fantastic* honey you've ever tried? Something *really* unusual.'

More rustling. 'Well, I always say that we like the honey we grow up with. Once I took some of my honey to an Aboriginal tribesman. I gave him some of mine, he gave me some of his. And he tasted mine, a lovely white clover honey, and he went, "It's a bit too floral for my liking." And then I tasted his and went, "Well, it's awfully bitter, isn't it?"' She tittered. 'So English honey is my favourite.'

Looking back on it, I should have cut my losses then and there. But I wittered on, desperate to convey some sense of what I hoped to achieve.

'I'm interested in the role of the beekeeper, on a metaphorical level, as a kind of mediator between man and nature,' I said. 'Do you think there is such a thing as a man or woman who has a natural affinity with bees?'

She gave a short laugh. 'Poppycock, I'm afraid, dear,' she said. 'A good beekeeper is someone who has achieved a sound scientific knowledge of the job. I've never subscribed to all those fanciful notions of beekeepers. It's a myth.'

She retrieved the papers she wanted and laid them on the side-table where she'd been sitting. 'Before we continue,' she said, 'how about a nice cup of tea?'

'That'd be very kind,' I said. 'Can I help?'

'No, no, dear, you stay there. I shan't be long.'

I sat in silence for five minutes, morosely reading the spines of the books on the shelves. Soon she came back with a pot of Darjeeling tea, two Staffordshire china cups and a bowl of white sugar lumps. I helped with the tray and she sat back down, poured the tea, and then picked up her papers again.

'Right, where were we? I'm getting *so* absentminded these days. Oh yes, I remember. You're not a beekeeper, are you? Of course that's going to make it difficult. But I suppose you've set your heart on all this, have you?'

I returned to London browbeaten. Eva Crane had failed to grasp my idea entirely and had scooped much of the wind from my sails. But I would not let that dispirit me. Rather, I looked upon it as a learning experience. I had discovered that beekeeping is an insular world, with its own habits and customs, somewhat resistant to outsiders. I had also discovered that there are two separate schools of beekeepers, as there are in life itself: those who think with the left half of the brain and those who think with the right. Eva Crane was a consummate left-brainer: logical, rational and analytical. Gunter, on the other hand, was, to the same degree, a right-brainer: holistic, subjective and intuitive. Needless to say, my sensibilities lay with Gunter – but it was important that I recognise Eva Crane's camp. I would meet both sorts on the road ahead.

The following day I went back to the British Library. There I retrieved a copy of *The Georgics*, a book by a right-brained beekeeper, namely Virgil, which would, I hoped, inspire me onwards.

Virgil was fascinated by apiculture and espoused many colourful theories about bees in his work. He kept bees in the hills above Naples among orange and lemon groves and with a view of the snow-capped Apennines to the north. Like most of the ancients, he believed in the divine origin of bees.

> Some say that unto bees a share is given
> Of the Divine Intelligence, and to drink
> Pure draughts of ether; for God permeates all –
> Earth, and wide ocean, and the vault of heaven –
> From whom flocks, herds, men, beasts of every kind,
> Draw each at birth the fine essential flame.

Virgil wasn't alone in his belief. Many religions hold bees separate from the rest of the animal kingdom, believing them to have a special intelligence, or to be in touch with supernatural forces.

Some tribes, considering beekeeping a spiritual practice, allow only their shaman to take honey from the hive. In Western Nepal, the local *dharmi* determines when it is most auspicious for hives to be made. Equally, if a menstruating woman touches the hives, he will perform a *puja*, by sprinkling the hive with cow urine and reciting mantras, so that bees will not abscond.

In other parts of the world, such as Malaysia, Sufi 'magicians' protect women in childbirth by choosing an auspicious place for the birth and surrounding it with thorns, nets, rays' tails, and bees' nests to keep the spirits of evil away. In India, the influence of evil is especially feared at weddings, so honey is used to deter the spirits. For Siberian and South American Indians, the bee represents the soul which flies away from the body. In France beekeepers follow the mysterious practice of placing hives over underground water veins. Such hives can produce up to three times more honey than hives positioned a few feet away, but according to these beekeepers, the life span of these bees is considerably shortened and they are more aggressive.

Absorbed in such thoughts, and in the scholarly quiet of the British Library, I quickly regained my enthusiasm. This was, after all, a very personal quest. Apiculture itself was unlikely to benefit from my journey, and that was perhaps what had baffled Mrs Crane – like most scientists, she had a horror of and contempt for speculation. But for me the way ahead seemed as clear as anything in my life had for a long time.

THE MIDDLE EAST

CHAPTER FOUR

THE MIDDLE EAST seemed a good place to begin. If my calculations were correct, the bees would be at the height of their productivity just now, and the hives thick with new honey. I was already planning a trip to Nepal in October, with the hope of seeing honey-hunting in the wild, so it made sense to concentrate now on hive beekeeping, and the ancient methods that had first brought bees into domesticity.

Much of the earliest archaeological evidence about honey stems from the ancient world. There are references to bees in Egyptian creation mythology, the Koran, the Talmud and the Bible. Inside the tomb of Rekh-mi-re at Thebes in Upper Egypt, a well-preserved relief from about 1450 BC shows a group of men filling and sealing honey jars.

Honey, in ancient Egypt, was used by all classes of society, not only as a sweetening material in most households, but as a part of the marriage contract, by physicians and magicians, and even for the preserving of the dead. Of this last habit, one account relates an incident of grave robbers looting tombs near the Pyramids. Coming upon a sealed jar, they broke it open and began to feast on the honey within. One of the men soon noticed, however, that there was a good deal of hair mixed in with the honey. Peering into the jar, they discovered the body of a child, still in a good state of preservation.

Straight from the hive, honey is thin and liquid. But as time passes, its molecular structure changes and the honey granulates. Under the microscope one can see that the particles within granulated honey lie much closer together — so close, in fact, that bacteria are unable to multiply. This is the reason why, technically, one could eat a spoonful of honey straight from a jar found within Tutankhamen's tomb, and why honey is so useful as a preservative and embalming agent.

In the 500s, a famous Arab runner, Thabit ibn Jabur, recorded an extraordinary description of hunting honey in the wild. The poem describes how the author was lowered down a rope in order to gather honey from a cave. But while occupied with the bees, his companions were set upon and captured by enemy tribesmen. Emerging from the cave mouth, Thabit was confronted by armed men, shouting down for him to give himself up as their prisoner. It was then that Thabit conceived of one of the most daring and bizarre escape plans in all of human history. Thabit 'poured forth the honey upon the rock from the mouth of the cave, then he bound upon his breast the skin in which he had stored the honey, and spread himself out on the slide thus prepared. And he did not cease to slide down thus, kept from slipping by the tenacity of the honey, until he reached the level safe.'

It is an astonishing account. A reckless, sugar-propelled mountain get-away, which deserves its place in the history books if only for its sheer idiosyncrasy. Visualising the event, it is not hard to imagine the fugitive gleefully striding away from the bottom of the cliff, licking the last of the honey from his hands in triumph.

After a journey filled with dreams of dramatic honey-enabled escapes, I disembarked at Beirut airport. I was tired and enervated after forty-eight hours without sleep, and more than a little uncomfortable as the result of the oven-blast of heat that was intensifying my already entrenched headache. Not yet eight in the morning and already it was like the furious interior of a kiln.

I was thus in little mood to deal with the story given to me by Akram, the embodiment of all dodgy taxi drivers, who accosted me as I left the airport.

First we endured the usual round of haggling over what he would charge to take me to the centre of Beirut. It was a lengthy procedure, full of feints and theatrical gestures, but one in which I felt I'd held my own. I sank gratefully down into the cab, the windows of which were tastefully adorned with a lurid velvet brocade.

'Which hotel, sir?' said Akram, turning round to flash me a gold-augmented smile – the visible proof of his hustling skills.

I told him.

'Oh no, no,' he sighed, with an admonitory shaking of the head that seemed to imply I had the intellectual capacity of a turnip. 'That is a *very* unhealthy place. Dirty. The staff are stealing everything.'

'It's fine, thanks,' I lied. 'I've been there before.'

'When?' he said scornfully. 'Now *new* management. Bad people. *Criminal* people. I take you to a good place. Very clean. My cousin. He is making best falafels.'

'No thanks,' I said, thinking fast. 'The owners of the hotel are actually friends and they're expecting me.'

'Ah . . .' There was an uncomfortable silence while Akram came to terms with this. Then there was an angry bout of horn-blowing, followed by a couple of stentorian attempts to excavate some phlegm from the deepest recesses of his lungs. Finally, he lit himself a cigarette as a consolation prize, his failure to wind down the window a rather transparent gesture of recrimination. 'Fine, sir,' he muttered gruffly, sparking the engine. 'I take you there. But you will soon see that Akram is right and be wishing you had listened. *Stealing*, you will be experiencing. And my cousin will be getting very nasty with me.'

The hotel which I had so bravely insisted upon turned out to be a gruesome relic of Beirut's past. My room was approximately the size of a single bed and had a wire mesh instead of a window. Six feet from the mesh was a view of a concrete wall strafed with machine-gun fire. Billions of dollars have been spent rebuilding Beirut in the last ten years, but some parts remain just as they were, a memory bank of crumbling stone and mortar.

Despite their intimations of a violent history, part of me was glad that such vistas remained. After a few days spent wandering the streets, my first impressions of Beirut were singularly mediocre. It had little or nothing of the old-world charm that had made it famous. Instead, I saw a modern, featureless metropolis, a gleaming hotchpotch of concrete developments and American-style boutiques. For a city with such a fabulously rich history – an Ottoman port less than a hundred years ago, and before that a centre of classical civilisation – it seemed awfully keen on securing a sterile, American future.

It was hard, however, to blame the Lebanese for embracing the modern world. The past had been full of bloodshed for Lebanon, specifically because of the civil war which had raged for the fifteen years preceding 1990. The spark that first ignited the war occurred when an attempt was made on the life of the Lebanese military commander, Pierre Gemayel, on 13 April 1975. In defending Gemayel, soldiers killed four Phalangists, members of a Lebanese Christian political party. Believing the assassins to be Palestinian, the Phalangists quickly retaliated by attacking a bus carrying Palestinian passengers across a Christian neighbourhood, killing around twenty-six of the occupants.

In a country already racked by religious tensions, the fighting spread quickly. Many Muslims had considered themselves unfairly treated since 1943, when the National Pact established a dominant role for Lebanese Christians.

Within weeks the war had escalated to a national level. Various groups took sides, primarily on religious grounds. Soon Syria got involved, then Israel, who supported the Phalangist/Maronite militia. Fighting would continue in various forms until 1990, when the Taif Agreement, allowing increased Muslim representation in the government, finally resulted in an uneasy peace.

It had been a war with no winners, however. Almost 150,000 people had been killed, more than three-quarters of whom were civilians. Just under a million people had fled the country. Lebanon's environment was perhaps the greatest victim of all.

Habitats were destroyed, water sources contaminated, many species eradicated. As for the economy, by the year 2000 Lebanon was 20 billion US dollars in debt.

I wandered around Beirut. In the decade since the end of the war the Lebanese government has attempted one of the most ambitious reconstruction projects in human history. All of the great landmarks, the Grand Serail, the Al-Ornan Mosque, the Maronite and Greek Orthodox Cathedrals, have been rebuilt. And yet there is still no reliable electricity, no proper telephone system; many schools remain in ruins. The divide between the rich and poor is increasing.

It was into this confusing sprawl that I had come. A city with, reputedly, the highest proportion of Mercedes and BMWs in the world yet at the same time a place where the shells of old buildings contain whole communities of Palestinian refugees, makeshift washing lines strung across the rubble.

On my second day I made contact with a man named Kamal Mousawak, a food writer and Lebanese representative for the Slow Food Movement. Slow Food celebrates traditional cuisine, sustainably produced, and now has some 80,000 members worldwide. Without exception, Slow Fooders are people who love time-honoured recipes, convivial company and a chance to wax lyrical about their local dishes. I hoped Kamal could provide me with some contacts, not to mention an insight into real Beiruti life.

What I had *not* been expecting, when I arrived sweating profusely after a two-hour walk through the back streets, was the degree of elegance in which Kamal lived. I was wearing olive combat trousers, a grubby T-shirt bearing the mantra 'Think Global, Act Local' and a pair of hiking boots which had seen better days long before I bought them from a thrift store in California, two years before.

The man who opened the door was immaculately clad in a Japanese kimono, wore a pencil moustache which had been groomed with a topiarist's precision, and instantly struck me as a man who concerned himself only with life's most genteel activities. Like most of Beirut's moneyed class, he spoke French as a first language, Arabic second, his perfect English marred only by the faintest of Gallic tinges.

Some time later I found myself sitting in Kamal's exquisite sitting room, eating chocolate éclairs with a silver fork. The day had certainly taken an unexpected turn.

'Zees pastries are as good, if not better, zan zose of Paris,' remarked Kamal, noting my appreciation.

I nodded in agreement, unable to actually speak due to the concentration required not to sully my reputation further by dropping cream on Kamal's chaise longue.

'Zo of course London has some contenders – particularly Pâtisserie Valerie, don't you think?'

I nodded again. If the truth be known, I was slightly awestruck by my surroundings. Muted by wooden-slatted fans, the burning sun had become an irksome memory. My gaze took in a mosaic-tiled floor, abstract paintings, a dining-room table of antique mahogany. Our every whim was catered to by Kamal's Sri Lankan maid. It was a lifestyle I felt sure I could get used to.

To his credit, Kamal seemed undaunted by my dishevelled appearance. Over green tea, we discussed the demise of traditional Lebanese cuisine while the city's youth rushed to embrace a fast-food culture. Kamal and his friends were championing organic agriculture, artisan foods, and thus reclaiming, not just their taste-buds, but a sense of cultural identity. It was grass-roots activism at its finest.

As for honey, Kamal felt sure that some of his friends would know who to ask. He was having a little soirée that night, he told me, and would be honoured if I would attend.

Weighing a return to these idyllic surroundings against an evening spent battling prehistoric insects in my room, it was not a difficult decision to make.

I returned at 8 p.m. sharp, a jar of honey in hand. It was a dinner party such as could occur only in Beirut. The guests were in turn a fashion designer, a jeweller, a Hollywood make-up assistant, a restaurateur, a banker and a photographer, all of whom ate 'slowly' in their spare time. Conversation flowed seamlessly from French to Arabic to English, often within the same sentence. As for the location, we sat at a full-length table in the roof garden which covered the top of Kamal's house. It was, without a doubt, the most beautiful piece of urban space I have ever seen.

Firstly there were flowers in their hundreds. Vines, orchids, damask roses, wild herbs. Jasmine grew across a metal trellis, its scent pouring from the open trumpets like some invisible yellow fog. One corner of the roof even had a bed, a minimalist white futon under a mosquito net, where Kamal could sleep on the muggiest of summer nights.

The wine, perfectly chilled, was of a vintage and calibre such as I have rarely drunk. The food was a testament to Kamal's Slow Food credentials: tahini-rich *hummus* flecked with parsley, white mountain cheese, crusty breads, *mojadara* – a lentil-based dish –

and *keshk* – yoghurt with bulgur wheat. Beeswax candles glittered along the table. And at the head, Kamal was in full spate, declaiming the virtues of Slow Food.

'When ze Lebanese diaspora spread around the world,' he announced, 'our people forgot many sings about their heritage. Zey forgot zeir history, zeir language, zeir clothing, but zey rarely forgot zeir *tabbouleh* or zeir *kebbeh*. Food is our one remaining connection to the past.'

It was with these words, which had struck a deep chord in me, ringing in my ears that I wove my way later, somewhat drunkenly, through the narrow alleyways on my way back to real life. I had several good contacts scrawled in my notebook, a pleasantly full stomach, and I had glimpsed, if only for a short while, a little of the world which had once made Beirut 'the Paris of the Middle East'.

CHAPTER FIVE

TWENTY-FOUR HOURS AFTER the dinner party, after eating in somewhat less salubrious surroundings than Kamal's rooftop (i.e. a roadside stall), I came down with chronic food poisoning. Lying in my room, munching acidophilus capsules like Tic-tacs, I flicked through the notes I had made so far. There was a glut of it; my notebooks were bursting with facts about bees and honey. And since I was incapacitated, now seemed a good time to review them.

To begin with there was the basic question: just how is honey made? I had photocopied several pages of notes on this before leaving.

It all starts with nectar,* a sweet, sticky substance produced by flowers, and loved, above all, by bees. Probing inside the flower, the bee sucks up this sugary substance and stores it in a 'honey sac' – essentially a second stomach. Flitting from flower to flower until the honey sac is full, the bee then returns to the hive.

Back in the hive, the honey-making process begins. The bees masticate the nectar for some time (a process in which enzymes released from their salivary glands change the complex natural sugars of the nectar into simple sugars) and the nectar becomes honey. It is then expelled into the honeycombs – still in a somewhat liquid condition.

If the honey is to last without decaying, however, the water content must first be lowered. To increase the rate of evaporation, the bees flap their wings very fast, creating a warm flow of air against the honeycomb. (Nectar is 30–90 per cent water, but honey should be only about 17 per cent.) When enough water has evaporated, the worker bees close up the honeycomb cell by covering it with a wax cap. When the honeycombs are capped, the beekeepers know that the honey is ready to be collected.

All this, however, is a staggeringly labour-intensive process. Considering that the average bee will produce only about 1½ teaspoons of honey in its lifetime, it takes about 5,300 bees to gather enough nectar to make a pound of honey. One jar of honey is also the result of about 80,000 trips between flower and hive, the result of about 55,000 miles of flight, and the nectar from about 2 million flowers.

I have always hated science. At school I botched every

---

*From an evolutionary perspective, the plant's main purpose in life is to ensure propagation of its species, and the bees' unwitting pollen transfer is essential to this. Nectar may therefore be a convenient lure by which plants attract insects towards themselves.

conceivable experiment, exploded things with alarming regularity, and managed to exasperate every teacher unfortunate enough to find me in his laboratory. And yet, that day in Beirut, as I began to understand the processes of the hive, I found myself afflicted by a strange phenomenon. These facts and figures, the like of which had once filled me with so much dread, now enthralled me. Even though I was a passionate honey-eater, I had not fully appreciated how much effort goes into the production of honey. It was miraculous.

Having recognised the sheer toil involved in honey's creation, it also became easy to see why so many religions consider it such a sacred substance. For the Jewish people, the word honey has especially powerful connotations – it was after all one of the principal factors by which their Promised Land was described to them. In Hebrew the word for bee, *dbure*, has its origins in the word *dbr*, speech. Because of its honey and its sting, the bee is also considered to be an emblem of Christ: it represents his mildness and mercy on one side and his justice on the other.

But while we know that the former Hebrew kingdoms are often referred to as 'flowing with milk and honey', does the word refer to the honey from wild colonies, from hives, or from something else entirely? The historian R. J. Israel, in his wittily titled essay, 'The promised land of milk and date jam' (*National Jewish Monthly* 87), has made a persuasive argument that these references do not speak of bee honey at all but of a syrup made from crushed dates.

Samuel, however, contains a passage which seems clearly to refer to true honeycomb.

There was honeycomb in the countryside; but when his men came upon it, dripping with honey though it was, not one of them put his hand to his mouth for fear of the oath [Saul had forbidden eating until nightfall]. But Jonathan had not heard his father lay this solemn prohibition on the people, and he stretched out the stick that was in his hand, dipped the end of it in the honeycomb, put it to his mouth and was refreshed.

The famous manna which appeared to sustain the fleeing Israelites was described as tasting like 'wafers made with honey'. But since the Bible also likens it to 'dew', it may be that manna is actually 'honeydew', which is the sweet sap excreted by certain insects on to the surface of leaves and twigs. Bees often collect this instead of nectar for it is extremely sugar-rich as well as containing many beneficial vitamins and amino acids.

In the case of the biblical 'dew', it is now widely believed that this refers to the tamarisk tree manna, exuded in June and July from the slender branches of *Tamarisk gallica*, var. *mannifera*, in the form of honey-like drops, which in the cool temperature of the early morning are found in a solid state. This secretion is caused by the puncture of an insect, *Coccus manniparus*. In the valleys of the peninsula of Sinai, this manna is collected by the Arabs and sold by them to the monks of St Catherine, who dispose of it to the pilgrims visiting the convent under the name of *gazangabin*, which means 'Tamarisk Honey'.*

The sun reddened; halyards in the harbour snapped against their masts with the onset of an evening wind. And in my room, a wisp

---

*Botanical.com, Mrs M. Grieve http://www.botanical.com/botanical/ mgmh/a/ashmno75.html.

of coolness arrived, rustling the notes upon my bed. My stomach appeared to have calmed enough to attempt a brief foray into Beirut. It was time to brave the city again, to thread a path through the dirty streets in search of adventure.

I thought of Joan, now back in her home town of New York, pursuing her own dreams while I pursued mine, and wished, for a moment, that she was here to share all this. Typically, she'd never once tried to dissuade me from my quest, for she recognised that it was something I needed to do, a necessary exorcism.

And yet the distance was taking its toll, was weakening those supports that the accident had welded so tautly between us. I tried to ring her on an ancient pay-phone but the line was as silent as the grave.

I didn't feel like being in Beirut for much longer. It certainly didn't fill the prescription for wilderness that I'd determined on back in London. And besides, I'd already seen a Dunkin Donuts and, worse still, a Starbucks, outside which the chic Beirutis were eschewing their Arabic coffee, habitually served in elegant glasses, for a bland American import in styrofoam. It was time to move on.

But before then, I had a meeting to attend. Away from the city centre and the Place des Martyrs, in the back alleys smelling of sweat and smoke, an old Lebanon lingers on: a place of glass-fronted cafés and vegetable barrows. And somewhere there I knew there to be a beekeeping shop. 'Bees for Development', the helpful NGO I'd discovered in London, had sent me the address and wished me luck on my quest.

It was the end of my third day when I set out. I could hear shutters clanking open now that the sun was losing its ire, shops preparing for evening trade. There were hints of a salt breeze moving in from the harbour. I could smell roasting cumin and the oily tang of a recently peeled orange. Beneath my feet, the macadam gave way to baked mud as the streets grew poorer. Blue lilies thrust their roots through the oxidised grille of a drain.

At last I arrived at the place in question. It was situated prominently on a corner, but I would not have found it without the assistance of the taciturn old man, with a white beard and crimson *tarboush*,* who left his tea steaming to help me. Grasping my upper arm, with a delicacy that I used to reserve for leading my grandmother around her roses, he shuffled me forward until the shop sign itself was visible, Arabic lettering above a graceful depiction of a bee.

Entering the beekeeping shop, I felt a tremulous thrill. It was the kind of place in which one might find a treasure map, a labyrinth of untended shelves and boxes. A patina of dust lay over cedar crates, swathes of folded canvas, moth-eaten burlap sacks, an empty paint tin full of galvanised nails. And everywhere there were piles of old-fashioned beekeeping equipment: significant-looking apicultural tomes, rust-mottled smokers, queen-excluders, bee brushes, comb-holders, apiary barrows. There were feeders, travelling boxes, drone and queen traps, robber-screens, pesticide sprays. On the wall there was a fine old map of Lebanon in which the various sources of honey and pollen were marked in both French and Arabic calligraphy.

'May I assist you?' came a resonant voice.

---

*A fez-style wool cap commonly worn in much of the Middle East. It was introduced to the Arabs with the Ottoman occupation.

'Wadih Yazbek?'

He peered at me through his spectacles. He was a diminutive, pleasantly ugly man with startling sage-green eyes. His large jowls, which bristled with a hoary three-day stubble, gave him the appearance of a minor character from Dickens, a usurer or an owlish Scribner. He spoke a beautiful, almost formal English.

'*Al-salaam 'alaikum*. Peace be with you. You are the man looking for honey?'

I nodded.

'You will take tea?'

'Please.'

Wadih walked to the doorway of the shop and clapped his hands together. A grubby urchin darted obediently into view, accepted the proffered note, then ran off. Wadih dusted off two chairs, pulled out a small mosaic table and sat down with the unhurried grace of a man for whom watches have little importance.

'Tell me, sir. How long have you been working with bees?'

Shades of my meeting with Eva Crane flashed before my eyes. 'I'm afraid not at all,' I said hesitantly. 'I'm intending to write about honey, though. I've heard that Lebanon has the finest honey in the world.'

The plump mouth curved into a smile. 'Well, that is without doubt the reality. Lebanon is blessed with a climate and plant life that the bees like very much. Of course we do not produce a lot – barely enough for our own, let alone surplus for export, but this honey is of the very *first* quality! A liquid gold, my friend.' He took off his spectacles and polished them with a scrap of mauve silk. 'And may I ask who told you that our honey was so good?'

'There was a famous beekeeper in England called Brother

Adam,' I explained. 'In one of his books he speaks very highly of
Lebanon – particularly the variety of flora here. In fact I believe
he wrote that, in principle, Lebanon provides the best conditions
for honey production that he had ever seen.'

'Anyone who works in bees professionally knows the name
Brother Adam,' said Wadih matter-of-factly. 'A simple monk who
achieved pioneering work in bee breeding. And, of course, his
great genetic masterpiece: the Buckfast bee.* I have ordered queens
from the monastery in the past.'

There was a brief pause while the boy returned with the tea
on a silver tray. Wadih accepted his glass delicately between
thumb and forefinger. 'Well, let me tell you about honey here.
There are three main types. In the spring, an orange-blossom
honey – very superior. Deliciously white and dense. You will
find this easily around the country. Then, at a higher altitude –
around eight hundred metres – one may also find an oak-tree
honey. A pronounced flavour. Very prized here because it never
crystallises.'

'But what's wrong with crystalline? I prefer crystalline honey,'
I said.

Wadih held up his palms in meek acceptance of God's over-
sights. '*We* know it is good,' he said. 'But the Lebanese think that
if it is not liquid, it has gone bad. So they will not buy it. That is
why the oak-tree honey fetches a good price. Believe me, we have

---

*The Buckfast bee was the culmination of Brother Adam's work in bee
breeding – a good pollen gatherer, of gentle temperament, resistant to
disease and an excellent honey producer. Buckfast queens are now sold by
Buckfast Abbey in Devon and are prized by beekeepers all over the world.

tried to change their minds over the years. It is no good trying to convince such simpletons.'

'And the third honey?'

'Wild honey,' said Wadih with some reverence. 'That which is made above fifteen hundred metres. For myself, this is the more special. Different every time, you see. A bright honey of flowers and bitter herbs. The honey of my youth.'

'I understand your father, Rachid Yazbek, was a famous Lebanese beekeeper?'

Wadih smiled. 'He was a pioneer with the modern methods. And the last to document the old ways. He organised the first Arab Beekeepers' Union Congress in Beirut.' A flicker of sadness passed across his face. 'I would suggest you meet him but . . . since his heart attack he is not so talkative.'

'I have something drawn from his correspondence here,' I said, taking a sheaf of papers from my bag. 'It's quoted in *The World History of Beekeeping and Honey Hunting* by Eva Crane. Your father talks about the ancient honey-gathering that used to go on here in the mountains.'

'Ah, of course!' said Wadih. 'Mrs Crane! Another great beekeeper. President of the International Bee Research Association. A scholar and a friend. Read it to me.'

In the Baruk mountain forests of Lebanon, few colonies nested in trees, but many in fissures in rocks, most of which were horizontal. Every year specialist honey collectors went there and harvested honey. They were let down from the top of the rocks by a rope, latterly wearing a metal gauze face mask held in position by the customary

headcloth, and socks over the hands. The smoker consisted
of glowing charcoal on a flat piece of tin, and the smoke
produced was directed by blowing. If the entrance to the
nest was too small, the man might enlarge it by using a
charge of dynamite. When his bucket was filled with
honeycombs it was raised to the top by a rope, which left
the honey collector without any safety line and, on several
occasions, mass attacks by bees from a harvested nest
resulted in his falling to his death on the rocks below: one
of the places where the nests were found is named Sannine,
'valley of skulls'.

'Does such a practice still exist?' I said. 'I was very much hoping
it did.'

Wadih shook his head. 'Not for a long time, my friend. That
was a practice of before the war.' He glanced out of the window
reflectively. 'Happier times.'

'Is there any wild-honey hunting left at all?'

'I very much doubt it. It is not just us, the people, who have
suffered in this last century. The land itself has taken many
savage blows. And the wild bees, in consequence, have grown
quiet. Of course, we beekeepers make sure that the bees
survive – but in the wild, in caves and trees, they no longer
make their homes as they used to. The varroa mite has hit us
badly here.'

I was very disappointed. That passage had been one of the
principal reasons I had chosen Lebanon as my first stop. And this
mention of the varroa mite, so soon in my journey, was bad news
too. Varroa* was the worst thing ever to happen to the honeybee,

a parasite that has spread to almost every country in the world, decimating bee populations.

'So varroa is *all* across the country?'

'Alas. My biggest sellers are these strips,' he reached behind him, 'so amusingly called "Check Mite". They provide some protection against the disease but they are very chemical. I do not like being so reliant on them.'

'And what of the old ways – people keeping bees in clay cylinders or jars – do they still exist?'

Wadih rested his chin on his hands. 'Before the varroa, I would have said yes, certainly. In the mountain villages these practices have been going on for several thousand years. But this mite has caused so much trouble – it is everywhere – and it is only the modern beekeepers who know how to treat it. The oldtimers would not know to come to me for medicine, and anyway, it would be very hard to apply in those old cylinders.'

This was appalling news. 'So I'm too late,' I said disconsolately. 'No wild honey, no traditional methods. I'll have to move on to Syria.'

Wadih's face darkened. 'Syria!' he exclaimed. 'There is surely no hurry. Wait a few days. I will see what I can turn up.'

While Wadih was making his inquiries, I made some of my own.

---

*The varroa mite (*Varroa jacobsoni*) is an external parasite of honeybees that attacks adult bees and their developing larvae, or brood. It causes decreased brood, deformed bees, and a general weakening of the entire colony. The mite can spread quickly to other bee colonies by travelling with swarms or migrating drones, and by the movement of infested equipment. It is not harmful to humans or livestock.

I needed a guide, someone who could speak Arabic, a man who could take me into the wildest reaches of the country. One of Kamal's Slow Food contacts soon led me to Nabil Khouri, who ran a small eco-tourism company out of West Beirut.

Nabil, the only son of a middle-class Beiruti family, spoke accentless French, Arabic and English, and drove a thirty-year-old military-issue Land Rover with desert camouflage. He had the easy-going stride of an outdoorsman, was about my age, and smoked Bedouin tobacco from a camel-skin pouch. His scalp, shaved smooth to the skin, was burnt dark from his hours in the mountains and high passes.

We met in the Café Gemayze, a cool, tiled Lebanese institution where every evening the same coterie of greybeards cluster around the *tawleh** (backgammon) board, gambling, it is rumoured, for extravagant sums of money. Here the traditional clay oven still burns from dawn to dusk, producing steaming trays of flaky cheese and swiss chard *fatayers*, or the traditional Lebanese *mannoush* flat-breads baked with olive oil, thyme and sumac.

Over *mezze*, Nabil and I discovered many common interests. He

---

*Backgammon is thought to have originated in the Middle East. Gaming boards of 3 x 10 squares have been found in Egyptian archaeological sites. The game was known to the Egyptians as the Game of Thirty Squares or *Senet*. In Asia the game of *Nard* appeared some time prior to AD 800. The earliest variant of the game, though, may originate in the ancient civilisation of Sumer which flourished in Southern Mesopotamia, now Iraq. In the 1920s, a British archaeologist named Sir Leonard Woolley excavated Ur of the Chaldees, the biblical home of Abraham. In the royal cemetery he found five game layouts made of wood and adorned with a mosaic of shell, bone, lapis lazuli and red limestone.

was a nonconformist, deeply committed to environmental reform, and exuded an air of resilient optimism. He had a dry, iconoclastic wit which soon had me in stitches. We formed immediate bonds over such unlikely subjects as the poetry of Gary Snyder – he had a battered copy of *Riprap* in his bag.

Considering our closeness in age, it was also fascinating, to me, to compare our differences in experience. While I had been ensconced in rural England, reciting Latin grammar from outdated textbooks, Nabil had been crouched under a stairwell to avoid the incoming mortar fire.

'My father had the idea of rigging up a microphone on the outside window frame,' Nabil explained, his *arak* turning milky as the ice melted. 'If we listened carefully, it was possible to discern the differences between incoming and outgoing fire.' He grinned. 'Our ears became very sharp.'

'It's hard for me to imagine,' I confessed. 'Did any kind of normal life continue?'

'A surprising amount. There were periods of respite. For a few weeks there'd be no fighting, people would return to the streets, shops would begin to open. There'd be talk of my sister and me going back to school. And then, for seemingly no reason at all, it would all begin again, the night sky full of rockets and tracer fire. But life goes on. One learns to take pleasure in small things.' He held up his glass in illustration.

'But your family survived?'

He cocked his head. 'We were lucky. There was one particular night, though, when things might have gone differently. Crouched under that stairwell, we heard the unmistakable sound of an incoming mortar. From the first we knew it was going to hit. It was so clear. I still remember the tone of it. A kind of hollow whistling – like a "child's voice" my mother said afterwards. And then there was a huge explosion, white heat, smoke and flames, pieces of plaster raining on our heads. Thank God my father always insisted we sleep under that stairwell – it was the strongest part of the building. We huddled there all night, too afraid to move. And when it grew light the next morning, we opened the door to where my bedroom had been to find it was gone completely – torn from the side of the house like a strip of paper.'

There was a long silence. Nabil slowly stirred a cube of ice, floating in his *arak* like a miniature berg.

'So what got you interested in nature?' I asked eventually. 'I can't imagine you had much time for it while all that was going on.'

'That's just it. When the end of the war came, I felt a burning desire to see every bit of this country. To find trees and rivers; to meet those who were still living the old way of life. My generation in Beirut is so disconnected that way, growing up as we did. So I began to spend weeks with friends camping up in the Holy Valley, or in the mountains watching raptors. Many others were doing the same – trying to get back to the land, I suppose, in order to heal some part of themselves that the war had damaged. And while I was doing this, I realised that there were not a lot of wild places left in Lebanon, that unless something was done to protect them, ours would be the last generation that would have any kind of nature. That was a powerful sense of calling for me.'

I nodded. I had already told Nabil something of my own motivations for being here. What he was saying now felt like something of a reciprocation, a baring of the soul for want of a better phrase.

'Do you get much call for eco-tourism in Lebanon?'

Nabil laughed. 'Hardly. No, I barely break even in the best months. All of my customers are usually foreigners. The Lebanese don't give a damn about the environment. And now, of course, the Americans have invaded Iraq, which pretty much puts a stop to any remaining tourism in the Middle East. Lean times ahead, I think.'

'Bloody politicians,' I grinned, raising my glass. 'To hell with them all.'

'To hell with them,' said Nabil, raising his. 'And may the penis of George Bush shrivel to the size of a chickpea.'

We began to get quite drunk. Some Lebanese musicians struck up in a corner of the restaurant. There was a corpulent, flamboyantly moustachioed fellow on the pear-shaped *'ud*, a fleet-fingered *tablah* player, and a tiny, earnest man blowing a kind of double-reeded flute called the *mijwiz*. The empty tables filled up and the room grew thick with fragrant smoke.

'So tell me again,' shouted Nabil above the racket, 'you've come all this way to taste some Lebanese honey?' He roared with laughter. 'If you'd called me I could have just sent you some. Contrary to what you may have heard, our postal service is really quite reliable.'

I grinned. 'No, the plan is to taste it from the source. It's like you getting back into the mountains after the war – just something I have to do.'

'Well, I can make some calls,' said Nabil. 'There are environmental projects in some of the wildest areas of Lebanon. I've friends there who can make the necessary inquiries. And since I've not much going on right now, we can make a trip of it. You'll need a car like mine to get there.' He sat back in his chair and spread a cigarette paper on the table in front of him. 'Ah, it'll be good to get back out there. I haven't left Beirut in a month now – this heat makes everyone a little crazy.'

'Glad to hear it's not only me,' I said. 'I've never experienced anything like it.'

'This heat starts way down in the Egyptian desert. It moves up here on the back of a wind called the *khamsin*.* Beirut gets so hot sometimes people forget what day it is. Actually, I *have* forgotten.'

'Wednesday, I think.'

'On Friday I'm heading up to the Cedars, if you're interested. I've a conference to attend on soaring-bird conservation – but if you like I could drop you in the village of Baruk. From there you can spend the whole day in the mountains, get a feel for the country-side here. I'll pick you up when I'm done.'

'Sounds ideal,' I said. 'What are you up to tomorrow then?'

He looked down at his *arak* glass and signalled to the waiter for a refill. 'Since you are a first-time visitor to this country, it's my duty to get you drunk this evening. With that in mind, I have put tomorrow aside for sleeping off my hangover. May God make it a gentle one.'

---

*Blows from the Sahara Desert to Egypt for about fifty days each spring; called '*rih al khamsin*' (the wind of fifty days) by Egyptians.

CHAPTER SIX

FRIDAY. AFTER A 6 a.m. start, we drove south along the coast road. A strong swell from the east was ruffling the sea, pushing waves towards the shore like fluid blue steps. Even at that hour the tarmac was putty-like in the heat, causing the jeep tyres to squeal at every twist in the road. It felt good to get out of Beirut.

By eight we were in sight of the long elevated ranges of the Barouk. By eight-thirty I was standing in their shadow, suddenly alone. Nabil would not return for almost twelve hours. I was in the Al-Chouf Cedar Reserve, a 50,000-hectare section of protected mountain range, and I had all day to myself. There were wolves here and caracal lynx. And recently there had been a reintroduction of Nubian ibex, a large kind of mountain goat with powerful scimitar-like horns.

As I began to walk, sharp morning air in my nostrils, I felt more alive than I had done in a long time. Some distance to my left, a stream gurgled in its descent. Wild flowers glinted like fallen gems between rocks. The slope rose up steeply before me as a kind of challenge and I quickened my pace, anxious to gain some altitude and leave the road behind.

My first excitement was the sight of a golden eagle riding thermals at the crest of the gully. Through field-glasses I watched its sharp outline against the sky, the breadth and flex of its wings. It was a rich mud-brown, with spatters of gold across its tail feathers and on the crown of its head. It floated away to the west and then suddenly wheeled back towards me, its wings catching the updraught of warm air rising from the valley. For a second, I saw its eyes, cold and ochre-yellow, returning my gaze.

Thrilled, I walked on, increasing the pace, enjoying the feeling of my lungs working hard. A poem of Rilke rose to the surface of my mind – I'd copied it into my journal the previous winter during a particularly difficult week. Running away had been so much in my mind at the time. I had dreamt endlessly of leaving the city, all cities, for good – of getting back to the hills and the streams, of reconnecting with things. And now I was here.

Ah, not to be cut off,
not through the slightest partition
shut out from the law of the stars
The inner – what is it?
if not intensified sky
hurled through with birds and deep
with the winds of homecoming.

And here I was! Not, for the first time in many months, cut off.
The mountains beckoned me upwards. To the east, there were
glimpses of distant buttes, dark canyons and coulees, stands of wild
plum and juniper. There wasn't a soul about. I had a litre of water,
a hearty lunch, and a feeling of lightness that was more valuable
to me just then than anything in my existence.

I was wearing my usual walking gear: Old Patagonia trousers
with pockets on the sides, Lowa hiking boots (which see me through
metropolitan streets and craggy passes with equal facility), an old
T-shirt, no watch. On my back, a daypack containing a waterproof
smock in case of sudden rain, a compass, and my trusty Laguiole
shepherd's knife, with its handle of worn olive wood, which has
pared fruit, sliced bread and cheese, and performed minor surgical
operations in many locations across the world. Also bread, some
pistachio nuts and a notebook.

After a few hours' hike I came to a stand of the famous Lebanese
cedars, a representation of which adorns the Lebanese flag. Five
thousand years ago, large tracts of the Middle East were swathed
with dense cedar forests. Today there are only a few stands left.
The tale of this demise is recounted in *The Epic of Gilgamesh*, written in Mesopotamia somewhere in the third millennium BC. The
Epic remains a fine parable of human greed and an early plea for
wild nature.

It tells of a famous ruler, Gilgamesh, who, despairing of human
mortality, wishes to make for himself 'a name that endures' by
building a great civilisation. To fulfil his plan he requires large
quantities of timber and for this, he looks to the great untapped
cedar forests. The chief Sumerian deity, Enlil, however, having no
trust in humans, places a guard in the forest. Gilgamesh and his

companions, consumed by their desire for the timber, attack and kill him.

Then there followed confusion; for this was the guardian of the forest whom they had struck to the ground: he at whose words Hermon and Lebanon were used to tremble. Now the mountains were moved, the ranges of the hills were moved, for the guardian of the cedar lay dead.

With no one to stop him, Gilgamesh begins his terrible felling, an act which will change the geography of the Middle East for all time. Incensed, the gods respond by killing Gilgamesh's best friend, an act that further propels him in his futile search for immortality, and finally results in his death. As he lies dying, Gilgamesh mourns his own stupidity and wishes he had not cut down the trees.

Like all great stories, the truths expounded by *The Epic of Gilgamesh* retain a great deal of relevance today, especially in their proscriptions for human interaction with the natural world. The extensive deforestation caused by Gilgamesh led to the erosion and salinisation that would eventually turn much of the land into a desert.

Today, the few cedar stands left in Lebanon remain some of the country's most visited tourist attractions. In Lebanese folklore, cedar pitch is still valued as a cure for toothache, whilst cedar sawdust is said to put snakes to flight. In times gone by, the mountain people even believed the trees to be half human – a wholly understandable anthropomorphism, in my view. It is hard not to feel awed in the presence of such ancient and compelling beings.

A secluded meadow suggested itself to me as a fine lunch spot, so I hiked down through the trees, leaping over roots and boulders, towards the inviting grass. Once there I stretched out my legs and took out my lunch, a large *mannoush al zatar* (flatbread with thyme and sumac) that I'd bought on the way. It tasted of strong, clean grain, pungent thyme, olive oil, with a faint aftertaste of wood smoke from the oven. There is surely no meal so fine as one eaten at high altitude, alone, after a hard morning's walk.

At this height, the blood-curdling heat of Beirut was halved, and when I'd eaten I lay on the soft grass for some time, enjoying the tranquillity and the sun on my face. In such a place, away from all the competitive bustle of the city, it was hard to fathom how I could have fallen so low in London. What was it that had pushed me so near to the edge?

Several things became clear. The city itself was partly to blame: the pressures of too many people, too much stimulus and data-smog. Hadn't the accident and my subsequent confinement made me a victim of a deep isolation? Denied any truly intimate contact with the natural world, I was withering.

Wilderness, the perfect antidote, provides an escape for the mind in the same way that its landscapes provides a physical escape. Even a morning out here had proven as much. The act of walking appears to me a kind of meditation. It forces one to concentrate on the task at hand, narrowing the mind's arena and essentially resulting in an altered state of consciousness. 'I have two doctors,' remarked the British historian G. M. Trevelyan, 'my left leg and my right.'

I knew, deep down, that I wasn't the same person as I had been before the accident. The trauma had overwhelmed not just what

could be termed my 'self' but also the grounds of the self: I had
lost my faith in the world. Psychological studies of Vietnam vet-
erans show that even years after their return to normal life, they
are neurologically still at war.

And yet the hills were working a slow magic on me. I listened
for a moment to the gentle wind, and behind that the call of
bird-life and the whirring of cicadas. I felt like a clockwork toy
that had been grossly overwound, suddenly released of its
tension.

CHAPTER SEVEN

FROM THE FIRST, honey was considered a food of divine origin, a holy substance. While the Bible contains numerous references to honey, the Koran goes so far as to name an entire book 'The Bee'.

The Lord has taught the bee saying, 'provide thee houses in the mountains, and in the trees, and in the hives which men do build for thee. Feed, moreover, on every kind of fruit, and walk the beaten paths of the Lord.' From its belly cometh forth a fluid of varying hues, which yieldeth medicine for men. Verily in this is a sign for those who consider.*

Around 1371, an interesting book on animals was written by a

---

*Koran, Sura XVI.

man named Kamal Aldin Al-Amiri. In this he comments that 'honey-flies' are the only flies which go to heaven; all other flies go to hell. Another writer, Ibn Magih, quotes the prophet Mohammed as saying, 'Honey is a remedy for every illness, and the Koran is a remedy for all illnesses of the mind, therefore I recommend to you both remedies, the Koran and honey.'*

In Finnish myth, the bee was the creature chosen as the one animal emissary, whose task it was to transport the prayers of the people to the Creator. In the twelfth century BC, Ramses III offered fifteen tons of honey to Hapi, the god of the Nile. The ancient Egyptians believed bees were created when the tears of the Sun God, Ra, fell to earth. Even Plato expounded the theory that bees were the reincarnated souls of the righteous.

Of the many references to honey in the Bible, one of the best-known is that of Samson finding honey in the carcass of a dead lion. The subject of whether bees *would* ever naturally make their nest in a carcass is something beekeepers love to debate. Some say it could never happen, while others surmise that if the desert critters had picked the carcass clean enough, and the sun baked it hard enough, it might indeed be somewhere in which a colony could nest. This incident is the origin of the phrase: 'Out of the strong came forth sweetness.'

Whether the story of Samson is true or not, were one to find an untouched honeycomb within the emptiness of the desert, it might be reason indeed to suppose a miracle: what better food to sustain the weary traveller? In the 1300s, King Seti I of Egypt actually rationed his men with it when he sent a thousand of them to

*Hilda Ransome, *Sacred Bee*, p. 73.

the Silsileh quarry to fetch sandstone blocks for the construction
of his temple.

Full of energy, honey has long been considered as important
food for physical well-being. All Greek athletes were given honey
as part of their training regime, while Pythagoras and Hippocrates
both advocated it as an important ingredient for prolonging life.
Democritus also held this view and was in fact so successful that
he lived to the age of 109, at which point he craved death.

I was particularly intrigued by this link between honey and
longevity – I'd no doubt be eating a lot of it in the coming
months and wondered, optimistically, whether I might live to a
great age as a result. Further investigation told me that in
Hinduism a substance called *panchamrit*, used in many religious
ceremonies, is known as 'the nectar of immortality'. It consists
of milk, yoghurt, ghee, sugar and honey. Greek myth makes refer-
ence to a drink called *kikeon*, made partly of honey, which grants
eternal life. In the ancient Indian medical text *Yadjour Veda* (The
Book of Life) it is written that it is possible to prolong human
life by up to 500 years by adopting a diet of pollen-filled honeycomb. The great sage of Central Asia, Abou Ali Ibn Sina, also
known as Avicenna, suggested honey to be the reservoir of eternal youth.

Well, even if I didn't reach immortality, the outlook was good.

In the spirit of things, I took a jar of honey with me on what
would probably be a fairly strenuous trek. A week after my trip to
the Cedars, Nabil drove me to the Wadi Qadisha. This wild, inaccessible gorge, a kind of Lebanese Grand Canyon, marks the start
of a deep geological fault along whose floor a snow-fed river

hastens towards the sea. Looking down from the ridge, one can just make out the river's glint through the trees, as if a silver snake were scrambling for cover. And on a quiet day one can hear its rush, the sibilant hiss of rapids moving over smooth stones.

Because of this water source, and the natural facility of the valley as a catchment area, the Wadi Qadisha remains lush and green even in midsummer. From the moment of entry one feels something of its isolation, as if this were a hidden world it might never be necessary to leave. It feels like a rugged Garden of Eden – and one can see why its earliest visitors felt that such a refuge could only be heaven-sent.

The Holy Valley, as it translates, is so called because it has provided asylum to monks, anchorites and ascetics since the early Middle Ages. From the start it was a place where people went to hide from something, the Christians from their persecutors, the hermits from the temptations of the world. Maronites found their way here, as did Nestorians, Monophysites, Chalcedonians and even Muslim Sufis. They inhabited and deepened the tiny crevices in the high limestone cliffs, the Maronites even building a monastery there, Deir Qannoubin, which became the seat of their patriarch.

We had been hiking for about four hours when we ran into Ramonos, the heavy-bearded ranger with the enviable job of patrolling the Qadisha valley. Aside from his Arabic skin tone, flat nose and piercing mahogany eyes, he seemed the epitome of the woodsman everywhere, wearing heavy tan work trousers and muddy boots and carrying a thick staff.

'Kif alak,' said Nabil, who knew Ramonos of old.

'*Kif alak*,' replied Ramonos. 'Peace be with you. Is your health good? What brings you to my valley?'

Nabil explained that he was showing me round Lebanon, alluding also to my interest in honey. Ramonos listened patiently, then led us through the trees to a nearby clearing. A frail old man whittling a piece of wood gave us a wave as we arrived.

'This is Omer,' said Ramonos. 'My friend. He has lived here for more than seventy years. There is nothing about this place he does not know. He comes down here to the valley sometimes on his mule – to tend his vegetables, he says, but I think he likes to tell the old stories. I am a good listener.'

'More than eighty years,' said the old man, his eyes crinkling with amusement. 'I have never been sure of my age but it is more than eighty. I came into this world just after what you Britishers call the Great War.'

We sat down next to Omer, who had a deeply weathered face and pensive blue eyes. He was wearing a threadbare shepherd's greatcoat. Something about the old man struck me at once. He seemed to possess a manner completely uncontaminated by artifice. I felt, by some strange impulse, that a sage, if I were ever lucky enough to meet one, might give off a similar impression.

The old man withdrew a leathery piece of sausage from his pocket and used his knife to slice off a few chunks. Nabil accepted a piece, then repeated the details of my honey quest in Arabic. Omer listened, chewing dogmatically.

'Honey,' he said wistfully. 'A fine thing to look for. We don't get so much any more. But when I was a child there was always honey. Although we had many other ways of making things sweet. My mother would take grapes or figs and cook them down to make a compote.' He let out a high-pitched laugh. 'Even an old man remembers such flavours!'

'Where did your honey come from?' I asked.

'Sometimes from friends who kept a jar or two of bees behind their house. Sometimes from the cliff below the village. I can point you in the right direction. Cheer el Nahal – the cliff of the bees, we call it. There were always nests there at the right time of year. Men from the village would climb up there with fire and take it. It was a dangerous business.'

'Are there nests now?'

'One,' he said. 'I have seen it from the cliff top. But one is *nothing*! One is less than nothing. One is not worth risking one's life for. And besides, there is no shortage of sweetness now.' He cleared his throat. 'I'll tell you a little. About the old times. Back when honey was important to us. When I was young, this valley was a lively place. Everyone was friendly. We knew every family for miles because we all lived here. There were no cars – only mules and donkeys. People were strong and healthy.' He clutched his biceps. 'Big muscles. Life was very harsh but we were content. These days, of course, we have so much and no one is content.' He spat out a piece of sausage rind in disgust.

'For example, when a couple got married and they wanted to build a house, the whole village would come to help them. And equally in the preparing of food – we meet in the evening and share our dishes with each other and tell stories. And in this way, the passing of time was nothing – the blink of an eye. Now, even in the high villages, most of the houses are watching television. No one is talking any more.'

'What did you eat?' I asked.

'Well, there were not peaches or apples, to begin with. We ate
what we grew, what was in season. Even honey we only ate once
or twice a year. Even one spoonful was a great luxury for us. My
brother and I once fought viciously over one spoonful left in a jar
– I gave him a black eye.'

'I imagine people lived to a great age!'

He waved his hand dismissively. 'Psshh – cancer! If someone
got cancer in Beirut, the whole village was talking about it! And
now it is everywhere, in every place. Actually, we are in a bad
position here in the valley because the chemicals everyone is
using now on their crops wash down on to the valley floor –
they come to us. I have always said that the using of chemicals
was a bad idea.'

Omer rose to his feet and ambled over to the other side of the
clearing. With some difficulty, he reached into the lowest branches
of a walnut tree and gathered a handful of the unripe nuts. They
were the size of grapes and a pale reed-green.

'Hold these,' he said, handing me all but one of them. Then he
used the flat of his blade to prise open the shells. 'A Lebanese
delicacy,' he said. 'One of the tastes of my childhood. My mother
would preserve these in honey for feast-days.'

The walnut was sweet and milky. There was only a faint aftertaste of the flavour I was expecting. The old man nodded as he
watched me, smiling as he discerned my enjoyment. He retrieved
the nuts from me, one by one, and continued to open them and
place the meat in my upturned palm.

'And now I'm going to talk religion,' he said, stamping his boot
emphatically on the ground. 'In the old days the women were at
least covering themselves up when they went to church. Now, it's

skirts up to their thighs, tops with no sleeves. Where do they get such ideas? Am I the only old man this offends? My God, the young people these days. They know nothing! One tells them something from the East and they answer from the West.'

Ramonos gave a great booming laugh, so loud that several birds flew startled from the tree above us. 'I like that. Didn't I tell you Omer could talk! No one can talk like Omer.'

'Come and see my vegetables,' said the old man. 'I have a nice patch here. Carrots, tomatoes, potatoes, mint. They grow very happily in the Holy Valley. I think the soil is blessed by God.'

We followed him, beyond the walnut tree, to where a square of earth had been beautifully cultivated, lines of green arranged with geometrical precision.

'I love this valley,' said Omer quietly. 'We who live here love it because it has always provided everything we need – our food, water, community. We had no need of another world.'

'You were born here?'

'Yes. My mother was Brazilian – she came here shortly after 1900 to work, met my father and decided to stay.' He cupped his two hands in front of him, as if to indicate a woman's breasts. 'Children were all breast-fed back then, of course. Now they feed the babies some kind of powder. I do not think it makes them strong. What kind of world is this when a mother's teats no longer suffice for her own child?'

I nodded sincerely. The old man could not know what a chord his indignation was striking.

'And when they grow up, they do not want to stay here,' he continued, his voice trembling with emotion. 'The village is almost empty now. They go the cities, to the coast. They work in casinos and fancy hotels. They return only in summer – in their pickup trucks.' He sighed.

'Now you must see the cliff,' he said. 'It's a steep climb but the view from up there is perfect. Would that my old legs could carry me there one last time! And there's a hermit's cave with some paintings on the wall that you should see, too. I am sure those old hermits used to take the honey from that cliff – perhaps they even named it. And they would have made candles, too, from the wax. They needed light to read their holy books – and to keep away the wolves!' He laughed. 'Oh yes, there were wolves here in the old days. Lots of wolves. Come, I'll show you the way.'

After bidding farewell to Ramonos and the old man, we began the steep climb. Half of me wondered why we were doing this, considering it was no longer a practice to take honey from the cliff. But another part of me wanted to see it, as one might visit a long-uninhabited house – just to trace one's fingers along the old panelling, to listen for the ghosts of the past. If there was no wild-honey hunting left in Lebanon, perhaps I could envisage how it might have been, what exactly we had lost in making the transition from cliff to market, from forest tree to corner store.

Despite the greenery that shielded us from the worst of the sun, it was still almost forty degrees outside and within minutes we were drenched in sweat. Nabil set a fierce pace in front of me, immediately displaying his fitness in just such terrain as this. I followed as best I could, enjoying the trickles of water that dripped soothingly from the overhanging cliffs. Sometimes the way led us over small, fast-flowing rivers, or natural springs bursting out of the rock. Once we crept through a narrow tunnel, a dark slimy short cut smelling of mould.

As the gradient steepened, the rocky path narrowed to a slender ribbon. There was no question of surviving a fall from here – already the trees below looked like models, the mighty oaks like green florets of broccoli thrust into a sandbox. Ahead of me, Nabil was leaping from rock to rock like some sprightly ibex, while I followed up behind, feeling a burn in my lungs such as I remembered from compulsory cross-country runs back at school – a dreaded annual ordeal.

What was particularly amazing were the terraces that stretched away on either side of the path. Even in such inhospitable terrain, people had found a way to coax food from the soil, a patient levelling of the steepest mountainside for the sake of parsley, chickpeas or potatoes. I picked and ate wild figs as we climbed, and fished handfuls of watercress from the streams.

But there was no time for the contemplation of Lebanese agricultural skills: Nabil was now almost out of sight. I stopped for a swig of water from my flask, put aside the demands of my aching limbs, then set off at a cracking pace to try to catch him up. Around the next bend the path ended; from here on it was necessary to scramble up an uneven stairwell of rocks. I felt like a Lilliputian ascending the steps of a giant's castle. But at last I could see the cave mouth, a dark entrance at the cusp of a vertical ravine. It was just possible to make out some kind of structure, too – the crumbling remains of a Maronite hermitage.

As I reached the cave, the sun withdrew from the valley, bequeathing us a moment of blessed shade. The whole Qadisha valley stretched out below us, a wilderness of caverns and wild

roses beneath a limitless sky It was a haunting spot, inaccessible
to any but the most daring spiritual athletes.

'There it is,' said Nabil breathlessly, appearing behind me to
point to the cliff which faced us. 'You see those small nooks in
the limestone? That must be what the old man was talking about.
And *there* – near the ridge – there's the nest.'

So here I was, finally within sight of my first wild bee nest. It
was about the size of a car tyre, a dense brown swathe of insects,
and through my binoculars I could make out tiny flickers of movement. It was like a pool of oil disturbed by wind, trembling with
energy. But as for anyone descending the cliff to get at the bees,
it seemed an unlikely feat, or at least one which could never be
attempted without modern rock-climbing gear.

'You're wondering how they managed it,' said Nabil, reading my
thoughts. 'So am I. But how these mountain people are tough!
Even now, they live day to day, with great risks. If they wanted
the honey badly enough, they would have found a way.'

I nodded, saying nothing. If the truth be known, I was disappointed. My intention from the start had been actually to hunt honey
from the wild. But as this instance made clear, we live in a world in
which the value of life has changed. No family would risk a father
or a son for the gathering of honey, when they might just as well
make do with sugar, or buy a jar from a nearby town. Something *had*
been lost in the transition though – and not just the purity of the
honey. As the old man Omer had illustrated so eloquently, the modern
world has little room for rituals, songs or stories. Already these things
are fading into the past. And with them go the honey-hunting ladders
passed from father to son, the tools, the people, and finally the knowledge, the self-esteem – even the way of life.

We turned to explore the cave. The ruins I had caught sight of on the way up turned out to be those of a small chapel built into the existing structure of the cave.

'This is called Deir-El Salib,' said Nabil in a hushed tones, 'the Monastery of the Cross. The last hermits lived here in the thirteenth century. A very holy place.'

I drew closer to the walls to examine the paintings. They were flaking from the rock before my eyes, ruined by centuries of wind and damp and the cooking fires of long-dead hermits. They weren't masterpieces – even my untutored eye could see that – but they were beautiful, none the less, in their sharp-lined honesty, in the muted Byzantine lustre of their colours: lapis blue, copper green, saffron yellow. One showed the Archangel Gabriel, another a group of five saints. The third was too damaged to make out.

Closing my eyes for a minute, I pictured the artist at work up here, alone with his solitude and his visions of the divine. Like me, he had sought out this remote cleft in the rock in order to draw closer to something fundamental to his worldview – in his case God, in my case the landscape itself.

Kahil Gibran, author of *The Prophet* and perhaps Lebanon's most famous literary son, lived not far from Qadisha. His childhood was steeped in the countryside here and it would continue to inspire him, even after his departure for America. In one of his Arabic pieces entitled *Before the Throne of Beauty*, Gibran pictures himself taking refuge in a quiet valley.

My God state is sustained by the beauty you behold wheresoever you lift your eyes; a beauty which is Nature in all her forms. A beauty which is the beginning of the shepherd's

happiness as he stands among the hills; and the villager's in
his fields; and of the wandering tribes between mountain
and plain. A beauty which is a stepping-stone for the wise
to the throne of the living Truth.

For Gibran, expounding a worldview that is almost Buddhist
in its credo of interconnectedness, there *was* no difference
between God and nature – one was simply a manifestation of
the other. In every brook, cloud or mountain he found confirmation of the divine, and in this light he might be termed an early
ecologist.

I sat on the cliff top, looking out over one of the most extraordinary vistas I have ever seen. Is there a common thread, I thought,
between the hermit painter, Kahil Gibran and myself? All of us
are trying to make sense of the world we live in. All of us are trying
to articulate the relationship between the internal and the external.
All of us are simply looking for a way of being in the world.

Bees – some thoughts

From an evolutionary perspective, the bee is a masterpiece. A flying
insect with at least 22,000 named subspecies, it is capable of surviving at an altitude of almost 15,000 feet, on the periphery of deserts,
in burrows as deep as sixteen feet within the ground, or in the
hollows of trees. After humans bees are the most studied creatures on the planet.

Despite this body of learning, the relationship between the bee
and the natural world seems almost to transcend what science can
explain. We know that bees are integral to the process of pollination.
We also know that pollination is integral to the food chain, enabling

regeneration of about three-quarters of the staple crop plants that feed humankind. But which came first? How did flowers know to tailor their colours in order best to attract insects? How did the bees' eyes develop so as to receive ultra-violet light and hence see markings on flower petals, invisible to humans, which guide them into the centre of the flower?

And what of honey's place in all this? Honey is the energy source which sustains the colony throughout the winter. But it is also prized as a food by other creatures: bears, mountain gorillas, honey badgers and many more. All these animals, like humans, are drawn by the sugar, but how did their taste receptors become so sensitive to sweetness?

The love of sweetness, in fact, is almost universal among mammals. A scientist named De Snoo succeeded, in 1937, in getting foetuses still in the womb to drink more amniotic fluid if he injected saccharin into it, thus proving that taste receptors, and the human love of sweetness, are active before birth.

Part of sugar's appeal may be that glucose, the body's most important sugar molecule, is the only energy source that can be utilised by the brain. Sweetness also generally indicates a high-energy food. For animals in the wild (Neanderthal man included), the sustaining of energy levels is a fundamental concern. The association of sweetness with good-tasting, high-calorie foodstuffs is therefore extremely important. The opposite, i.e. the instinct to avoid most sour and bitter-tasting fruits because they are likely to be poisonous or not yet ripe, also holds true.

Today, of course, in a world overcome by candy bars, fizzy drinks, cakes and ice-cream, sugar certainly does not seem in short supply. In fact, on average, Western Europeans consume about

100 pounds or 45 kilos of the stuff each year. Many children eat more than their own body weight in sugar per annum. With that in mind, it is difficult really to imagine the value of honey to those early hominids. But we *should* imagine it.

Imagine a world in which sweetness is extremely rare. Especially ripe fruits contain a healthy dose of fructose, but aside from that, sweetness barely exists. Sugar cane is indigenous only to the Asian tropics, and the refining of corn or beet for its sugar will not be discovered for thousands of years. And then one day, you and another caveman stumble across something glistening, some syrup trickling down the rock. You're curious. You reach out with your finger and touch the strange stuff with your tongue.

Boom!

Your tongue, which is specifically designed to detect sugars – energy being close to the top of the list of evolutionary survival needs – goes berserk! Alarm bells are ringing in your head. Your brain reacts to the sugar by producing a wave of endorphins, pleasure signals, which burst in your cerebral cortex like fireworks.

What is this magic? Where does it come from? Is it from God?

Thousands of years later, the questions raised by all this remain almost overwhelming. The study of nature is so complex, meeting science at one corner, philosophy at another, religion at another and so on, that at some point it is tempting simply to give in to wonder.

But wonder aside, we should realise that this infinitely sophisticated chain, which makes up our planet, is not immune to breaking down. The consequences of human interaction with the natural world are well documented, so I'll concentrate on just one thread: bees.

Currently, we are experiencing something of a crisis in pollinating insects. In the late 1940s there were 5.9 million colonies of commercial honeybees in the United States. By 1995 there were only 2.7 million. This has happened for a number of reasons: exposure to pesticides, parasitic mites, the invasion of Africanised honeybees, climatic fluctuations and so on.

The situation is made more serious still by the fact that domestic honeybees service only 15 per cent of our crops. The remainder are pollinated by wild bees, wasps, moths, butterflies, beetles, geckos, hummingbirds, flying foxes, fruit bats, opossums, lemurs and many more. Most of these wild species are facing some form of threat.

And if the wild species go, then so will the plants. What would our planet be like without them? What if there were no meadows, no rainforests, no woodland? What if we could not pick and eat an apple on a summer afternoon, or have a glass of orange juice, or crunch peas straight from the pod?

As I gather these dispiriting facts from scientific tomes and the internet, I reflect that at least we still have honey. Despite our faults, the ingenuity of man has led to some undoubtedly beneficial inventions, not least of which has been the modern portable beehive, the invention of one Reverend L. L. Langstroth of Philadelphia. His refinement of existing 'bee boxes' in 1851 enabled a radical increase in the amount of honey produced per hive.

With the invention of removable-frame hives, beekeepers could also inspect their colonies throughout the season, and manipulate them to their own ends. Honeycombs can be detached with ease and the frame simply returned to the box to be refilled. Queens can be taken away to prevent swarming. Perhaps most importantly, in the absence of wild bees, honeybee colonies can be loaded on to trucks and rented out as 'managed' pollinators.

All this is good news for agriculture and a testament to human ingenuity. Despite the things we destroy, we keep coming up with solutions. And yet we are also the inhabitants of what is becoming an increasingly managed world. The 'wild' – that is, those parts of the world in which human presence does not play a part – barely exists.

I'm as enthusiastic as the next man about a good jar of honey bought at a village fête, or a punnet of berries grown at my local fruit farm. But I also believe it will be tragic when this is *all* there is. The best berries are the ones stumbled on by chance on a woodland walk, picked with stained hands and at the cost of a few scratches. By inference, the best honey must be that gathered from a wild colony, scrambled for up flimsy bamboo ladders, nature's gift for those who dare to try.

The magic of these experiences is at the heart of what it means to be human. They're about rootedness and connection to place. They're about economic self-reliance, and the inherent value of tuning the mind to simple pleasures. If we do this, if we savour the breath, the field, the stream, we are re-establishing our humanity step by step.

CHAPTER EIGHT

M Y CHILDHOOD LOVE of honey smeared on brown bread from our village bakery soon extended to a broader culinary arena. I first ate a baklava when I was about seven, after my father's return from the Middle East. This tiny rectangle of pastry, impossibly sticky and dense with nuts, was certainly the most exotic thing to have ever passed my young lips. I ate it before my father had even unpacked his suitcase, sporting the Arab headdress which was his second present, my impressions of the mysterious East unfolding simultaneously through taste-buds and flowing *kaffiyeh*.

Since then I have sought out variants of the baklava in numerous different locations. There is a greasy halal butcher's on the Earls Court Road where they make the baklavas themselves, packing them in tin foil in direct contravention of any number of EU regulations, and labelling them with ornate calligraphic post-it notes whose meaning I have never discerned.

Eight years ago, there was the gypsy stall in the mountains of central Greece, where an improbably bejewelled grandmother plucked a single square from a groaning wooden table and pressed it into my hand, her eyes alight with pride. Starving, after a three-day journey with no proper food, I washed it down with water from a nearby spring, arctically chill, and marvelled at the aftertaste of thyme in the Greek honey and the crunch of the almonds under my tongue.

I have since eaten baklava from Cyprus, Corfu, Turkey, Israel, Saudi Arabia, Egypt. Each country has its own version of the sweetmeat, its own cultural stamp of authenticity. And since the origins of this many-leaved delicacy remain unclear, most countries have their own legend of how it was invented.

One story credits the Coptic Christians of Siwa with its invention, in particular a man named Atemius Theodorus Calinkos who concocted the first baklava for the festival of the 'Thirteen Bikinis', principally as an aid to sexual performance. Its great energy-giving properties, combined with the aphrodisiacal effects of honey and nuts, made it the perfect food to accompany bedplay. It has even been suggested that the festival of the Thirteen Bikinis is the prime reason why the Arabs have more than one wife.

The Assyrians, *circa* eighth century BC, also have a good case for being the first to layer honey and nuts between a few layers of thin bread dough and bake it in their primitive ovens. If this thread of the culinary detective story is true, it may be that Greek seamen, travelling to Mesopotamia, brought the recipe back to Athens. There it underwent an important transformation, its pastry becoming thin and leaf-like as the Greeks perfected their 'phyllo' or leaf technique.

From there the baklava took on still more guises. The Armenians, through whose kingdom the Spice Route passed, added cinnamon and cloves. The Arabs, perhaps to refine baklava's existing potential as a confectionery viagra, added rosewater and cardamom. By the eighteenth century, baklava was long established as one of the staple luxuries of the Turkish harem, where specific male and female versions were offered in order to tailor its effects better. In Turkey to this day, a common expression, 'I am not rich enough to eat baklava and boerek every day', is still used by country people, testifying to its place as a food of the privileged.

The Lebanese, like all of baklava's myriad exponents, will tell you *they* invented the delicacy, that theirs is tastier than anyone else's, and that in fact the recipe was stolen from them long ago and deviously adopted by other countries. Whether or not this is indeed true is anyone's guess, but I can testify that Lebanon offers some spectacular examples, not least of which can be found at Abdul Rahman Hallab & Sons on Riad Al Solh Street in Tripoli.

I was in Tripoli for the day, still on the honey hunt, and actually en route to an old pottery studio, whose proprietor had been recommended to me by Kamal as someone who still shaped the large terracotta jars which are the traditional Lebanese housing for bees. After a frustrating week in Beirut, making endless telephone calls to beekeepers, NGOs, government agricultural offices, friends of friends' grandfathers, it was becoming increasingly clear that not only had wild-honey hunting totally died out in Lebanon, but so had traditional beekeeping. As Wadih Yazbek had pointed out, the oldtimers' method of keeping bees makes it very difficult to apply the necessary chemicals against varroa, the bee mite. Ten years ago, I would have found an example within a few days. Now it was all but obsolete.

But at last Kamal suggested that to find men who kept bees in jars, one should first look for the jars. He knew a man in Tripoli, he said, who still used a manual wheel and dug the clay himself from the mountains. If anyone was likely to make the traditional bee jars it would be him. And so it was that Nabil once again fired up the ancient combustion engine of his Land Rover, picked me up from my hostel in the pre-dawn, and commenced the 85-kilometre drive north to Tripoli, once a key centre of the Phoenician empire. And seeing as we hadn't had any breakfast, and both of us shared a marked partiality for sweet things, the conversation soon turned to baklava.

A visit to Abdul Rahman Hallab & Sons is the Lebanese equivalent of tea at Fortnum and Mason. Established in 1881, it is an ornate, polished sort of establishment, crammed with smartly dressed families, Lebanese old maids peering over their horn-rimmed spectacles; plump, cherry-lipped children resentfully wearing their best. The sound of noisy chatter hums in the air, an overtone to the cordial slurping of tea. And now and again, like a treble note piping over the thrum of the orchestra, one catches a smacking of sugar-dusted lips. On all sides, mounds of *knafeh, wared al sham,* or *halawt al janna* are masticated by happy customers. A hypoglycaemic stupor keeps the children from behaving too badly.

Nabil had come here first as a child and boasted that the baklava was the finest to be had in the known world. What's more, he was friendly with the manager (one of the aforementioned Sons, no less) and would therefore be able to engineer a behind-the-scenes glimpse into this Aladdin's cave. I was intrigued.

'You have, naturally, heard of Abdul Rahman & Sons,' asked our designated guide, Carroll, who was wearing a green and gold suit which made him look like a doorman from Harrods.

I was embarrassed to say that I hadn't.

'But we are sending *many* of our delicacies to your country,' he said, incredulous at my ignorance. 'Just yesterday, I shipped several kilos of *jazarieh* to a gentleman in your St John's Wood. And he has *already* called back to thank us and to request a bottle of pomegranate molasses.'

'A man of taste,' I agreed. 'You ship all over the world then?'

'Every corner,' he said. 'We are using the DHL to make sure our confections arrive in the freshest state.'

'I look forward to tasting them,' I said, scanning the room to take in the sheer numbers of immaculately turned-out staff and the mounds of heaped pastries which shone under the lights like cut gems.

'And now, if it would please you, a glimpse into our kitchens? I understand you have a special interest in baklava.'

I nodded.

'Well, I trust we will not disappoint. Our baklava is world-renowned. And we have been making it in this establishment for over a century.' As he beckoned me forward towards the swinging gilt-edged doors, I felt like the recipient of a golden ticket standing at the entrance to Willy Wonka's factory.

We entered a giant room. It was the size of a tennis court, and filled with enough people to form two separate football teams complete with linesmen and referees. Everyone was suited in white: white coats, white trousers, white chefs' hats, white gloves. Even their skin was white, as the result of a light dusting of the Syrian wheat flour that hung in the kitchen air, never quite extracted by the twin turbine fans.

The place was sheer madness, like a London restaurant during the peak of a Saturday night service; everyone was immersed in their work, manipulating giant spinning wheels, cracking and chopping nuts, shunting chrome trolleys stacked with spices and sugar syrup and pats of butter the size of telephone directories. A rich smell of baking pastry filled the air.

'As you can see,' shouted Carroll above the din, '*this* is the nerve centre of our business. Our staff are *masters* of their trade – which is important because the pace is very swift in here and they must continuously work, not only at speed, but to the standards laid down by the great Abdul Rahman himself, a baklava maker of *legendary* prowess. It is said he could roll phyllo so thin one could read the newspaper through it.'

An angular-faced giant strode into view, a 25-kilo sack of wheat hefted casually under each arm. Small jets of flour snorted through the hemp as his heavy-booted feet struck the ground. He grunted respectfully at Carroll as he passed.

Our first stop was the phyllo section, where a team of about ten chefs mixed and kneaded the flour, and purified water and fat to the exact, highly malleable consistency required. A trio of heavy two-horsepower whisks circulated through pewter bathtubs of dough mixture, making a low roar like the revving of a World War I bi-plane.

'Over here we melt and clarify the butter,' continued Carroll.

'Our butter is a very special variety brought straight from the dairy. As you know, each layer of the pastry for a baklava must be brushed with some kind of fat — principally to stop it cracking — so we go through many tonnes of it here. From there we add the fillings. It may be pistachio nuts — most of which we get from Syria — or ground almonds, or walnuts, or dates — most of which come from Iraq.'

I watched excitedly. I've worked in a few kitchens in my time, some of them the busy domains of well-known chefs with tempers to match. But none of them came close to the sheer energy and productivity of this place. A young girl scurried past us with a wad of towels, then a young man staggering under a 90-kilogram saucepan full of molten sugar. His face was puce, with exertion no doubt, but also with the sure knowledge that hot sugar is among the most dangerous substances to be found in a kitchen — we could hear it making little *tssh tssh* noises as it sloshed upwards.

After the butter station, important for richness and texture, came the sweet filling. By now the phyllo was drenched in butter and ready for its overlayering of sugar syrup, liberally drizzled from a copper ladle. Select varieties of pastry are also anointed, at this stage, with costly rosewater, for its subtle floral aftertaste.

Next, the assembly deck, where a line of workers who reminded me of tobacco rollers in a Cuban cigar factory transformed the trays of flat phyllo, nuts and sugar into perfectly formed parcels. By the look of things, all of them were gunning for repetitive strain injuries, their fingers moving in a series of well-executed flashes: a nip here, a tuck there, before the baklava was rushed on to a steel baking tray ready for the oven.

At the final stage, the entire parcel was brushed with a further dose of butter, spices or nuts were sprinkled on to the surface, and the baklava was then rushed straight into the giant deck and windmill ovens which filled up the far side of the room.

I was ravenous merely from watching all this, and by the time Carroll had shown us round the packaging room and the on-site laboratory, in which spot-checks for hygiene are regularly carried out, I was more than ready for an actual taste. Nabil and I returned to the seating area where Carroll promptly met us with two laden platefuls. 'A little gift,' he said, 'for you to try.'

Needless to say, they were delicious. Sweet and crunchy, a little buttery, they struck my taste-buds like a timpanist's drumsticks, an explosion of sweetness and decadence with the aftertaste of a sultan's kitchen. 'Exceptional,' I said, as Carroll waited expectantly, hands clasped behind his back.

'You're too kind, sir, too kind,' he beamed. 'But you must try also the *Faysalieh Kashta*, the *Mafroukeh*, the *Ghazel el banet*.'

I tried them.

'And now you cannot *possibly* leave without sampling the *Ghraybeh*, and the *Barazek*, and the *Namoura Extra*.'

I confessed that I was getting a little full.

Clearly, this is what Carroll had been waiting for. 'Full already? Impossible! Sir, in that case, let me offer the latest thing, created exclusively for those wishing all the taste of an Abdul Rahman baklava but *without the calories*! Very modern, very healthy. This we are *particularly* proud of!'

'A baklava in which *every other* layer is drenched in butter?' I suggested meekly.

'No, sir. Close. We called it *Hallab lite*. A selection of pastries made with Nutrasweet! They are selling very well with *toutes les chics dames de Beirut.'*

'I can well imagine,' I said, inwardly boggling at the concept. 'Another time, I'm afraid.'

'Just the one?' he begged. 'I promise you, you *will* not tell the difference. And your waistline will be becoming very slim!'

I shook my head. Having only ever previously consumed one baklava at a sitting, and now having just put away about eight, I felt a little unwell, if the truth be known. It was time to withdraw with as much dignity as possible.

Abu George's pottery is a musty, pleasantly cool building, situated on the waterfront near El-mina harbour at Tripoli. The man himself, the current master potter in a line that stretches back, unbroken, for three hundred years, is a stocky, mole-like fellow, with a hooked nose and tufted eyebrows. His complexion is terracotta-brown, he wears glasses with black frames. His upper body is not muscular but lithe, a potter's build: the arms always in motion, illustrating some facet of a story with wide, expansive gestures.

Sitting beneath a framed picture of himself with an enormously bosomed Miss Lebanon, George was delighted to entertain us. He sent his apprentice out for fresh orange juice, swept the clay dust from some chairs, and began.

'Tripoli, as I'm sure you're aware, has a long history of potters. I believe it was the Phoenicians who first introduced the skills of firing clay. And then, as it became a great trading port, under Alexander the Great, the Crusaders and the Mamluk Sultan Qalaoun, the potters here were able to refine their skills through their interaction with many different cultures.

'A long time ago there used to be seven great towers here, for defence, built by order of the Mamluk sultans of Egypt to defend their inland city of Tarabulus from sea attack. One was called the *Fakhoura*, or pottery tower, because the ground floor housed a pottery workshop.' His eyes twinkled with pride. 'In the 1970s a journalist called our workshop "as big as the British army" because we had so many staff!' He looked mournfully around the now empty space. 'Alas, these days there is just myself, my three sons and one apprentice. There is little demand for the artisan work these days, little demand, if I may be so bold, for *quality*. The market is flooded with Syrian rubbish – cheap imitations. And the people buy them because they do not bother to think about the long term, if their pots will last. All they see is that they are cheaper than mine. All they care about is money.'

I asked him about the traditional jars for beekeeping.

His face lit up. 'Ah! Well, this is another thing for which we are famous. Throughout history, people would keep their bees in clay jars. I suppose it started when someone found a swarm of bees in one of their empty jars and realised that they made a good home for bees – cool and with the right-sized entrance to allow proper air flow. But of course, at the end of the season there was the problem of getting out the honey.' His face beamed. 'You can imagine that one cannot spend all day scooping out the honey through this tiny hole – they had to be smashed. But it is a very dangerous pastime to be smashing jars full of bees. My God, this is most hazardous. In fact, in the old days, there was a man in each village whose job it was to do this smashing – an expert. And in return he would be given a share of the honey, which he would then trade. So it was a fine arrangement.'

'Good for you too,' I pointed out. 'They needed to buy new jars every year.'

'They did. That was until my father's invention. A fine thing for beekeepers, to be sure, but one which turned out to be very bad for business! He came up with the idea of making the jars in two pieces. It was the same as the original water-jar shape – but with a break in the middle. Ingenious, no?'

I agreed. 'And how would you make the pots?'

'Well, we have in Lebanon a clay which is like no other.' He reached behind him and picked some off a nearby wheel, kneading it in his palm lovingly, as if it were a woman's breast. 'There are four types to be found here: yellow, red, white and brown. We mix them all to make our secret blend. When I was a child we would go on mules to the mountains for it. In Lebanon, almost ninety per cent of our mountains have soil which is good for pottery. And not just on the surface – it goes down seven or eight metres!' He beamed with pride.

'What do you fire the kilns with?'

'Now we use logs. But only since the last fifty years. Before that there were no machines to cut wood and we simply could not get the amount we needed. In my grandfather's time they used wild bamboo. People who trusted him would give him the keys to their gardens and he'd get up at dawn every day and go into these beautiful gardens and collect what had fallen. Also he would collect twigs from the *bellan* bush – like what you call "besom". The cooking of the clay benefits from this type of wood, giving the finished pot a white colour. In this infernally hot country, people need white pots to keep their water cool.'

'The crucial question,' I said, 'is whether anyone still uses those jars to keep bees in.'

George picked clay from the back of his hand and let out a long sigh. 'My friend, we used to make two thousand of those a year. Then a thousand, then five hundred, then two hundred. This year I made only fifty.'

'Who for?'

George nodded. 'There is one man whom you should meet. He lives in Ham at the end of the Bekaa valley, right on the Syrian border. That is really a wild place. A Hezbollah stronghold. And he uses my jars for his bees. That is where you should go.'

Back on the road. This time we headed east over the high passes of Mount Lebanon, the rugged massif that forms the western perimeter of the Bekaa valley. At the eastern end, the Anti-Lebanon range forms the border with Syria. And lying between the two is the Bekaa, a fifteen-kilometre-wide strip, stretching for almost two hundred kilometres in length, which the Romans called 'the bread-basket of the world'. Quite recently (in March 2004, in fact, during the writing of this chapter), the *Washington Times*, expressing a more contemporary view, called it 'a hotbed of evil . . . one of the most dangerous places on earth'.

'The Bekaa has always been very isolated,' explained Nabil as his old Land Rover rattled over the potholes. 'It's trapped between mountains so, until recently, there was no easy way in or out. That's one of the reasons it became famous for its hash.'

'Hash!' I said, probably sounding a bit too excited for my own good.

Nabil grinned. 'That's right. As you'll see, it is still a very poor place. The only wealth they have here is their soil – very fertile. But Lebanon has been in economic chaos for so long that they were never able to make money from traditional crops. Every year there'd be promises of UN subsidies but they never materialised. So the farmers just planted what they knew they could sell. Of course you don't see it so much now – the government's made a big effort to get rid of it – but when I was a student we used to drive down here and see great fields of plants, seven feet high. Lots of guys with guns standing around.'

'George said that the valley is a Hezbollah stronghold,' I said. 'Were they involved in the drug business?'

'Without doubt. It's always been thought that the Hezbollah were the ones making the real money out of it – to fund their military activity. And of course they have the connections to distribute it.'

I asked, as offhandedly as possible, if there were still many Hezbollah in the Bekaa.

'Of course. While Israel is still fucking with us, there'll be Hezbollah.'

'Are you saying you approve of the Hezbollah?'

Nabil shrugged. 'Of course not. I'm from a Christian family and the Hezbollah are Muslim, so we were on opposite sides during the war. And I'll never support people who use violence. But the fact is that Israel is a country which has behaved without any morality, which has forcibly occupied Palestinian lands, and which continues to use aggressive military force against the Lebanon. Hezbollah's stand against that I can understand, if not condone.' He sparked one of his strong roll-up cigarettes and exhaled thoughtfully. 'In our first conversation, we spoke of a mutual love of the poetry of Gary Snyder. That was an unlikely coincidence – not many people read him in Lebanon. Someone once asked *him* if he had a political position and his reply struck me very deeply. *My political position is to be a spokesman for wild nature*, he said. Now that's an attitude I've adopted for myself. Everything else I leave to other people.'

I gazed out of the window at a wilderness of shale and sun-baked earth. As we penetrated further into the Bekaa, ragged shanty towns of plastic and animal skins sprang up on either side of the road. Wild-looking children peered at us as we passed, their faces covered in flies. Emaciated mules scraped their hooves through the hot dust. These were migrant farm-workers, said Nabil, who arrived from Syria every summer to harvest sugarbeet, sunflowers, grapes or tomatoes. I could see them in the fields as we sped by, clad in black and with cloth drawn tightly over their faces, bent double under the scorching sun.

'Are they Bedouin?' I asked.

'Some. Others are *Dom* – gypsies – although they would probably tell you they were Bedouin if you asked them. There are thousands of them here, principally in the Bekka. Some people call them "Nawar" – a term of contempt in Arabic. They are an insular tribe, mostly nomadic. They have their own language, customs, their own music.'

'Out of curiosity, how much would they earn per day out here?'

'About seven dollars. Maybe ten.'

'Christ, how do they stand the heat?'

'I really don't know,' said Nabil. 'Hell, you should be here in winter. It's almost as harsh. There can be deep snow here. And a north wind comes down which the locals say can break nails. I believe them.'

Up ahead we saw an army checkpoint. Nabil braked to a crawl as we approached.

'Syrian army,' he whispered as a sullen boy who looked about eighteen strode towards us, shouldering his RPK machine-gun. 'They maintain a strong presence in the valley – always with an eye on Israel, of course. They long to reclaim the Golan Heights.'

There was a tap on the window. The boy, his eyes glazed from the intense heat, peered suspiciously into the Land Rover, as if he half-expected there to be a grenade-launcher strewn casually across the back seat. Nabil wound down the window and explained (he later told me) that I was a beekeeping expert visiting Lebanon to learn about Middle East apiculture. The soldier looked suitably placated by the response and waved us through.

We drove on, brief glimpses of the barren Anti-Lebanon range (outlines of burnt hills) appearing through the haze. We stopped for water in a one-horse village, desolate in the midday sun.

'I have to admit this is a somewhat frightening place,' muttered Nabil. 'I've never been out here before. I believe there used to be Hezbollah training camps out here, run by the Iranian revolutionary guards.'

As if in confirmation, my eyes caught sight of a crumbling wall graffitied with a yellow and green flag: a fist brandishing a Kalashnikov against a globe. The symbol of Hezbollah.

'I'm sure you know this,' muttered Nabil, 'but make sure you are never identified as an American out here. The Hezbollah have a slogan, "Death to America". And I'm not saying that applies to tourists or even . . . beekeepers, but one never knows.'

'Hell, Nabil, I'm just looking for honey,' I said humorously, more for my own reassurance than anything else. 'Perhaps we should get back on the road.'

Nabil went into the only shop that appeared to be open, found out exactly how far away we were from the village of Ham, and brought us some water.

'We're not far,' he said, 'only half an hour away.'

Evening was almost upon us as we reached the small village of Ham, a striking patch of green within an otherwise beige landscape. The light was drawing apart in large grains as the sun dropped, the spectrum of colour narrowing. Pulling over a declivitous ridge, there was a moment of panic as our wheels lost purchase on the track. For a second I seriously thought that we were heading over the cliff edge. While I invoked the gods of every faith, Nabil expertly guided the Land Rover back on course, never once losing his cool.

A stone bridge marked the beginning of the settlement. I was dismayed to see the sparkling river below – surely a lifeline for such a community – choked with plastic bags, leaking detergent tins and rusting pipes. In fact, in all my time in the Middle East, I couldn't help but notice an almost complete absence of environmental sensibility. Even on the most pristine hillsides, locals dump their old televisions and the wrecks of cars. And when a can of drink is finished, the only logical place for it to go seems to be out of the car window. It suggests a mental distinction between their own spheres and wilderness – as if nature was in some way 'other' to their own existence. How to explain this? Is it a legacy of the times they've lived through – some recalibration of priorities in the wake of conflict?

But we were not here to ponder culturally specific litter habits. We were here to find an ancient method of keeping bees that stretches back through history to the time, perhaps, when man first evolved into domesticity. The paintings and drawings at the Sun temple of Ne-user-re near Cairo, dated at 2500 BC, show workers blowing smoke into hives resembling large clay jars. At the rock tomb of Memi, located at El Hawawish in Egypt, archaeologists unearthed thirty-six coarse jars with small holes in the bottom – a bee entrance – from 2400 BC. These are the earliest proven documentations of such a practice but it is likely that it stretches back a great deal further.

We stopped by an almond tree laden with nuts. Many of the branches draped right over into the road and it was just too tempting not to pick a few. The green or unripe almond is a great delicacy in the Middle East, appearing on the trees as a small green bud after the blossoms fall in March; one often sees barrows of them wheeled through the streets. Inside the soft shell is a translucent jelly sac that tastes like a lychee with a faint almond flavour. Somewhat embarrassingly, we were busy munching on our illicit hoard when a wiry fellow in his early twenties, wearing a *kaffiyeh*, caught sight of us.

'*Masaa al Khair*,' he said, coming breathlessly up to the window. '*Al-salaam 'alaikum*.'

Nabil swallowed the last of his almond with a gulp. '*Wa'alaikum asalaam*. We have a meeting with the mayor,' he said in Arabic. 'Which way is his house?'

'I'm his nephew,' said the man. 'I would be honoured to take you there.'

He hopped into the back and we drove slowly up the track, stopping for scraggy chickens. A young child was leading a mule laden with water-pots.

The mayor's house was over the next hill. At least six men were sitting at a rickety table in front when we arrived, sipping coffee from small glasses, catching up with the latest gossip and blowing clouds of smoke. Three of them were dressed in the traditional tribal garb, long robes and headdress. They all rose to their feet.

'We've come about the beehives,' said Nabil.

'Of course you have,' said one of the men, 'we have been expecting you. A great honour to have you here.'

The formerly tranquil scene became frenetic. Women flocked from the house like birds and cleared away the ashtrays and coffee. Others carried the furniture back into the house, promptly as stage-hands, and swept the area clean with besoms.

'Let us sit inside,' said the mayor graciously. 'It will be cooler.'

We reconvened in the front room of the house – a large building to be sure, but architecturally sterile; it looked like a disused hospital with its long clinical rooms and cast-iron furniture. I made the mistake, in fact, of voicing this thought to one of the men.

'Hospital!' he spat. 'No, my friend, this is the mayor's house. A very important man.'

'Absolutely,' I agreed. 'I just meant that it looks like it was built for some functional purpose.'

'Certainly not,' repeated the man coldly. 'This has always been the mayor's house.'

I was directed to the sofa, where I sat nervously, flanked by two of the tribesmen. Both of them took out worry beads and began to draw the worn cedar through their fingers. Everyone but myself was smoking. The mayor, perhaps as an indication of rank, favoured American Marlboro reds, while the others pinched loose tobacco from their hip pouches. The gentleman on my left seemed to have perfected a technique which would allow him to roll a cigarette in a hurricane. He laid the paper in the crack between his thumb and forefinger, added a pinch of leaf, then rammed both tobacco and paper down into it, as if he were trying to force it through the gap. A flick of the tongue, then the finished article dropped through into the palm of the hand: a perfectly rolled cylinder. Nabil, a fairly hardy smoker in his own right, accepted one, then broke out into a fit of coughing. 'That's like smoking straw,' he wheezed. 'Straw soaked in petrol.'

'Yes, *first-quality* tobacco, this,' said one of the tribesmen, grinning. 'From my farm.'

'Let us talk about honey,' said the mayor, with the air of an interviewer opening proceedings.

'How do you eat it traditionally?' I asked. It seemed a harmless enough question.

He smiled. 'There are many ways. To ask which is best is like asking which weather is best – they all have their uses.' He conferred briefly in Arabic with his friends. 'One way is *very* special – usually a practice of winter. My friends agree that this is particularly good. In fact, my wife must get you some to try. One cannot really describe this – it *must* be tasted.' He clapped his hands and barked some commands towards the other room.

Shortly afterwards, a stout, red-faced woman with a cigarette stub jutting from the corner of her mouth entered the room carrying a vast, somewhat dirty-looking honeycomb and a bowl. I will never forget my first glance at its contents. It was a gelatinous grey, shiny, with the consistency of wet cement.

'*Samne*,' announced the mayor proudly. 'This is Arabic fat – from the lamb.' Around the table, previously sober faces broke into expectant smiles at the sight of it.

My heart sank. So here it finally was – the moment which every traveller dreads (and which has assumed a clichéd though hallowed position in travel writing) – the confrontation with alarming foreign foodstuffs. My grandfather would proudly recount his encounter with a fish eye in the Far East. ('The key in these situations,' he would always caution, 'is to maintain a stern English resolve.') As a vegetarian, I had been lucky in escaping thus far anything that I could genuinely not stomach. But there is always a first time . . .

'*Samne*,' I enunciated, perhaps with somewhat less gusto than the mayor. 'And you eat this with *honey*?'

'With honey, yes. And some bread if you like. This will make you very strong for the ladies!' He gave me a knowing Monty Pythonesque wink.

Pitta was produced, the honeycomb dissected into fist-sized chunks. I reached forward, took a large piece of bread, a reasonable-sized piece of comb, and then, I'm ashamed to admit it, a rather conservative amount of the *samne*.

'No, no, *no*!' said the mayor, snatching the bread from my hand. 'Like *this*!' He submerged the entire parcel into the fat and then held it dripping before me. It looked like a bloated slug which had fared rather badly against a gardener's boot.

'Really, I'm not sure if . . . that looks much too generous . . .' I held up my hands in protestation.

In a trice, the mayor had pushed the entire thing into my mouth, an act so swift and insistent that there was nothing I could do but accept my fate. No more grotesque thing has ever passed my lips. It tasted – unsurprisingly – of rank mutton grease, and I could feel it inching down my gullet.

The whole room erupted into laughter. Had my horror been so obvious? Or was it merely a jubilant shout that I was finally lucky enough to have discovered *samne*?

'Another,' called one of the tribesmen. 'You *must*. It is *too* good.'

The mayor was like a runner on the starting-blocks. Quick as a flash, he grabbed a huge piece of bread and a titanic piece of honeycomb, and was once again dipping the whole ghastly package into the bowl of fat. Once again he forced it down my throat. I felt as though I was engaged in some sort of human foie-gras enterprise. Out of the corner of my eye, I noticed that Nabil was laughing so hard he was about to have a hernia. I quickly pointed out that it seemed unfair that he should not also get to try it.

'You mean to say this Arabic boy has never tried *samne*?' shouted the mayor. 'This is an *outrage!*' Nabil's face began to pale but it was too late. Already the mayor was reaching forward . . .

How long did it last? Despite the fact that honey remains a delicacy to them, reserved mainly for feast-days, I had to eat seven or eight pieces before they would eat some themselves. Honeycomb itself, don't forget, is formed predominantly of wax – a highly fatty substance. I could feel my stomach bubbling, restless as a lava pit. Would they force-feed me until I vomited? It was a distinct possibility. Finally, their attention moved away from me a little and they began to roll more cigarettes and talk among themselves. I have rarely felt so relieved.

Still queasy, I broached the more palatable subject of the mayor's smallholding. I had noticed a well-tended garden around the back, olive and carob trees, a few spindly vines. The house itself cascaded with pink hibiscus trumpets.

'We grow everything here,' he said proudly. 'Fruits, vegetables, cucumbers.' He blew a thundercloud of smoke. 'And every week we make the *anayi* – Arabic cream. We make this from the milk of goats. In fact, my niece is cooking some as we speak – you may have noticed the cauldron boiling as you came in.'

More cigarettes – I have never seen such committed smokers. Then we trooped outside to meet the niece, who was wearing a *hijab* and was stoking a roaring blaze under a large witch's cauldron. She giggled demurely beneath the veil.

'I milk the goats by hand in the morning,' she explained. 'From this milk we make *anayi* and also *halloumi* cheese. For the *anayi* I simply bring the milk to the boil. As it heats, the curds rise to the surface. We skim these off and serve them warm, with carob syrup. Or sometimes cold and eaten with honey.'

I felt a moment of blessed relief as I realised that *anayi* was actually ricotta. I had seen a similar process in Cyprus some time before. One more taste of anything resembling *samne* and things could have got ugly.

At this point one of the sons, hungry perhaps, or merely feeling a little left out, offered to lift the cauldron from the heat. But in his eagerness, he failed to consider that a cast-iron cauldron will have reached some considerable temperature after hours over open flames. With a shout of pain, he dropped it from a height, ran off screaming, and left us in a cloud of lactose steam, the coals hissing viciously, and my hiking boots smelling faintly caprine. The mayor, demonstrating the agility which he had previously exhibited when ramming fat down my throat, let out a string of obscenities and searched frantically for something to protect his hands with. There was nothing. He swore some more. Finally, alighting upon a lettuce in the nearby vegetable patch, he uprooted it, tore it in half, and used the wilting leaves as a slightly outlandish oven mitt. It was an extraordinary sight, and one of the mayor's friends couldn't resist a snort of laughter. One glare from the man in charge pursed those lips in a nanosecond.

When the commotion had died down, we returned to the matter in hand. *Anayi*. Fortunately, some had been saved. A bowl of curds and sweet carob syrup was thrust into my hands. And, though I didn't much feel like it at the time, it was delicious. Rich and sustaining, with none of the cloying aftertaste of cow's milk, it wasn't too much of a hardship, despite the protestations of my digestive tract. As I finished, however, a cup of warm milk was pressed into my hand.

'I simply can't,' I began. 'Impossible, I'm afraid. Very full.' I patted my stomach.

'NO! Very good. You drink! Very special!'

I had not drunk a glass of milk since my days at kindergarten. But it looked as if I was going to be drinking one now.

As we stood there in the evening light, the mayor finally remembered the reason we had come.

'The beehives!' he shouted, throwing his hands up. 'You have not seen them yet! *Quickly*, while it is still light.' He was off.

We trooped after him, leaving the womenfolk to clear up the mess, and came to a cluster of rather unassuming terracotta jars, towards which the last bees were reluctantly returning, like furry commuters coming home after a long day.

'My father kept bees,' said the mayor, 'and his father before him. As children we would look forward to the time of the smashing. Some years they would be full to *bursting* with honey! We would even pick up the shards of clay from the ground to scrape off the sugar. Our tongues could not get *over* the sweetness!'

'I've looked all over Lebanon,' I told him. 'I've made many phone calls – you're the only person I've been able to find still doing this. You must never give these up.'

He looked sceptical. 'The only one! You have not been talking to the right people, my friend. All of us out here have the jars. Are you talking about the boxes – is that what people are using these days?'

I nodded. 'One gets more honey, but the work is more.'

He shook his head scornfully. 'I have no time for such affairs. With the jars, the bees give me honey and I do nothing. It is a good arrangement. A mayor is far too busy to do anything else.'

'And this disease . . . varroa . . . has it affected you?' I asked.

The mayor looked philosophical. 'That disease has affected everyone,' he muttered. 'It's not like the old days any more. If I start the season with fifty jars, I end with fifteen. One of my friends has been helping me with some medicine – but it is difficult. I wonder what is happening . . . the bees seem to get tired, then they fall down.' He coughed up a wad of phlegm. 'I have lived through many things,' he began. 'Through wars, through much bloodshed, through acts of God.' He shrugged. 'But never have I taken sweetness for granted. One must be thankful for what God bestows.'

I nodded solemnly.

A bell rang some distance away. 'At last,' said the mayor with a grin. 'Dinner is ready. I am truly hungry this evening. That *samne* has given me quite an appetite.' He slapped me warmly on the back. 'I hope you have room, my friend. My wife has made something *very* special!'

CHAPTER NINE

A FEW DAYS later I was sitting in my hotel, sharing some coffee with Ibrahim, the ancient desk clerk, when Wadih Yazbek, proprietor of the beekeeping shop in Beirut, called me. I was grateful for the interruption actually – Ibrahim was insisting on a fourth glass of his violently strong coffee, and I wasn't sure if I could take it without risking some sort of cardiovascular failure.

Over the crackling telephone wire, I understood that Wadih had found someone still keeping bees in the old way. Since he'd clearly gone to a lot of trouble, I didn't like to tell him I'd already found someone still using the bee jars. In any case, as it happened his contact was in the far north and wildest part of the country, reputedly stunning, so I was happy to have an excuse to see it. What I craved above all was a cool breeze, a clean puff of air, a moment of silence.

Nabil, with customary goodwill, immediately offered to drive me. We had spent a lot of time together over the past weeks and become good friends. Many fruitful discussions had arisen on our long journeys: stories of girlfriends won and lost, tragedies borne, great novels we'd once read. In many ways we were very similar: born in the city but gravitating towards wilderness, politically conscious, scared of what the future might bring. I was impressed by his refusal to make compromises in his life, something which I was only just figuring out how to do for myself.

Some hours afterwards we were driving north to the mountains, past Tripoli, through medieval villages where men gutted sheep by the roadside, slitting them end to end with long curved knives, the viscera slopping from their bellies like jellyfish. Here simple mud-brick buildings with no doors or windowpanes were the places where people lived and died. Between the villages, the landscape would reclaim its grip, asserting in the visitor that feeling which is wholly lost in the modern city: that we are but a tiny part of a much larger entity, upon whose skin we are little more than fleas amusing ourselves in the void.

Tiny waterfalls trickled from the hillsides, licking past the stumps of anorexic trees stunted by the altitude. Ancient orchards exploded with cherries whose blood-red flesh often decomposed among the crumbling Roman ruins of which Lebanon has too many to maintain. Children as young as ten roared past us on motorbikes, or on one occasion behind the wheel of a car.

'Aside from mules, it is the only way to get around up here,' Nabil said simply. 'These kids are working for their living, they have to drive.'

We drove on. It was all uphill. The wheels of the jeep bounced heavily in the dry ruts. The axle protested like a wounded cat, its mew driving birds out of the dead brush like handfuls of tossed stones as we passed. In one village, a man waved us over to his melon cart where he pressed a dripping crescent of fruit into our hands through the car window.

'You Britisher,' he asked me, 'or American?'

'British,' I said. 'From time to time.'

He grunted. 'Tony Blair is not liking Arabs.'

I didn't know what to say. 'Not a big fan of Mr Blair myself,' I said. 'But at least he's not as bad as Bush.'

The melon vendor seemed to understand. 'Yes, Bush is worse,' he agreed. 'But Blair is also bad.'

I nodded. 'Excellent melon,' I said brightly. 'Are they grown near here?'

He grunted and strode off.

The road steepened, narrowed, and finally ended altogether. We entered the Chamois valley along a track which brought us to another Syrian army checkpoint. As we showed our papers, the guard instigated a rapid exchange with Nabil.

'There's a mobile phone mast up here,' explained Nabil after we were waved on. 'Or I should say, there *was* a mobile phone mast up there. Last week it was blown up with plastic explosive. Took out half the hillside. They're a little on edge.'

'Who did it?'

'They don't know.'

'This war's got everyone riled,' I said. 'American officials are beginning to refer to the Syrians as an "occupying force" again in Lebanon – I don't think they've done that for ten years.'

Nabil shrugged. 'It makes little difference to Lebanon if America pushes out the Syrian army through political pressure. Their real influence here is all through undercover: plain-clothes secret police and networks of political patronage.'

'Yes, but up here there are a lot of Maronite villages, aren't there? It can't make them happy to see armed Muslims everywhere they turn. It can't make one feel free.'

Nabil conceded as much. 'In one respect you're right. But much of this land up here is tribal. Feudal really. People's affiliations tend to lie with a local leader rather than with any broader political hierarchy.' He paused for a moment, then said, 'After all, what use are borders to them anyway? The animals they eat don't recognise borders, nor does the soil they grow their potatoes in, or the rivers from which they drink. Borders are for other people to worry about.'

It was mid-afternoon when we arrived; the mountain sun was casting elongated shadows on to the pasture. We would be staying that night at Al Jord, Lebanon's only eco-tourism project, a wild and far-flung place but conveniently close to the beekeeper I hoped to meet. Al Jord is an NGO, set up to help reinvigorate mountain communities weakened by the tide of Lebanon's recent history. Intricately woven Bedouin tents dot the mountainside, intended to house hikers and nature enthusiasts as a way of bringing revenue back to this inaccessible spot.

It would be hard to describe my first impressions. I was startled by the ambition it must have taken to set the project up. It was in such a secluded spot, needing four-wheel-drive vehicles to gain access, that the likelihood of it ever really making money looked slim. I soon realised, however, as I got talking to the men responsible, that money was the last thing on their minds. Like many in the green community they were idealists – they had chosen to swim against the current knowing full well that there were easier, less painful options, but the process itself had value to them.

'We all had regular jobs in Beirut,' explained Philippe, whose jovial face seemed at odds with his weary grey eyes. 'Some of us were volunteering on the side with rural literacy groups and so on and that was how we got to know some of these tribes. They brought us up here first about four years ago, to show us where they pastured their flocks in summer and' – he swept his hand across the landscape as if he were polishing a vintage car – 'well, you see for yourself. I mean, we did not know there were places like this *left* in Lebanon. This is the fourth summer I've been up here and I wake up each day just *marvelling* at this place, the kindness of the people, the richness and strength of the soil, the smells which the wind carries. All of us agreed there and then that we had to do something to help these people.'

I had to agree. It was utterly perfect. We were sitting in a large Bedouin tent on the cusp of a hill, seated at an old wooden table. One side of the tent was open to the elements, providing a view of verdant pastures, long sandy slopes studded with juniper trees, clouds tangible as chiffon. At one end the mountains rose up like a file of stalagmites piercing the veil of the sky.

'And it took you three years before you opened it to visitors?'

Philippe nodded. 'Three summers. No one can live here in winter – the climate is too harsh. Drifts of snow a man could drown in. This is the traditional summer home of certain tribes. They have another place, down in the villages, for winter.' He refilled my glass with sweet mint tea. 'But yes, it has taken a long

time. Tribal lands, you see. Many tribes. Initially we were working
with Ali and Hussein over there' – he pointed them out – 'from
the Allaoh tribe. They are actually from the sub-tribe, Minjid, which
is connected to the Allaoh tribe, and they gave us permission to
set something up. But the tribal boundaries do not begin and end
with any line on a map.'

'I was saying as much earlier,' interjected Nabil.

Philippe lit a cigarette and blew a dismissive cloud of smoke.
'I mean, half of the time the tribes divide land by some particular landmark – a white rock here in the north, a gully in the south.
And there is no paperwork, no titles or deeds to any of this – it's
word of mouth, or from some conversation many generations
back between two grandfathers. Everyone knows, basically, who
owns what but these are oral contracts. So you begin to see what
we were up against, trying to establish which land we could use.
We were not after ownership, but we wanted to make sure that
once we had built this place we would not lose it again. And that
meant taking a lot of time to get to know everyone, and assuring
them that they would benefit from all this.'

'Are the tribes friendly to each other?'

Philippe looked evasive. 'Well, we don't like to talk about it. But
in the first year there was some trouble. A knifing incident. Some
old vendetta. But little since then. And, to be honest, that is *nothing*
compared to the stories we have heard about the past. They are
strong, proud peoples. They remember feuds, as well as who their
friends are, for *ever*. Their sense of honour is extraordinary.'

After lunch, a salad of bitter herbs, radishes fiery as *wasabi*, and a
delicious paste of bulgur wheat, potato and basil known as *kebbeh*,

we set out to meet the beekeeper. Philippe knocked on the car
window as we were leaving, handing us an ice chest.

'You'll be passing snowfields,' he said. 'Fill this with ice if you
have a chance — for our drinks tonight!' He grinned. 'Up here we
live like ancient kings!'

Al Jord itself is at an altitude of 2,100 metres. Half an hour in the
jeep and we had gained another 500. The temperature felt almost
ecstatically cool after the furnace of Beirut. The beekeeper, Habib,
lived in a sheltered spot at the base of the steepest incline in the
area — one could see a dirty band of ice striped across its cap.
Despite the altitude, his place seemed to have something of its own
microclimate: there were an unusual number of wild flowers dotted
about. Two plants in particular seemed more than abundant:
sunflowers and the stocky purplish-green *Cannabis indica*.

'Are they what I think they are?' I said to Nabil.

'They are,' he grinned. 'Ten to one he tells us he's a goat herder.'

'And the sunflowers?'

'When the government clamped down on the drugs trade, they
tried to promote the growing of sunflowers instead. They're both
plants which are relatively easy to grow without a lot of chemicals. But of course the profit margins cannot really compare.
Sunflowers soon became little more than a useful disguise. It's an
old joke actually in Lebanon. Fayrouz, a famous Lebanese diva
from the 1970s, had a song. How did it go? "I'm being persecuted
by the government. I planted sunflowers, which grew into
cannabis."'

A small boy wearing a bright red shirt and a sequinned hat clopped
up to us on a donkey. He seemed to think he was in the Grand

National as he was switching the poor creature mercilessly. The donkey, its eyes impassive as a Buddha's, maintained its own pace.

'*Marhaba!*' said Nabil. 'We've come to meet your father.'

The boy smiled shyly and shouted for his father. A well-built fellow with an unusually prominent Adam's apple peered out of the stone doorway. His eyes appraised us cautiously.

'Habib,' shouted Nabil. 'We're friends of Wadih Yazbek – we've come to talk to you about your bees.'

'*Ahlan wa sahlan.* What bees?' shouted Habib back somewhat suspiciously.

'This man here, an Englisher, is writing a book about bee honey,' bellowed Nabil. 'Especially the old ways. You still use the jars, no?'

'Ah, *bee* honey!' said Habib, walking towards us. 'Why did you not *say* so?' He beamed kindly. 'You can see them from here – down there in the valley. Not much to look at. Just old clay jars.'

I peered at them through my binoculars. Not much to look at, he said. Well that depended on whether you were interested in the field of cannabis plants or not.[*]

---

[*]The relationship between insects and narcotics is an interesting one. Many of the toxins which humans so value for their recreational use are actually produced by the plant as a defence mechanism against predatory insects. Some plant toxins, such as nicotine, cause muscular paralysis in pests that ingest them. Plants such as datura literally drive their predators insane, while others, such as wild parsnip, cause the animals that eat them to become hypersensitive to sunlight. Bees, like humans, are better equipped to deal with such problems, principally through the detoxifying mechanism of their digestive tract. Unlike pigeons, whose flight paths become distinctly skewed after snacking on cannabis seeds, the bee seems unaffected by its encounter with narcotic pollen.

Habib was a rather savvy hash farmer, I thought to myself. With wild bee populations at an all-time low in the Middle East, he had taken matters into his own hands to ensure a healthy crop. Similar practices occur in America – albeit on a much larger scale and with more conventional crops. Modern 'cowboy'-style beekeepers migrate with their bees, following the bloom north in summer, south in winter. Beekeepers rent their pollinators to the highest bidder: for apples in Wisconsin, South Carolina for berries, .Maryland for cherry and tulip poplar.

'Come in, come in,' said Habib. 'Our house is simple but a horse of good breed is not dishonoured by his saddle.'

Taking off our shoes, as Middle Eastern etiquette dictates, we entered a low room of the utmost simplicity: white walls and a floor of baked mud spread with carpets. Habib barked some orders and several small children staggered in bearing worn cushions.

'Sit, sit,' he said. 'Please be comfortable. It is not often we are blessed with visitors up here.' His voice had a soft and melodious quality, and his eyes flashed with intelligence. The veins which stood out from the lean skin of his arms and neck testified to an enormously active life.

'Cherries, Abdul. Bring us cherries in great quantities. I have an immense thirst.' Habib lay full-length across the cushions. Another son placed his cigarettes and a lighter within reach. Habib cleared his throat of phlegm. 'So, Britisher, what shall I tell you?'

I asked whether he saw wild bee colonies up here.

'I know wild bees,' he said, spitting a fleck of tobacco from his tongue. 'Last year I took three kilos from a nest I found in a juniper tree. Ahh, that was too good. And the year before I found a nest

in a cliff near here. But it was too far in to reach so I had to use
. . . a special technique to get at it.'

I was intrigued. Was Habib about to confide in me some traditional Lebanese method of extracting honey from small crevices?
'What method?' I said eagerly.

Habib drew close to me. 'Dynamite,' he whispered through his
teeth.

I couldn't stifle a chuckle. 'And was it effective?'

He grinned. 'Well, let's just say I will not be getting honey from
these bees again. I was perhaps a little . . . ambitious with the charge.
In fact I was lucky to escape some personal injury.'

Abdul now returned carrying the cherries, but in his right hand
there was something a bit more surprising: an automatic pistol in
a holster. He handed it to his father who laid it casually on the
cushion beside him.

'So your principal business is . . . making honey?' said Nabil,
suppressing a smile.

'No, my friend, I am . . . a goat herder.' He grinned.

'And the pistol,' I said, resisting the temptation to look at Nabil
after the goat herder comment. 'To keep away wolves?'

Habib patted the barrel and flashed me a wink. 'Jackals,' he said.
'Who come up here at night to try and take what is mine.'

I couldn't quite tell if he was being serious or making a veiled allu-
sion to the marijuana. 'Have you fought them off in the past?' I said.

Habib nodded. 'Many times. But there is also this.' He clicked
his fingers in the direction of his sons and pointed to something
behind the door. Abdul retrieved a well-oiled AK47 loaded with
a full clip of rounds. 'In actual fact, *this* is more effective against
the jackals,' he said. 'Why don't you try it for size?'

I shook my head. Guns have little appeal for me.

'You *must*, Britisher. Every man should know what it is like to hold such power in one's hands.' He gestured to Abdul who carefully pressed the AK47 into my grip. It felt very odd – like much too much responsibility for any man. I wondered if the safety catch was on or if a sudden movement might send a spray of bullets through the roof. 'And the pistol too,' urged Habib. 'Let's see how you look.'

I shrugged my shoulders at Nabil who was eating cherries like they were going out of fashion. 'You will be a very dangerous beekeeper,' he pointed out. I buckled on the holster reluctantly.

'*Wait* a second,' said Habib, leaping to his feet and peering at me. 'With that gun and beard, I *finally* recognise you. You are Hezbollah, Hezbollah!' He was jumping with delight, tears streaming down his face. He wiped them away with the back of his hand. 'That was too funny!' he muttered, still wheezing with mirth.

I was thankful to divest myself of the arsenal and sit back down.

'I've noticed a lot of cannabis plants around here,' I said. 'Do the bees like these flowers?'

Habib studied me with friendly intensity. 'Why not?' he said simply. 'After all, they are from God.'

'And does the honey have any . . . *special* properties?' I asked.

Habib shook his head. 'Perhaps in paradise, my friend! No, here one has to smoke them to achieve that. If you wish I could provide a little?'

I hadn't smoked since my student days. But in this high mountain room, with the doorway open to expose snow-capped peaks, wild flowers in the foreground and a bowl of magnificent high-altitude cherries from Habib's own orchard, who was I to refuse?

Habib clapped his hands – more children came in. He must have sired an entire clan for we never seemed to see the same one twice. He muttered something to one of them who vanished briefly before returning with a veritable brick of hash, which he pressed into his father's hands.

'Mother of God!' I exclaimed. 'Do you have any idea what that would be worth in England?'

'What, this tiny piece?' Habib chuckled. 'By Allah, I could smoke this in an afternoon.' He looked interested though. 'How much then?'

I made a reasonable guess. Habib began to splutter. 'Impossible!' he muttered. 'But if what you say is true, we must go into business together, my friend, *immediately!*'

I began to explain that there were certain risks involved, some fairly unpleasant penalties, too, if the truth be known.

But Habib was already counting his profits. 'No, my friend. God sells knowledge for labour, honour for risk. Nothing is insurmountable. Besides, I have very strong contacts – you will take no chances.'

I seemed to be digging myself deeper into a hole. 'Well, the first problem is that I will not be back in England for at least a year,' I said. 'Maybe longer.'

Habib's face fell. 'Ah. I cannot wait that long,' he sighed. 'Perhaps you have some friends who might . . .'

I shook my head. Habib cheered himself up, now that he was no longer to be a millionaire, by rolling an immense joint. We sat and smoked in silence, sipping tea, munching cherries. I became aware that I was holding tension in a number of places around my torso and slowly let it go. Motes of dust rotated in the day's last slanting beams of sun, like miniature planets in their own tiny orbits.

Time slipped by. Before long, dusk was upon us and I found myself blinking back geometric patterns from the gloaming. The marijuana was having a powerful effect on me – either because I hadn't indulged for so long or because Habib's crop was very strong. I seemed to remember reading somewhere that altitude has a marked effect on THC production.

Despite the stereotypes about hash, that it makes you dim-witted and obtuse, I've always found it brings me great clarity. One retreats into a personal realm, of course, and it may be this inherently anti-social aspect that has prevented it from ever becoming the social drug that alcohol is. But within that magical realm, of amity and intricate theories and sudden insights, the segments that construct us as individuals slide into focus.

I had a sudden sense of déjà vu on the floor of that mountain hut. Some element of this place seemed familiar to me. I racked my brains. And then I had it. I'd dreamt of a room like this during the first grim days after the accident. Back then, so frail and remote from the freedom I craved, I'd dreamt of a time when I could re-enter the world again, explore new realms, sit in far-off shepherds' huts with the clouds at my feet. And here I was.

'We should go,' said Nabil. 'Got to get that ice before dark.'

'No, no, NO!' said Habib. 'Now is the time for *eating*. My wife is just bringing it. There is no question of you leaving just now.'

I sank back down into the cushion. Once I might have been surprised by this, even made some attempt at protestation, but as any visitor to the Arab world will tell you, that urge soon wears off. The Arab sense of hospitality is overwhelmingly strong; refusal is nothing less than an insult.

A clucking, dark-skinned woman in a *hijab* bustled in, straining under an enormous silver tray. *Hummus, labne, baba ghanouj, tabbouleh,* sliced cucumbers and radishes, grilled *halloumi,* garlic in oil, bitter greens in garlic and oil, skewered chicken, yoghurt, steaming pitta, a sweet jam made of aubergines and sugar. I knew full well that this was an unusually extravagant spread, but delivered with such utter benevolence, such pride, such meticulous attention to detail, that I could do nothing but tuck in. An empty plate was the greatest honour I could accord them. And unlike the *samne* incident, to comply was nothing but pleasure.

We finished the feast with a simple square of honeycomb. Golden, fragrant with high-mountain herbs, it imparted a burst of sweetness that was very close to perfection. This was, in effect, marijuana honey, I thought to myself. But whatever the nectar source, no other food could have conveyed such a sense of place, or embodied with such precision the complex web of life that existed on this mountain landscape. Every flower was represented here, every patter of rain.

It was dark when we staggered out. The temperature had dropped rapidly and our breath made hoary vapour trails in the air. If we had arrived as strangers, we were leaving as close family. Habib made us promise to return soon, his wife pressing a package of fresh *halloumi* wrapped in mint leaves into my hand. I was deeply touched.

An egg-white moon was out. Weird shapes and forms swayed on the mountainside. I was pleasantly full, a little stoned, but as wide awake as I have ever been. We were driving higher still in our search for clean snow, Nabil wrestling with the wheel like the tiller of a ship during high wind. I listened to the revs carefully, and watched the gradient gauge on the dashboard through one eye – it would be all too easy to topple.

'Stop worrying,' said Nabil, sensing my unease. 'I've driven this jeep over ground like this before. Steeper maybe.'

'At night?' I ventured.

'Well, perhaps not strictly at night. Late afternoon, certainly.'

At last we reached a point where we could go no further. Just a few feet away lay a vast snowfield, curving upwards into the night sky like the plumage of a white owl beaded with rime. Nabil retrieved a shovel from the boot, I took the ice chest, and we stepped up together on to that mysterious plateau, as if we were astronauts broaching some new cosmos.

We could have stopped on the edge but we didn't. Instead, in unspoken agreement, we crunched on up into the night, slipping from time to time, enjoying the brittle sounds of the ice under our boots and the crusty texture of the frozen water molecules. The air was so pure and intense, each breath seemed to trigger small shockwaves in the cerebral cortex. Would I ever smell something this pure again? Would I ever again feel this alive?

I couldn't hold it in any longer. With all the power of my lungs I gave a great whoop of rapture that was just about the inexpressible delight of being alive. It gathered in a great roar and moved out across the empty valley where it echoed once and was gone.

CHAPTER TEN

I HAD HOPED for a revelation on the road to Damascus. Instead, I endured eight hours on a bus which threatened, at any moment, to come apart like a ball of poorly wound string. My seat was situated next to the bus's large double doors, permanently open due to a broken mechanism, so that every jolt threatened not merely to dislodge me but to toss me right into the traffic. Add to that a heatwave which put the mercury at forty-eight degrees and rising, a fifteen-year-old driver for whom the term road rage may have actually been invented, and an encounter with a customs official so gruff that I might as well have been George Bush himself, wearing an Uncle Sam hat in lurid Stars and Stripes.

To be fair, I didn't blame the customs officer for his attitude towards me. With the weapons inspectors in Iraq still empty-handed, the ideological machines of the West were turning their attention towards Iraq's southern neighbour. The charges against Syria also included developing biological and chemical weapons of their own, condemning the US occupation of Iraq, supporting international terrorism and succouring anti-US and anti-Israeli guerrilla forces. Officials were in the process of recommending sanctions which would include reducing diplomatic contacts with Syria, banning US exports (except food and medicine), prohibiting US businesses from investing or operating in Syria, restricting the travel of Syrian diplomats in the US, banning Syrian aircraft from operating in the US, and freezing Syrian assets there.

It was not exactly perfect timing on my part. Only a fool would thinking of going to Syria in midsummer under normal circumstances (it can be one of the hottest places on earth), let alone in the direct aftermath of the American/Iraqi war. But I was keen to continue down the honey trail, and craving the absolute emptiness which I associated with the desert. I had never seen desert before, but I thought of it as a kind of tangible absence, a landscape in which there was no need to invest meaning. I imagined myself standing alone under a burning cerulean sky, finally laying some of my demons to rest.

After the blandness of Beirut, part of me was also very much looking forward to a taste of the real Arabia, a land I'd read about in Thesiger and Freya Stark. Syria, I knew, had assiduously kept out American influence – banning Coca-Cola, McDonald's and their ilk, and even forbidding the use of internet sites like Yahoo and Hotmail. All this, in fact, boded quite well. But little had prepared me for the sense of isolation these barriers imposed. From the first, I felt this to be a country of extremes: climatic, political, religious, socio-economic. And although this, in part, was a legacy of the Western media on which I'd been weaned, and in many cases not true at all, I could never shake off a sense of unease in Syria – the heat seemed to magnify all my anxieties, as if the sky were a magnifying glass and I a hapless insect, pooled within a boiling centre.

I'd heard many rumours about President Bashar Al-Assad, of course – they were staple gossip on the backpacker scene – all of them unpleasant. He was a corrupt Ba'athist dictator, deeply hostile to the West, and with a fairly active *mukhabarat* (secret police) whose interrogation techniques were of an almost legendary inventiveness. Although he had made some efforts to give a gentler face to the regime he inherited from his father, the government's legacy of brutality in the face of internal challenges to its authority is largely unshaken. Its February 1982 massacre of up to 20,000 people in Hama, Syria's fourth-largest city, remains deeply imbedded in Syrian popular consciousness.

Damascus is a vast, overpopulated city, filled with too many cars and the kind of architecture which one commonly associates with refugee camps: all breeze blocks and stressed concrete. It is flanked on three sides by desert hills, and on the fourth by the desert itself: a long, unvaried expanse of scorching dry sand.

Finding a room turned out to be a nightmare. For some unidentifiable reason, all the cheap hotels were full, so I ended up on the eighth floor of a crumbling tower-block, tucked behind a boiler room which reeked alarmingly of petrol. As rooms go, it was one of the worst I have ever seen. Its nicotine-yellow paint flaked from the wall like a leper's skin in the final stages of the disease. Its skirting boards contained enough holes to allow free access to a

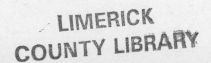

mob of exuberantly healthy cockroaches. The air-conditioning unit, a lifeline in this burning heat, sounded like a rusted Howitzer when I turned it on and, if anything, actually increased the temperature in the room.

It was early evening when I took my first stroll in the city. Visually, I struggled to find purchase here; there was nothing in the architecture to inspire or provoke the eye. Only the odd minaret relieved the skyline of its disarray – elsewhere there were rows of rotting tenements, the odd sand and mud box recalling a vanishing way of life. But, at least the day's heat was ebbing. And in the distance the muezzin was calling for evening prayer – a haunting refrain.

I stopped with the hot evening wind on my face and listened to it ringing endlessly around the rooftops, feeling the sudden hush descend on the city as the faithful hurried to the mosque. 'God is Great, there is no God but God.' Somehow it made me feel very much alone.

I drifted into a maze of streets, stopping for orange juice squeezed by hand. The juice was a deep marigold colour, perfectly balanced between sweetness and acidity, and cost me no more than about ten pence. I wandered on, past stray dogs who bared their plaque-encrusted fangs at me but ran off squealing when I bent to pick up a stone; past outdoor grills sizzling with the fragrant smoke of lamb sprinkled with pistachios and peanuts. 'Come in and eat,' entreated one chef after another.

Even at this hour, the traffic was of a staggering density, a pall of greasy brown smoke limiting the gaze. As I'd expected, almost all the women were veiled, some using the traditional *shedora*, a black, shapeless garment that covers all but their eyes. Part of me envied them their anonymity. As the only European in sight I found myself stared at with great curiosity. What on earth are you doing here, their eyes seemed to ask.

A fair question – although they might have been surprised by my response. In Syria, I hoped to find a beekeeping method even older than the terracotta jars of Lebanon. There was an outside chance of finding someone who hunted wild honey, too, but I knew that this was unlikely, given the spread of varroa. More probable was that I'd see the traditional cylinders of sun-dried mud within which bees can build up to five horizontal honeycombs. As for flora, I might just catch the end of the eucalyptus and anise honeys in the Golan region. If not, I'd look for the cotton honey, quite unique, on the Euphrates plain.

Before leaving England, I had copied some riveting facts from the ancient Syriac book of medicines. The book's unknown author was a Syrian physician from the Christian era and, though the system of medicine he follows is principally Hippocratic, it is distinguished by its references to the arcane: to astrology, omens, spells and divination. Bees and honey come up frequently.

A medicine to prevent the hair from becoming white – Take a handful of bees, roast them in oil and smear on the hair, and it will become black.

To prevent bees leaving – Heat water and wine and rub the mixture on the hives, or fumigate them with burnt ass's dung.

To keep moths from hives – Sprinkle fresh milk and the urine of children over the legs of the hives and the bees will make honey.

Bury the liver of a white falcon in a beehive, and the bees will thrive.

Whosoever shall place the eye of a bear in a hive of working bees, the bees shall prosper.

Armed with such invaluable knowledge, I wandered the narrow alleyways and crowded souks of the city. In the relative cool of evening, a busy trade was under way. An old man selling household plants – damask roses planted in corroded metal paint cans – knocked on the doors of the great courtyard houses in search of customers. Scent wafted up from open burlap sacks of violets, favoured as a *tisane* ingredient. I passed roaring bread ovens, vendors of bitter herbs, and the famed Yemeni coffee, first brought up on camels along the ancient trade routes. Before long I had lost myself in the dust and the bustle, swept along by the past.

My first night in Damascus was of an almost biblical unpleasantness. I woke in the small hours to find a giant cockroach nestling against my left cheek and after switching on the light found that I was almost surrounded by them. My personal credo of non-violence was quickly rescinded as I went on a mission of total annihilation with my hiking boot. Then I rolled up the rug from the floor and laid it along the skirting board to repel as many of the invaders as possible. Unsurprisingly, sleep did not come easily after that. I lay awake for hours, quietly dripping with sweat in the enormous heat, and listened to the scuttling of the enemy as they searched, desperately, for alternative ways in.

In the morning I was up early, anxious to be out of my room.

I found a café which seemed encouragingly full of locals and ducked in for a few flaky pies made from a wild green named *silek* (silverbeet), still warm from the oven, and a scalding glass of cardamom coffee. Arabic coffee is made by grinding the bean as finely as possible – one degree further than for espresso. It is then packed with cardamom pods, which quickly add their fragrance to the grounds, or in Turkey with pounded dried figs which add a sweetness and help to neutralise acidity. To brew it, one simply mixes a few spoonfuls into a jug of boiling water and waits for the grounds to settle.

I sipped my coffee contentedly. Around me, the first *narghileh* of the day were being lit with glowing coals. One boy actually had the job of circling the room with a brazier of coals and a pair of tongs. He stopped at each table to make sure the *narghileh* was burning properly – if not, inserting his own personal mouthpiece into the end and getting it going. It was the kind of improbably specialised job without which Arabic café culture would break down entirely. None the less, the notion of becoming what was, in effect, a professional smoker, held little romantic appeal.

The noise of smoke being drawn through water gurgled soothingly in the background. After several sweet coffees, I was more myself. I began to feel at home among so many dedicated caffeine addicts and to watch, with interest, what was going on around me. My reverie was broken by a gentleman on my left, a barrel-chested, shock-haired fellow in a grey suit, who tapped me on the shoulder. His questions reassured me that Westerners are not the only ones guilty of cultural stereotyping.

'Meester, you are American man?'

'Certainly not,' I said. 'English.'

'Have you many cars?'

'Not even one. In fact I don't even drive.'

He looked deflated. 'Have you nice wife?'

I shook my head.

'Then, Meester, what is purpose in our country?'

I explained my interest in honey. To my utter astonishment, his eyes brightened.

'I know minister in charge of bees very well. I am working in same building as this man.' He lowered his voice to a whisper. 'A very fat man.'

'Could you introduce me?' I said. 'What an extraordinary stroke of luck.'

'Not luck,' said the man matter-of-factly. 'God has willed this meeting.'

Hussein, as my new friend was called, was a junior clerk in the bustling offices of the Syrian Department of Agriculture. Part of the reason he had got his job, he told me, was his command of foreign languages, chiefly French and English, which he had perfected over a period of years by listening to illicit foreign radio programmes.

'They are also playing excellent heavy rock music,' he whispered. 'I like especially your Red Hot Chili Peppers.'

After insisting on paying my bill, Hussein led me to his office. It was a walk of no more than ten minutes at soon after 8 a.m., but by the time we arrived you could have wrung out my shirt like a sponge.

'Even we find this *fuckeeng* hot,' said Hussein, proudly displaying his grasp of Western slang. 'They say today it will be fifty. In your Fahrenheit that is more than a hundred and thirty degrees. Maybe we boil like chicken eggs!'

Inside the Ministry, it was little cooler. With an average of eight men in every office, each in an identical nylon suit and drab tie, there was an entrenched smell of sweat which hung in the air like incense. Each man had the same picture of Al-Assad above his desk, the same facsimile from the Koran staring up at him, and a near-identical stack of papers, face down, before him. No one seemed to be doing any work at all.

My luck looked set to continue – the minister himself was in and agreed to see me. He was a charming, shiny-pated giant who weighed, as Hussein had intimated, at least twenty stone. He sported the kind of gargantuan moustache one sees on figures of authority all over the world. When I arrived he was sitting at ease in a high-backed chair, a magnanimous smile poised between his pendulous trumpeter's cheeks. A cigarette smouldered in a cut-glass ashtray.

Over tea we discussed the problems of varroa, the falling price of honey on the world market, and the undoubted superiority of Syrian honey over all others. It was a cliché I was happy to hear again – I never tire of hearing how much pride a jar of honey can stir in people.

'What about the old ways?' I asked eventually. 'The clay cylinders.'

There was a long pause while his elegant fingers, strangely at odds with his bulk, tugged reflectively at the ends of his moustache. Then he reached into a drawer beneath his desk and pulled out an ancient ledger, spattered with tea stains from a bygone era. It was full of names and addresses, elegantly penned in a beautifully feminine script.

'I know about those pipes,' he said. His voice was rich. 'My grandfather had some. But, as I mentioned, we have had great

problems with this bee mite in Syria – many people have lost everything. Those who still have bees have had to change to the boxes.'
He wrinkled his brow. 'But there is always a chance. I will make
some inquiries. If it exists in this country still, I will arrange that
you see it. Leave me your number. And in the meantime, here is
my personal card, please ring me, day or night, if there is anything,
anything at all. We are at your service.'

Once again, Arab hospitality left me speechless.

That night I queued in a molten telephone office to try to speak
to Joan. Flies thronged the cramped room, settling on eyelids and
lips with horrific regularity. At last, squeezed within a booth so
hot I could scarcely breathe, the line clicked once, and I heard her
voice on the other end. Formal, at once familiar and disconnected,
this voice almost overwhelmed me with its intimations.

We spoke for half an hour, trying to connect through wires and
underground cables. She was struggling to pay the rent in New
York, and feeling like an outsider in a city she hadn't lived in for
years. She was looking for work as an environmental consultant
with little success. We spoke of friends in London, of my travels
and the search for honey, but rarely about the way we were feeling. We skirted around the subject, like two duellists sizing each
other up, then stepped back, lapsing into the meaningless banter
of everyday life. And when we rang off, at once thrust back into
our vastly separate worlds, I found myself biting back the tears.

CHAPTER ELEVEN

I QUICKLY REALISED, in Syria, that Eva Crane had been right about the problems of language. With French and English you can just about get by in Lebanon, and I'd had Nabil for more complicated questions, but Syria was a different matter entirely. If I was to get anywhere here, I would need a translator.

A few enquiries at the tourist bureau led me to Abdullah, who was short, moonfaced, and bore an air of cheerful directness. He was in his early forties and had recently married: a fine plump girl, he boasted, with excellent hips for bearing sons. He was a tour guide by trade, but given the complete absence of tourists since the Iraq war, he was happy to have the work. Together we hired a decrepit-looking Chevy and set out east from Damascus towards Palmyra, a desert oasis where the ruins of a once fabulous second-century city spread out for almost fifty hectares.

Two-thirds of the way to Palmyra, we stopped at the house of

one of Abdullah's friends, a Bedouin who occasionally helped him
lead groups through the desert. He was a quintessentially modern
Bedouin, one foot still firmly in the sand while the other made
regular forays to Damascus in order to buy such essentials as avia-
tor sunglasses and a mobile phone. Abdullah explained that Ali
was a true original, a highly erudite historian of his culture, who
had lived a life far outside the realms of most of his tribe. If the
Bedouin had any traditions concerning bees, he would surely know
them.

Even Ali's living arrangements combined both worlds. Half of
his property was made up of the traditional black tent constructed
from woven goat-hair, the other half of whitewashed cement
blocks. He greeted us wearing a sky-blue robe and white headdress, looking completely at ease in the immense heat, now at
fifty-two degrees. His hair was well trimmed, his teeth white, and
his skin absolutely flawless. Given that the traditional Bedouin
diet consists of camel cheese, camel milk and camel yoghurt, a
little meat, and almost no fresh produce whatsoever for most of
the year, he looked fantastically healthy.

He ushered us into the tent, which was several degrees hotter
than the most intense sauna I've ever been in. Sweat ran from me
like a fountain. A simple rug covering the ground was the only
furnishing. After the ubiquitous sweet tea and cigarettes, we sat
down to talk, with Abdullah translating my questions.

'As you will know,' Ali said cordially, 'there are no bees in the
desert. To have bees in the desert would be like having fish in
the desert. So most of our sugar comes from dates. In Islam, the
date is *very* special. Muslims believe that after Allah created man
there was some dust left over, from which he created the date

palm. There are hundreds of varieties: *medjool, deglet noor, zhahidi, khadrawi, halwai, barhi, hiani.*' Ali gave a thundering laugh. 'I must tell you that they are selling two *new* varieties of dates in the market. The plumpest best dates are called Bin Ladens! And the worst – the dry, cheap ones – are called Bush!

'But,' he continued, 'sometimes we graze our flocks near the mountains on the edge of the desert. It is still very dry there but there are bees. They make their houses in the rock where it is cool. Sometimes my brother and I light grasses and take their honey. Once, when we were doing this, we found a ball of wax, quite solid, within the comb. When we broke it open we discovered that it was a mouse, perfectly preserved. It must have got into the nest and been stung to death. And since they could not move it, the bees covered it with wax to stop it decaying. Such clever creatures!'

'Abdullah tells me you've travelled a lot – outside of the desert.'

He nodded. 'I am unusual in that respect. Bedouin travel hundreds of miles with their herds but rarely outside the desert. The desert is where we belong. But once, as a young man, I went to see the ocean.' He shivered. 'It made me very afraid to see so much water. I have never felt so lonely in my life.'

I was quite stirred by this confession. Having just driven for hours through the desert, I was experiencing something similar myself. The desert was an alien landscape as far as I was concerned; its silence seemed as loud as cannon fire. And that Ali should feel something similar by the ocean cast it all into sharp relief. Our landscapes define and nurture us. Gunter had found his in the Tuscan hills; Ali recognised that his was here. But I had yet to find my own place to put down roots.

Ali finished receiving a fourth call on the mobile phone and returned to the conversation. 'You know one of the books of the Koran is called "The Bee". They are *very* holy insects. My uncle lives in Aleppo now. When he dries apricots on his roof, the bees choose not to fly for flowers but simply take the sugar from the fruits! What other animal could make such decisions? Once I saw a battle between two hives. One of the bee armies had noticed that the other was much weaker. So they decided to steal their honey rather than make some of their own.' He grinned mischievously. 'Rather like Mr Bush is doing in Iraq, don't you think?'

We drove on into the Syrian desert – Badiyat Ash Sham in Arabic – an arid wasteland joining the cultivated lands along the Eastern Mediterranean coast and the fertile Euphrates valley. The sand extends north from the Nafud Desert in Saudi Arabia and comprises Western Iraq, Eastern Jordan and South-eastern Syria.

This was the driest season in a dry country. The landscape tones were ochre, umber, copper – not a hint of the one colour, green, which might signify water. A minute in that heat leaves you breathless and winded. After a twenty-minute walk in it you can simply not get enough water down your throat to quench your thirst. Inside the car everything had contracted and shrivelled: vinyl unsticking from the doors, the polyester seat-covers wilting like cut flowers. I felt very far from home indeed.

In the distance I saw a Bedouin camel train making a slow arc across the empty sand, like distant crows in a white sky. The last remnants of a closed, insular world. Full of formal courtesies and feuds.

Despite the apparent emptiness, Abdullah assured me that many creatures make their home here. Because the desert steppe is so sparsely populated by humans, some large vertebrates still survive. These include predators such as wolves, Asiatic jackals, striped hyenas, leopards, caracals, swamp cats, and large prey species such as Arabian oryxes, goitred gazelles, and wild boar.

But in the midday heat, anything living was in hiding. The stunning glare was like a halogen bulb trained on to the iris. A ghostly solitude persisted beneath it. It seemed as if Abdullah and I were the emissaries of some alien culture, penetrating into lands unknown within our metal pod.

The silence was the most absolute I had ever known.

After a few more hours on the road, we stopped for the night in Palmyra. The ruins stretched out for miles, golden and dust-swept in the evening light. It was hard to imagine that this sun-baked husk was once a vital stopping point for caravans carrying goods along the Silk Route between China, Persia and the Roman Empire. Now it was a desolate tourist spot, full of urchins selling tacky postcards, or offering camel rides on the backs of vicious, ill-tended animals. None the less, the ruins were impressive, despite the fact that concrete has been used to keep much of them upright – the equivalent of using Polyfilla to patch up the Sistine Chapel.

Early the following day, we continued our desert journey. One of the minister's assistants had left me a message with the address of a man in the far north-east who he believed was still using the bee cylinders. It was a long way to go, within a stone's throw of the Turkish border. To get there we would have to cross a large stretch of desert, then head north to a town called Qamishle.

Leaving Palmyra behind, we headed east towards Iraq. The desert swallowed us within minutes, so imposing in its vastness and in the ferocity of its climate that I found myself utterly mesmerised. The sun beat down without mercy on the red-tinted sand, its heat quickly playing tricks with my eyes. Abdullah pointed out what looked like a large lake on the horizon, chuckling to himself as it vanished into thin air.

'People love it when I show them this. It is the glare of the sky reflected against the sand,' he explained. In Arabic we say "sarab", which comes from the verb "to flow like water". You call it mirage.'

Later we saw a group of men far out below a stone bluff, staring upwards at a pair of falcons dancing on thermals.

'Bird traders,' explained Abdullah. 'They catch falcons to sell to the Gulf princes – one bird can make a man rich for life.'*

I said nothing. It is hard to deny a man the right to dream of great wealth, but the idea of capturing such a regal creature filled me with disgust.

As the day marched on, the desert began to peter out, finally becoming arid agricultural land. The weary Chevrolet reached the Euphrates at the town of Deir Ez-Zur where a 500-metre suspension bridge joins the two banks. It was a wide, ambling river, reminiscent of the Mississippi, and, like that American river, flanked by many miles of cotton fields. Just to see a stretch of water was a blissful relief. A small crowd of boys were climbing

---

*In the Middle East falconry is a high-prestige activity for the elite. The majority of falcons used by the Arabs are migrant sakers (*Falco cherrug*) from Asia. Sakers are a species that is rather like a slightly smaller version of the gyrfalcon. Gyrfalcons themselves, because of their long wings and large size, are especially prized. Members of the Middle Eastern royal families have reportedly paid up to 100,000 US dollars each for healthy specimens of these arctic raptors.

the metal suspension ropes and diving recklessly into the river some fifty feet below.

When we set out again, the thermometer hit fifty-five degrees. As often happens during long journeys, the conversation stopped, each of us succumbing to the pull of our own thoughts, the hypnotic sound of tyres scudding over dust. I sat in the passenger seat, facing the road ahead, but my eyes were gradually sliding out of focus. In the extreme heat, the unease which I had felt upon arriving in Syria was bearing down upon me with more and more weight. It was not merely that I struggled to feel at home here, or that the temperature sapped my energy more potently than opium. Nor was it the extreme political climate in Syria or the proximity of a war zone, just a few miles away.

I'd hoped that immersion in the vastness of nature would provide me with some kind of redemption from the psychological and spiritual malaise that had overtaken me. But it was still very much with me. Syria brought with it pressures I hadn't counted on: a sense of total isolation, a bleak austerity of landscape, which left me hollow. If anything, my ennui was magnified here.

All that was keeping me going was my goal – to see these simple clay pipes – but suddenly I struggled to see the point even in that. It seemed at once too academic, too theoretical a prize to bring a meaningful conclusion to the search. For the first time in months, I longed for England.

Arrival in the Euphrates valley provided some respite from my thoughts. This was, after all, the place in which anthropologists believe man first gave up his hunter-gatherer lifestyle for one of domesticity. For humankind, it was the beginning of a radically different way of life: the start of hierarchical societies, of religious elites, and, environmentally speaking, perhaps the beginning of the end.

Nomadic man had given up his freedom here for a safer, more rooted way of life; I could understand that. To use a relevant metaphor, he had chosen to seek his honey within the convenience of his own backyard, rather than scale cliffs and risk his life for it. But few tradeoffs come without a price.

Today we are still paying that price. A fearful wave of materialism is sweeping the world, fragmenting social groups, breaking down borders. This wave has long since reached Lebanon, engulfing its traditions without a glance back. And though Syria, sequestered from the rest of the world by Al-Assad's anti-American stance, is a few years behind in this respect, its people are certainly none the happier for it. Television has dangled the worm before their eyes and filled their dreams with consumer goods.

The Euphrates, wide and omniscient, trickled past. Standing on its banks, I wondered: was this the beginning of it all? The point at which man began to separate his life from nature, to subsume his sense of place beneath a worldview based on convenience and mechanisation? Was this the place where man lost touch with the network of wild systems, landforms, elevations, the distinctive web of flora and fauna which define us?

Qamishle. A border town in the old sense of the word. Streets crowded to the point of bedlam. People jostling one another. The air full of smells: sewage, rising yeast, the rank sweat of all of us in this heat. Everyone seemed to be shouting, bargaining, arguing. Pariah dogs snapped at random heels. I narrowly escaped being kicked by a mule overburdened with watermelons.

Christ, it was hot. Hotter than lava. It made one's head throb and stole all appetite for anything but water. My clothes grew damp and then dry again a moment later.

Abdullah ducked into a phone centre to ring our beekeeping contact, provided by the Minister of Agriculture. I leant against the wall and watched the goings-on. Barrows of dirty wool, rugs, blankets for sale. Bicycles flying past with a tinkling of bells. Urchins selling cartons of cigarettes – one of the most commonly smuggled goods from Turkey. Clouds of malevolent black flies. Car horns blaring. Hot spits of sizzling meat. Chickens clucking in undersized coops. Shoe polishers. Crackles of cooking fat. The hawking of traders. Sacks of henna and beans spilling into the dirt. Clicking of passing coffee sellers who advertise their passing with a treble retort of the castanets.

Abdullah returned and signalled to me with a thumbs up. 'We go,' he said simply.

It took us an hour to find the house in question: a ramshackle property on the outskirts of town. As senses of direction go, mine is awful: I can get lost anywhere, at almost any time. But compared to Abdullah, I felt like a human compass! His chipolata-like fingers moving boldly across the map, he would announce with complete certainty that this was the street in question. Turning the corner to find himself back in the main square through which we'd passed several times already, he would curse vehemently before muttering, 'This map is mistaken!' or some other self-exonerating remark.

But at last we found it. The beekeeper, magnificently bearded, but with a sallow complexion like a yellowing page, appeared at the gate as our feet crunched our arrival. Pulling out a giant rusted key, he opened his gate with all the air of Ali Baba conjuring aside the door to his fabled cave.

'So I am called,' he said, 'first by my local bee association and then by a man from the minister's office! I say what can this be – the minister calling *me* – on my ancient telephone? And he says there is an important man coming all the way from England – an Inglestan – to see my bees.'

We entered his garden, a dry and thorny paradise, dappled with a single pink spray of blossom.

'I thought he would be older,' he said rather frankly to Abdullah, who then translated with undisguised mirth. 'I would have thought an important Inglestan would be older. And with a longer beard.'

We sat down in the shade on some old plastic chairs. Naguib brought us coffee in chipped glasses.

'So you are looking for the old hives,' he said in his unusually cracked voice. 'Well, I am one of the last, you know. I could get the boxes if I wanted – yes, I could. But why should I want to? My honey is better. Everyone knows that my honey is the best. If you make tea on gas, it's not the same as wood, is it?'

I nodded emphatically.

'When I was a boy,' he said, 'my mother would give me honey with custard. She would make it herself with fresh milk and eggs and then mix in the honey.' His pale eyes narrowed. 'My father used to like honey with his eggs. You heat some *samne*, fry the eggs, let it cool, then add two or three spoons of honey. That is a fine breakfast.'

I asked him what flowers his bees liked.

'My bees like cotton, which is a very big crop here in Syria.

Also sunflower, fruits and olives. They wake up very early here before it gets too hot. We all do in this country. Explorer bees leave first to go and see which pollen is good. Then they bring this back for the queen who makes the decision what is best. I have developed a *special* method, however, of influencing their deci- sion. I go to a big tree or flower with a sheet. Then I knock the tree till all the pollen falls on to the sheet. I then shake this off at the base of the hive and the bees think that it is their lucky day – so much pollen, so close to the hive – and then when they have used that, they go in search of more of the same type. In that way I can control the flavours of my honey.'

'And wild bees? Are there any left?'

He rubbed his temples with his huge wrinkled hands. 'Few. Too few, Inglestan. When I was a boy there were many. Many! There was a famous nest in the roof of our church. They had found a way in and made a home among the bells. If one looked up one could see the wax, hanging down like stalactites. And throughout my childhood, they *never* rang the church bells because of that. No one wanted to disturb them. To have honey in the house of God – well, that was seen as a blessing.' He looked gloomy. 'It is this disease, Inglestan. It is everywhere and I think now it has reached my bees too. Come, I will show you.'

He took us to the hives. Ten adobe cylinders, the size and shape of large fire extinguishers, sat in the middle of a dusty yard under a corrugated tin roof designed to protect them from the sun. They were the sorriest, most primitive-looking things imaginable. At one end of each there was a small hole, about the size of a ten-pence piece, from which bees meandered, moving sluggishly as if they were drugged or exhausted. Even my untutored eye could see that all was not as it should be. A healthy-looking hive should seem as busy as a train station during rush hour, all comings and goings and focused activity. By the same analogy, this was a train station in the early hours of the morning, almost deserted, with only a few weary stragglers remaining.

'Some local people are using tobacco leaf in their smokers,' said Naguib. 'They say that the varroa mite does not like this. So I have just recently bought some. Perhaps today would be a good day to try.'

Naguib went off to find his smoker. While he was gone Abdullah jabbed me on the shoulder excitedly.

'Look at that chicken coop, Mr Piers,' he whispered. '*Special fighting chickens*. That one in the middle looks very fierce. Maybe Mr Naguib is rearing them for competition.'

'Is that legal?'

Abdullah shrugged. 'In Syria we do not worry about such things. But it is too exciting. Many times have I watched this.'

I peered at the chickens with their long curved beaks. One of them looked as if it had just come out of the ring with the Ali of the chicken world: it was scratched and missing whole patches of feathers.

Naguib returned with his smoker which was already lit and trickling dark smoke. 'Very nice tobacco, this,' he muttered. 'My bees are too lucky to be smoking this.'

He bent down at the rear of the cylinders and began to scratch away at the clay with his tool of choice: a machete as long as my arm. The end of the Syrian beehive is usually sealed with a simple adobe disc, loosely stuck with clay, so that it can be removed when it's time to collect the honey. Naguib, who was wearing no bee-veil and had bare arms, was going about it with a kind of mercenary vigour. Inside the bees could hear the sound of the attack and started to buzz loudly. Defender bees began to stream from the entrance and fly angrily around us. I took two steps back, ready to run.

Naguib, who was soon covered with bees, began to apply the smoke liberally. None the less, many of the bees had made it out of the hive and were looking for someone to blame. Several touched down on my face, buzzing angrily. I stood there, frozen with fear. I could feel their tiny feet pacing the skin beneath my eyes and it took every ounce of courage I possessed not to start flapping around in panic. I closed my eyes. One of them stepped lightly on to my left eyelid and paused there, in no hurry to move. I could feel my heart thumping like a piston, sweat running from my nose.

Eventually, the smoke began to affect them and they dispersed. I breathed a sigh of relief. The effects of smoke on a colony of honeybees are something that scientists do not yet fully understand. They grow sluggish and less aggressive, which is useful for the beekeeper. But more importantly still, most of them choose not to leave the hive. One theory is that this is an evolutionary response to a threat from forest fires.

Naguib had now prised the back off the hive and I drew closer to peer inside. Dead bees littered the hive floor, like a battlefield strewn with the fallen. There were five long spherical honeycombs within, in various stages of construction, but I could see at a glance that without treatment the hive was unlikely to last the season. Naguib puffed smoke as far into the hive as he could and resealed the end. Over the next half-hour, I watched him do the same to the others. It was distressing to see and I only hoped he could save the bees before it was too late.

When he was finished we reconvened in his barn, which doubled as a workshop for his carpentry business. A dead fox hung limply from the ceiling. Several partridges, which Naguib referred to as 'bobwhites', squawked mournfully from small wooden cages. Two assistants busily assembled a doorframe while listening to the muezzin's call on a portable radio.

Naguib cradled his tea disconsolately. 'What a disaster,' he growled. 'One more month and they will all be dead. I am embarrassed that you have come all this way to see only this.'

'Loath as I am to suggest it, you need to get the antibiotic strips,' I said. 'It's the only hope, I think.'

Naguib winced. 'Perhaps you are right. But you know, Inglestan, I like honey because it is the sweetness of flowers and only that. Never have I added sugar to the hive like others I know. Never have I used chemicals like the others. Never have I interfered with God's design. Why should I begin now? I would rather let the bees die, if that is His will.'

I looked sideways at him, at his deepset eyes so full of acidity. 'Or you could look upon it that the bees need your help. That you have some role to play in all this.'

Naguib downed his tea in a single draught. He met my gaze. 'I will think upon it. But in the meantime, I would like you to eat with me. In Syria we consider it our duty to feed a guest to the house. And since you have travelled so very far to be here, I would like it to be special.'

He led us to an outdoor table behind his house. It was a peaceful, chlorophyll-rich haven, which he obviously watered assiduously for it was blooming with herbs and exotic brightly coloured blooms I could not name. A veiled woman was laying the finishing touches to the table as we arrived: a cloth of pale cobalt, unglazed terracotta plates, small dishes of mauve radishes, sliced cucumber, tahini-rich *hummus* glistening with oil. There were also thin slices of grilled aubergine speckled with mint leaves, *labne* white as chalk, crusty falafels, lamb kebabs, stuffed vine leaves, hot pitta breads exuding steam from tiny cracks. I was deeply touched: this was a meal such as they would eat no more than once a year.

We sat down and quenched our thirst. Since Naguib was Christian he was permitted alcohol, and there was a bottle of ice-cold *arak* sweating in a bucket. I touched it with my finger: it was deliciously chilled, with a bluish frost on the glass. Naguib poured a generous amount, dropped several cubes of ice into it, and handed it to me.

'Welcome to my country, Inglestan,' he said. 'May God grant you health on your journey. May he provide you with a taste of his most wondrous honeys.'

'Thank you,' I said. 'May he give your bees new life.'

'May he ensure that I never again have to travel to such far-off desert places with strange Inglestans in search of bee honey,' said Abdullah, grinning as he held up his water glass.

'To all of us then,' I said, chuckling. Then, remembering Nabil's toast from Lebanon I added: 'And may the penis of George Bush shrivel to the size of a chickpea!'

Abdullah snorted water in two fountains from his nostrils and began a coughing fit that left him puce in the face. And even though Naguib hadn't understood the first half of the joke, he laughed so hard at Abdullah's reaction that I thought he was going

to fall off his chair. When Abdullah had mopped his face a little
with a napkin, he translated for our host. Naguib promptly collapsed
with laughter once again, using the edge of the tablecloth to wipe
his eyes.

'Inglestan, you know, of course, that the manhood of George
Bush is *already* the size of a chickpea,' cackled Naguib. 'Further
shrinkage may result in complete *invisibility*!'

He and Abdullah were now laughing so hard that they were
wholly incapable of normal speech. I was absolutely weeping myself
and the three of us went on for some time, utterly childlike.

We finished the meal, fittingly, with honey. Naguib put out three
bowls on the table, from his three most recent crops. The first
contained a citrus blossom honey: floral, intricate, zesty. The
second was a dark, smoky honey from tobacco flowers. The third,
clear and white, was from cotton plants. We dipped our spoons
from one to the other, smacked our lips, discussed the flavours
like wine experts. Naguib smiled as if all his birthdays had come
at once.

It was a welcome end to my time in Syria, which I had found
extremely difficult and intensely lonely.

As for what I had discovered, it would take me some time to
coalesce my experiences into any articulate whole. But what I *was*
sure of was that I had seen the last generation of beekeepers using
the old methods. For reasons of disease, convenience, and the
sharp thrust of modernity that is sweeping the Middle East, the
old ways are fading and may soon become little more than archaeological relics, to be analysed by future scientists, pondered over
by future beekeepers, and remembered fondly as the last bastions
of a former way of life.

NEW YORK

CHAPTER TWELVE

I T WAS EXTRAORDINARY to return to the muted cityscape of London after Syria. Sitting in the underground after a twenty-hour journey, my skin still tingling from the desert sun, I gazed at the soporific passengers all around me, beaten into a psychological submission by the pressures of modern life. What were they thinking behind those eyes? Were they thinking at all?

Travel has a way of making things seem glaringly obvious. What is hidden from our day to day self by habits of perception becomes clear when we step outside what we know. Back in London, it became apparent to both Joan and me that our relationship was facing its biggest challenge yet. My accident had evoked in me a powerful determination for adventure. It was not sated yet, nor would it be anytime soon.

Joan, on the other hand, was pursuing her career, seeking city life, stability and the company of old friends. She wanted children, a regular income, a roof that was not made of corrugated iron.

None of those things was I ready for. And yet to separate after all we had been through seemed impossible. We had seen each other at our worst and come through it. We had held each other's hands during moments of paralytic bleakness – so how could we fall apart when things began to go right?

In the end I decided to go to New York. We had to talk about this face to face – the telephone was only clouding an already muddy pond. Just a few days after my return from Syria I booked a flight.

It was late August 2003, early evening, the city steaming in the summer heat. Minutes after my arrival at JFK, New York was struck by the citywide blackout that would become the country's defining memory of that season.

Drained after our transatlantic flight, myself and the several hundred Virgin passengers slumped on the ground in the customs hall, waiting expectantly for the lights to flicker back on. We could not be processed through customs until the computer systems regained their power. I watched the red lights passing overhead in the darkening sky – planes unable to land. Beside me, an Indian family had removed their shoes and were sitting cross-legged, eating samosas.

Minutes turned to hours. We were told very little. People whispered amongst themselves about terrorist threats. Osama Bin Laden. Eye-raquis. Others pointed out that we were lucky to be on the ground. Scores of flights were now en route for other airports along the East Coast – miles out of their way.

At ten o'clock, customs officials found a laptop with battery power and began to process the elderly, and those with young children. It seemed an extraordinarily painstaking process for this supposedly hi-tech airport, in this most modern of American cities.

After several hours it was my turn. In my fatigue, I had naively thought that this would be the end of it, but the baggage hall was worse – a room in half-light, passengers from many different flights clamouring for their bags. Teams of baggage-handlers, sweating like miners, wheeled in trolleys laden with Samsonite, Gucci, Louis Vuitton, the odd ragged backpack like mine. But there was no telling where they were from – Delhi? Prague? São Paulo?

Each trolley that came in was greeted by a mob of haggard travellers, elbowing and jostling one another, a stampede of angry men and women, desperate for what was theirs, uncaring of who they trampled in the rush. I rescued an old English lady, all but mown down in the charge. 'Well, dear, they haven't organised this very well, have they?' she muttered with quite staggering understatement.

I sat back and watched it happen. The mob mentality. The sweat. People in tears. Baggage-handlers shifting mountains of luggage for an ungrateful rabble. Then, by some stroke of luck, I saw my bag lying in a corner. It had been torn open in the struggle, toothpaste and boxer shorts spilling on to the vinyl floor. I picked it up like a relay racer grabbing a baton and sped out into the night.

The darkness hit me like a wall. What was a New York night without neon: shop signs, billboards, LCD screens in shop windows? Emergency lights bled an orange glow on to the tarmac. But the city itself was a ghost town, that familiar horizon conspicuous by its absence.

'Any way of getting to Manhattan?' I asked a cop, his hair matted with sweat.

'Brooklyn Bridge is closed, fella – you ain't got a snowflake's chance in hell of getting there right now. Power's out up the whole East Coast.' I nodded a thank you and moved towards the taxi line – a queue two or three hundred long. Officials were walking up the line handing out bottles of water.

Two hours in the queue. I talked to my neighbour who was vowing to install his own generator.

'Goddamned if I'm gonna be tied to the grid after this is over,' he ranted. 'They got these wind turbines now which run at about thirty g's – put one of them bad-boys in and I ain't gonna depend on *no one* for my power. You just can't believe that a city like this is so unprepared. Hell, the airport should have full emergency powers systems and from what I can see it ain't got shit.'

He was right.

Another two hours. Taxis arrived sporadically. People grumbled, smoked, sweated. I was still a long way from the front of the queue when a cab driver shouted, 'Bridge is back open. I got room for one more for the Upper East Side.'

I held up my hands like a castaway signalling for a passing plane.

Driving through New York in total darkness was a surreal experience. For the first, and possibly last, time in my life I saw a modern metropolis reduced to a pre-industrial state. It was like seeing a life-support unit without a single electric heartbeat. And it was so quiet. No rattling subway cars. No TVs or radios. No air conditioners, electric blenders, coffee grinders. Not even a plane passing overhead. Every time I go to New York I'm amazed by the volume of it all, the pitch and velocity. And now it was hushed as in the aftermath of some cataclysmic event.

When we reached Manhattan the atmosphere was very different. Many of the bars were bulging with people, the event catalysing some new community spirit. Some of the revellers raised their cocktails at us as we sped by, their faces flushed and giddy in the headlights. Two people (avid seventies movie fans no doubt) were trying to jimmy the top off a fire hydrant.

Further up the road a huge crowd had gathered outside an ice-cream store. With the power off, the owner was taking the opportunity for a huge publicity drive.

'Free gelato New York,' he was yelling. 'Quickly before it melts.'

My cab driver, irate and wearing a Hilfiger cap pulled jauntily to the side, leant out of the window to add his own take to the event. 'Free gelato yourself out of the goddamn road then,' he shouted.

At Joan's apartment building, fifty floors of old brownstone overlooking Central Park, my troubles were by no means over.

'You the one stayin' with Joan?' said the concierge, a shaven-headed Puerto Rican with a weary smile. 'She's been down here waitin' on you. Gone back up now.'

'What floor is she on again?' I asked.

He grinned. 'That would be the thirty-fifth.'

'Can I call her?'

'No can do, pal. Phone's out.'

I nodded. 'I should have known. I don't suppose your lift is working either, is it?'

He shook his head. 'I tell you what, my friend,' he said. 'I'm going to help you out. I'm gonna give you my last candle.'

I wiped the sweat from my brow. 'Must be my lucky day.'

Half an hour later, my hand encrusted with wax, I arrived at Joan's door. Over the last thirty minutes I'd got lost three times, reached numerous dead ends, and at one point seriously considered bedding down for the night in the corridor. She opened the door, tired-eyed and thinner than I remembered. Now burned down to a nub, the candle sputtered in my palm, imparting a sulphurous light.

'It's been a long time,' she said.

A few days later, when some of the madness had died down and the electricity was restored, I began to find my feet in the city again. I had time to explore while Joan was at work and, since our problems didn't look as though they were going to be resolved anytime soon, I spent a lot of the time pacing the streets, breathing in the scents of the old fish market on 92nd Street, eating big breakfasts of pitch-coffee and eggs in cheap diners. Afterwards I'd just walk. Walking was the only way I could stop thinking.

This was my first visit to post 9/11 New York and I noticed the change at once. E. B. White called New York America's 'visible symbol of aspiration and faith, the white plume saying that the way is up'. A little of that faith was gone now; the nation's ideological figurehead had taken a beating and Americans were wondering if maybe they weren't the people everyone wanted to *be* any more. Several of them were realising that certain groups even hated them for what they'd become, and that quashed a little of their cheerful swagger, the brashness which the city cab drivers had made into an art form.

One day I ended up at the Union Square farmers' market, where farmers and homesteaders sell their wares from old plank and sawhorse counters: apples called Spitzenberg and Liberty. Potatoes called Nooksack and Red Ruby. Tomatoes the size of footballs – the Dixie Golden Giant or the Black Krim. And it was at this market that I came across a berry stand where some jars of honey caught my eye.

New York Rooftop Honey.

'Is that New York State or New York City?' I asked the stall-holder, a freckled, sun-crinkled lady wearing an apron.

'That'd be New York City, honey,' she said. 'David's got bee boxes stashed just 'bout all over the city. Roof gardens, old fire-escape units in Queens, office blocks in Harlem.'

It seemed a fantastic possibility. I asked if I could meet him.

'You come back in half an hour you might catch him,' she said.

I continued around the market, excited by this new prospect. It seemed strangely ironic that, although I was here to see Joan and work out my relationship, I'd ended up on the honey trail once again. Something in my life seemed inextricably linked with the movements of bees and the search for sweetness.

I was newly inspired; the day suddenly took on a hopeful slant. I have always felt New York to be a place where wonderful, unexpected things can happen and this morning appeared to be no different. I soon met a lady walking a pet iguana on a leash. She grinned at me as if to be walking a four-foot non-indigenous pet reptile with a personalised diamanté collar was the most normal thing in the world.

Later I witnessed an altercation over some basil that almost led to bloodshed. The two protagonists were both pensioners, the woman propped upon a Zimmer frame and wearing mauve horn-rimmed glasses, the man sporting a pork-pie hat and with an orange skin tone that indicated plenty of time on the sun-bed. Both, it later turned out, had pounced upon the last bunch of basil (pronounced bay-zil) at the same time. When I arrived the old lady was working herself into a frenzy.

'Goddamn putz, that's my bay-zil. Get your sticky paws off it.'

'Look, lady, I don't know who you think you are but I got your number. I saw that first and I *need* it!'

'I don't give a rat's ass what you need. First come first served, buddy!'

I left them to it, echoes following me across the square.

David Graves is a shy, affable man with a deep appreciation for his work. He and his wife run Berkshire Berries, a small organic farm growing and producing jellies and conserves, honey and maple syrup, and selling them at the Union Square Greenmarket and others around the metropolis. He has a tanned face and a placid smile, and he walks with the wide, regular pace of a man used to working outdoors.

He greeted me warmly at his stall, a gentle handshake belying heavy calluses and a tough woodsman's build. 'You're right on time,' he said. 'Load yourself up with some of these boxes and you can help me work on the hives. 'Bout ten or so blocks to the first one and we can talk on the way.'

He had always kept bees, he told me as we went, because he liked honey and because he found it was good for the berries. And being attuned to the amount of available nectar for bees, he'd got to notice how much there was around New York City: all those roof gardens, window-boxes, well-groomed city parks, urban green spaces and patios.

'A couple of years back I asked a friend if I could try a hive on his roof,' he said as we walked, loaded with beekeeping equipment, through Manhattan. 'We figured we could see how it went and in the meantime I could teach him how to look after bees. And then we'd split whatever honey there was. Seemed like a fair arrangement.

'I tell you what, we were surprised at how much honey we got, too. New York City is just *full* of available nectar.'

'Isn't the honey a bit polluted?' I asked.

'That's what everyone thinks,' said David. 'But there's two reasons it's not. Firstly, majority of stuff what pollutes the honey is agricultural pesticides. New York City don't have any of those because there ain't no agriculture. Secondly, the nectar which the bees like is well concealed inside the flower. Traffic fumes and so on might come into contact with the outside of the flower but the bee finds his way inside – to where it's clean. So as a matter of fact the opposite is true – New York rooftop honey is often better quality than what you might find in the country.'

'How about the dangers – people stumbling across the hives and so on?'

He shook his head. 'Well, there's been some talk about that,' he said with a chuckle. 'Strictly speaking, the New York City health code bans animals that are "wild, ferocious or fierce".' He raised his eyebrows. 'Some folks think bees fall into that category. That's crazy of course. There are millions of bees in this city anyhow – carpenter bees, bumbles, wood-borers. And there's yellow jackets, too – they're much more dangerous. And as for getting at the hives – as you'll see, they're totally inaccessible to the public.'

We'd now arrived at one of the sites – the pied-à-terre of a New Orleans chef who worked most of the year in the South. It was an old building, ten floors high and constructed of pink hand-moulded Hudson River brick. There were two windows to each floor, and one of those old fire-escapes popular in cop movies, upon which residents had potted up a few beleaguered plants, or hung their grimy vests to dry. Across the road was a coffee-roasting plant and the charred-bean smell wafted across the parked cars and tingled the nostrils.

David said that the owner was barely ever here and he couldn't see why he kept up his lease. But it was a good arrangement for the bees – they were left alone much of the time and had a nice quiet place to make honey.

As in many old New York buildings there was no elevator. We went up the narrow stairs, carpeted in a faded grass-tinted baize, squeezing past a couple of mountain bikes, an old vacuum cleaner and even an empty fish tank, a sunken plastic treasure chest poking out of some dirty sand.

After an exhausting climb, we came to a narrow round-runged birch ladder which led to a trapdoor. David went first so that he could unlock the padlock. Then he gave it a shove and a cloud of black dust showered down.

'Come on up,' he shouted.

On the roof I was greeted by the most spectacular view of New York City. Not the picture-postcard view of high-rises and chrome office blocks but a gritty insider's view, the little squares of green which the residents had carved for themselves out of the stone. Two houses down, some enterprising person had even planted window-boxes with small heads of lettuce, and there were nasturtiums and borage and even catnip against which a corpulent tomcat was sniffing.

The New Orleans chef had done nothing, however. He had a flat concrete roof upon which David had placed two beehives. Aside from that it was empty. I asked David how many hives in total he had around the city.

''Bout twenty all told,' he said. 'Fluctuates a little bit. Now and again people call me if they find a swarm and I get one more. But I been losing a few to varroa, too.'

'I was coming to that,' I said. 'Do you use the pesticide strips?'

He shook his head. 'Not yet I don't. Most people are but I just can't bring myself to. There's natural ones you can get now – they're strips impregnated with tea-tree and other oils which the mite doesn't like. Maybe I'll get those.'

Using an old screwdriver to jemmy up the lid, David lifted the top off one of the hives. He looked unhappy.

'Ah damn, I thought maybe these guys would have found a little more energy by now. Either there's a real shortage of nectar flow or this hive ain't doing so good.'

I drew close to have a look. Since we were in late summer it should have been thick with new honey. As it stood, it was barely a third full. The colony looked weak and seemed to be struggling.

'Well, let's taste some anyhows,' he said. He cut out a thick wedge for me. It was good – delicate, without the defining taste of a monocultural honey.

'Lighter-tasting, isn't it?' said David with a smile. 'Very sweet and floral. On a good year I can get fifty pounds of comb out of one of these hives. And varroa aside, they're hassle-free. Back on my farm I'm always losing hives to bears. They come in at night and there ain't much you can do about it. Here in the city my only real problem is transporting them. And since I only put one or two hives in a location, I also have a lot of walking to do. Out in the country you can put twenty or more in the same place because there's enough nectar. New York, you got to spread them out. I don't mind about the walking though – keeps me young.'

Later, when I had said goodbye to David, I stopped in an internet café to research the notion of urban beekeeping and see if there were others engaged in this unlikely practice. Amazingly, it turned out that both Paris and London boast similar projects, started by savvy modern beekeepers interested as much in educating disconnected city dwellers about the delights of apiculture as in utilising untapped nectar.

Such things can only be good news. Small rebellions against the overwhelming orthodoxies of our time. In bringing bees to New York City, and greenmarkets to the asphalt hubs of modern life, people like David Graves are providing valid alternatives to a processed and packaged culture.

An inner-city child may catch a first glimpse of an infinitely mysterious world. They may taste fruit actually grown in their own neighbourhood and not shunted halfway around the globe in some fuel-guzzling jet. They may eat the sweetness which bees have made and not that from a candy bar and before that a Petri dish. And if they follow those threads, they may even become alert to possibilities which, had the fates not intervened, might never have graced their lives.

The intelligence in an animal's eyes. The fact that a porcupine crumpled by a passing car has not strayed so much into our world as we into its. The reassurance of a human enterprise designed to augment and not to diminish the planet in which we live.

The day I left New York the temperature was still in the high eighties, the air so motionless it was as if the weather patterns themselves had been burnt up in the heat. Clouds had dissolved to steam. The wind dispersed.

I had woken early, and sat at the window for some time sipping coffee and watching the awakening city below: the mail delivery, shutters rattling upwards, the joggers, dog-walkers, rollerbladers whirring off a few hundred calories before their nine to five. My head throbbed with a deep, unsteady pain, the evidence of the alcohol drunk the night before in an effort to allay the inevitable – the conversation both Joan and I had postponed from the moment I'd knocked on the apartment door, sweating and haggard in the blackout.

But it had happened eventually – as we knew it must. A bitter, galling dialogue that I will remember until I am old and whose echoes would follow me around India like hungry ghosts.

In the end it was as if Joan and I were breaking apart not because we had fallen *out* of love, but because each of us wanted the other to live their life of choice. Perhaps that amounts to the same thing? Perhaps a mutual direction, by some definition, is a kind of love.

Either way, we came undone. Two people sitting in a small

apartment, high up in a city of many million souls, all of whom were living, dying, even breaking apart like us, and yet it seemed that no one could possibly be experiencing such unhappiness just then – there was simply not enough to go around.

As I packed my bag for England, from where I would quickly get myself together and leave again, this time for the honey-hunting expedition in Nepal which had always seemed the most important part of my quest, I felt as if I were going on a much longer journey than I had before. Everything was different now.

Thinking back, I could barely remember the invincible youth of that distant San Francisco summer. After the crash everything had changed. And this new person, the one with so much weight on his shoulders, had never known a reality of which Joan was not a part.

NEPAL

CHAPTER THIRTEEN

BEFORE LEAVING FOR India, an old friend had given me a sealed envelope. On the outside he had written in pencil: 'Do not open until arrival at New Delhi airport. Believe me, you'll need this.'

Fraught with preparations at the time, I had thought little of what the mysterious envelope might contain. But finding myself with a few moments to spare, waiting in the dusty customs line in Delhi, I opened it. It was a Valium tablet, cocooned behind a strip of tape. I grinned and swallowed it, mindful of the stories I'd heard which suggested arrival in Delhi to be one of the most intense of all travelling experiences.

By the time I stepped out into the blazing afternoon, the pill was taking effect. The world was retreating behind a soft cushion. But even thus bolstered, nothing could have prepared me for that first glance of India. It was as if I had previously been living in black and white, like Dorothy in *The Wizard of Oz*, and had stepped through a magic portal into a world of colour. And by comparison, that previous existence had also been without noise, without smell, without taste. India was truly life in closeup.

The sky was a searing lapis, the sun an orb of throbbing apricot light. The air was heavy with mustard, dirt, spice, shit. This smell would later coalesce to become my single defining memory of India: precise as a GPS system.

Several hours later, I was sitting outside my room, sipping piquant *massala chai*, the strong and sweet Indian tea flavoured with cardamom, cinnamon and black pepper. Mynahs, kites and a red-vented bulbul drank from an ancient bird bath on a strip of lawn. I maintain a deep attachment to my notebooks, which contain a myriad of information relating to my day-to-day life, from the profound to the utterly mundane. Looking back over some of them before my trip, I was struck by how many references to India had accrued in them over the years. Numerous interests seemed to have drawn me here: yoga, vegetarianism, Buddhism, and now honey.

It seemed strange, and somehow fitting, that now I was finally here it was to hunt wild honey. As with all my travels, honey seemed curiously equipped to lead me to the heart of things, closely intertwined with religious, culinary and medical folklore. 'Anoint me with the *madhu* of the bee,' says the Rig Veda, 'so that I may speak forcefully amongst men.'

The Sanskrit word for honey is *madhu* and the gods Vishnu, Krishna and Indra are sometimes called *madhava* – the nectar-born ones. Sanskrit names for the bee include: *madhva*, the honey-fly, *madhu-pa*, the honey-drinker, *madhu-kara*, the honey-maker, *madhu-lih*, the honey-licker, and also *brahmara*, the wanderer.

These gods also have a sacred plant called '*tulasi*', or holy basil. According to Indian legend, Krishna was once in love with a beautiful girl whom he transformed into the *tulasi* plant, so that her memory should live for ever. He decreed that no worship to him should take place without her presence. Because of this, and because Hindus hold honey to be the food of the gods, Indian beekeepers traditionally hold a piece of *tulasi* in their hand when taking honey from the hive. Might this not indicate, from a certain angle, that beekeeping is itself a kind of religious practice?

To steal honey in India is considered highly imprudent: honey thieves can expect to be reincarnated as gadflys. Fathers of newborn children feed their babies with honey, often from a golden spoon, saying: 'I give thee honey so that the gods may protect thee and that thou may live a hundred autumns in this world.' At a wedding, the bride may have her earlobes and the lids of her eyes smeared with honey to ensure a happy future. Conversely, to dream of honey is considered inauspicious.

Ayurveda, the ancient Indian system of healing, contains a great many prescriptions including honey; indeed it is believed that the addition of honey to any medicine makes it more effective. A famous Indian surgeon, Susruta, as far back as 1400 BC, recognised eight different varieties of honey, including honey from a form of stingless bee, and even wasp honey.

After a few days to acclimatise, I took the train north towards the Nepalese border. The honey-hunting season was rapidly approaching and I had a rendezvous in Pokhara, in the foothills of the

Himalayas, with a man who promised me an introduction to the Gurung, the legendary honey-hunters. After Nepal, I intended to return to India and travel by land to its southernmost tip, and from there to Sri Lanka, the final stop of my journey.

On the way north, I stopped at Varanasi, the holy city, where I watched a limpid sun rising over the Ganges. It was shortly after 5 a.m., utterly quiet, and around me the world was creaking into gear. Crackles of light hit the water like tiny electrical sparks. The water was murky, punctuated by votive candles and lotus flowers, even the odd corpse. Varanasi is famous for its burning *ghats*, where those who can afford it cremate their departed on sandal-wood pyres and sprinkle their ashes into the river. Sandalwood is prohibitively expensive, however, so many people simply float the corpses away, mere contact with the Ganges ensuring a benefi-cial rebirth.

In today's India, one of the most rapidly modernising countries in the world, rivers, and the Ganges in particular, retain a strong place in the popular imagination. Hindus consider water to be a powerful medium of purification and a source of energy. One religious text, the *Pravascitta Tatva*, makes the following recommendations regarding correct behaviour around the Ganges:

> One should not perform these fourteen acts near the holy waters of the river Ganga: i.e., remove excrement, brushing and gargling, removing cerumen from the body, throwing hairs, dry garlands, playing in water, taking donations, performing sex, attachment with other sacred places, prais-ing other holy places, washing clothes, throwing dirty clothes, thumping water and swimming.

On the morning I was there, however, this advice was systemati-
cally disregarded on almost all counts. I saw several thousand
people engaged in every possible human ablution. And as for the
'taking donations' phrase, I have never been so persistently
hounded for money in my life.

One man, however, did pique my interest. I was sitting on the
worn steps which lead down to the river's edge when he arrived,
a spindly Sikh with a French waiter's moustache.

'You want to know future, boss?' he whispered, his grey eyes
boring into me.

'By all means,' I said light-heartedly. 'Can you tell it to me?'

He drew closer. 'Not *me*, sir. But in Varanasi there is one man
who can. A holy man. Many peoples are coming to see him.'

'What kind of holy man?'

He looked bewildered. 'A *very* holy man, sir. He is reading the
stars *and* the palm. Never is he wrong!'

'What about you then? Does he pay you to bring him
customers?'

The man's face dropped. 'Oh *no*, sir. I am being *freelance*. Actually,
I am living in Delhi but I have come to Varanasi to see him.' He
lowered his voice. 'I am having some problems in my family. We
are hoping that he will see some change of fortune coming for
us.'

My new friend, Raja, agreed to take me to the holy man. Usually,
fortune-telling exerts little pull on my imagination, but something
about Varanasi made me curious. It seemed a place in which many
normal rules might not apply: certainly, the strict barriers between
life and death, so rigidly maintained in English society, did not
exist. I had seen scores of dead bodies since my arrival, bodies on

pyres, bodies swathed in bandages, decaying bodies gruesomely inflated by too long an immersion in the river. This constant reminder of the inevitable might have made Varanasi gloomy, but instead it seemed more filled with life than anywhere I had ever been. Death's presence seemed to magnify the need to live in the moment – and that was something I could identify with.

Raja led me with great purpose. Within minutes I was totally disorientated, hopelessly lost in these labyrinthine streets. We passed bullocks, rickshaws, barber's shops, vegetable stands, scores of beggars, skeletal dogs, shoemakers, sweet vendors, ancient sweat-soaked men bent double under impossible loads. The alleys became narrow, a little quieter, threaded with untended bougainvillea and a creeper which Raja called *madhumalati*.

After some fifteen minutes, Raja halted outside an arched entranceway.

'Now I must tell you a few things to remember when dealing with such a holy fellow,' he began. 'Firstly, you are not doing the talking unless he is asking you something. Secondly, you are think-ing *only* holy thoughts in his presence. And thirdly, you must be very honest with him if he is to tell you the real occurrences of the future.'

We went in.

Inside we were met by an elderly retainer who had the most elegant hands I have ever seen. He was wearing a well-starched white kurta pyjama and a simple cotton cap.

'Which country, sir?' he asked.

'England.'

'Ah,' he smiled. 'Nasser Hussain! A very fine man.'

I couldn't help chuckling. It was refreshing to know that even such mystical establishments as this were permitted the joys of cricket. Later I would realise what a defining feature of Indian life this is: Indians make no distinction between the spiritual and the mundane as we do in the West.

'You will wait upstairs,' said the retainer. 'He will see you shortly. At this moment he is in deep meditation.'

Raja turned to me. 'I will be going,' he whispered. 'Best of luck, sir. I hope you find the right answers.'

'Did you?' I called after him.

Raja smiled cryptically, and clasped his hands together in *namaste*, that versatile Indian gesture meaning simply: 'I salute the God within you.' Then he turned on his heels and was gone.

I waited for almost an hour in the upstairs room, which was the size of a cell, without a single piece of furniture, and with a narrow, paneless window through which the morning sun flooded. The retainer brought me a glass of milkless *chai*, then left without a word. I watched the world below: India with all its wonders and woes. On an adjacent terrace a small boy flew a homemade kite, tugging on the string so that it rose higher above the roof of the city, like a bird struggling to reach clean air.

This was something of a diversion from the honey trail, I knew that. But I couldn't shake off a curiosity about what he might say. And since one facet of this whole journey had been about rede-termining the course of my life, there was perhaps some relevance to it. If the fortune-teller could give me an inkling into the karma which had brought me this far, I might be better equipped to face the future.

At last, the mystic was ready to see me. He was sitting cross-legged on a small Kashmiri carpet when I entered, a pinch of sandal-wood smouldering in a *neti* pot. He was about fifty, with a shock of bushy black hair, the requisite thick beard, and flashing black eyes. I was immediately struck by his presence, which seemed to fill the room to its edges.

He gestured for me to sit down.

'You have been in some accident?' he asked, pointing to the scars on my forehead.

I said that I had.

'This can happen for many reasons. Problems from a past life. A karmic debt. Someone may have *cursed* you.'

It was a grim possibility. 'Can you find out?'

'Why not?'

He began a long series of questions. Time and place of birth, profession, parents' names. He scrutinised my palms for some minutes, then my feet. He placed his hands on my scalp. He made some complicated calculations using a quadrant and some ancient Sanskrit texts. Then he began to write furiously on a piece of paper, drawing circles within squares, joining separate symbols with lines.

If I had expected rolling eyes, a frothing mouth, some theatrical demonstration of connection to the arcane, I was wrong. The mystic worked as if he were an office clerk perusing the tedious entries of a civic ledger.

I watched with interest, only becoming alarmed as I recognised a dark frown appearing on his face.

'Is something the matter?'

He stared at me. '*Problem* is there, sir. Oh yes. Big problem is there. As I thought, someone has *cursed* you!'

I looked suitably morose. 'Any good news at all?'

He tilted his head from side to side in that quintessentially Indian manner. 'Yes, sir, not all bad. You will have one child before the age of thirty, out of wedlock. Then you will break with that woman, find another one, marry her, and have a second child after the age of thirty-five, a son.' He beamed.

Well, if that was his idea of good news, what in God's name was the bad?

'What can I do about the curse?'

Another head tilt. 'Well, curses are an extremely *frequent* phenomenon, sir. Many peoples are suffering from them. Yours is nearing end now, actually, but it is a *very* bad one. Tell me, sir, before this recent accident, has there been other bad luck?'

I mentioned a burst appendix some years before that had been quite serious.

He tutted excitedly. 'Yes, sir, as I thought, I am *never* wrong about these things. But when the curse ends you will find success. Great success, sir. Although you will never be rich. Not too poor, but never rich.'

Success: this sounded more positive.

'Although this success will only last until your sixtieth year,' he furthered. 'At that point life will be more difficult again. And then, of course, your death will come at the age of eighty-two. A sudden death.'

'That's very precise.'

'Oh yes, sir, I am very precise. It is my gift.'

'Can you help me lift the curse a little early?'

He nodded. 'I have a small orphanage, sir, and in such cases as this I ask for little donation for childrens.'

'Naturally.'

'And in return I am providing lucky amulet! You must wear this next to your skin at *all* times. Never be showing this to anyone or it will not work! I sense you are on a great journey. You are seeking answers to many pressing questions.'

I said that I was.

'This amulet will help you find what you are looking for. It will dispel enemies and evil spirits. And if we are lucky, it may help with curse. Only you must not be eating spicy food, sir. Not too many onions. That will make things difficult.'

'But almost all Indian food has onions,' I protested. 'I may starve.'

'No, sir,' he smiled, 'you must be asking for Jain food. Jains do not eat onions.'

By the time I left the fortune-teller, he was in meditation again and made no sign of farewell. I pondered on the experience as I took a rickshaw to the train station. He hadn't been after money – of that I was certain – for he'd asked me for a pittance, even by Indian standards. But the precision of his answers made them hard to find credible. Dead at eighty-two! That gave me fifty-four years to play with. Well, only time would tell.

The train dropped me at Gorakhpur from where I took a bus to Sunauli, a popular crossing point for travellers moving between India and Nepal. As I walked over the border into Nepal, I reflected that I was now in the province of Lumbini, the birthplace of the Buddha. I had been a somewhat lazy Buddhist since my early twenties, philosophically in tune with the teachings but without the discipline for daily practice.

I had got into Buddhism, funnily enough, through the writers of the so-called Beat Generation. Writing in the America of the 1950s, they'd found an antidote in Buddhism to the paranoia and conformity of the atomic age. Later, I felt a secondary pull towards the teachings through the Buddhist conception that human beings are not separate from the natural world (as in the Christian view in which man is given 'dominion over all things') but part of a complex network of connections with every beast, plant and river. That struck me very deeply.

In the course of my research, I discovered that Buddhist doctrine actually makes several references to honey. In the *Uttara Tantra* there is an analogy in which a comb of honey is surrounded by many bees. Honey represents the sweetness at the heart of the human condition. Bees represent our mental defilements, the constantly buzzing distractions which prevent us from tasting it.

Another of the Buddha's teachings mentioning honey cautions against sensory indulgence.

Wise men control themselves and do not indulge their senses but guard them like robbers who must not be allowed freedom from restraint . . . Indeed, you ought to fear indulgence of the mind's desires more than poisonous snakes, savage beasts, dangerous robbers or fierce conflagrations. No simile is strong enough to illustrate this danger. But think of a man carrying a jar of honey who, as he goes, heeds only the honey and is unaware of a deep pit in his path![*]

* * *

[*]*The Discourse of the Teaching Bequeathed by the Buddha*, translated into Chinese by the Indian Acarya Kumarajiva sometime prior to the year 956 Buddhist era. (http://www.sinc.sunysb.edu/clubs/buddhism/sutras/foyijiaojing.html)

Well, I had two jars of English honey in my bag – a present for any beekeepers I might meet – but what about this deep pit? It worried me to think that Nepal itself might qualify: the political situation was deeply unstable at the moment and both the British and American embassies were advising travellers to keep away.

It was a difficult state of affairs and one on which the foreign press seemed little able to shed light. Since February 1996 the Maoist Communist Party of Nepal had been engaged in a 'people's war' against the government. The fighting had flared and receded at intervals since then, with brief periods of ceasefire, then renewed outbreaks. Recent months, however, had brought the worst fighting yet. I'd read more than one comparison between the Nepalese Maoists and another well-known group of Communist insurgents: Peru's Shining Path. Both groups recruited from the poor and the dispossessed; both provided their members with a sense of self-worth and pride within a country losing itself to modernity, an alien system of knowledge and values derived from the West. Worst of all, both groups displayed mind-boggling cruelty towards their enemies.

Despite the advice of people who knew better, I resolved to go to Nepal anyway. The one thing I had hoped to find above all others in the past months was an opportunity to hunt honey in the wild. I knew for certain that this happened in Nepal and I was damned if I was going to turn back now.

I'd also recently seen a stunning set of pictures by a *National Geographic* photographer, Eric Valli, which had further convinced me that I was on the right path. Some years before he'd documented a honey-hunting expedition on the southern slopes of the

Himalayas. His shots showed enormous cliffs down which men lowered themselves on ropes of woven bamboo. The honeycombs they sought were as big as wagon wheels. It was the stuff of legend.

Pokhara, a sleepy mountain outpost, is the final piece of civilisation before the Annapurna range and has been popular with trekkers and climbers since the sixties. From the Indian border it takes a bus ride of eight hours to reach it. The journey, traversing some of the most ill-kept mountain roads in the world, can be a perilous form of Russian roulette. The drivers overtake on precipitous blind turns, skim their wheels over cliff edges, drive at speeds which would be madness on flat ground. Passengers do best to grit their teeth and pray, for a glance out of the window shows crumpled bus carcasses littering the rocks below. On that first journey, I counted five.

I arrived in Pokhara as the sun was dropping, genuinely thankful to be alive. It was a mild, cloudless evening and the mountains were perfectly silhouetted against the skyline. I could see Annapurna and the feared Machhapuchare, the fish's tail, still never climbed. Its white summit, irradiated by a pink evening light, is believed by Hindus to be the home of the gods Vishnu and Shiva. Other views deem it the abode of Tara, the Saviouress of Tibetan Buddhism, or that of Amitaba, the Buddha of Boundless Light.

In the foreground, white egrets roosted in the trees. Wizened Tibetan ladies wandered along the edge of the vast Lake Phewe, selling their handicrafts to the smattering of travellers who, like me, had ignored the warnings. It seemed very peaceful. None the less, it was hard not to notice the strong military presence here. Nervous young men stood by roadblocks at various intervals throughout the town, knuckles white over their machine-gun hilts.

Halfway along the lakeside, I made out the summer palace of
the Nepalese royal family. Aside from the Maoist crisis, they'd had
other woes in the last few years. In 2001, a bizarre shooting led
to the deaths of nine of them, including King Birendra and Queen
Ashwarya. It was the worst mass killing of royalty since the 1918
murder of Tsar Nicolas of Russia and his family by Bolshevik
revolutionaries.

Over the following week I waited expectantly for my honey-hunting
contact to arrive. Chitra, as he was called, was a member of
the tough mountain Gurung tribe, the largest ethnic group in the
Annapurna region. Like many young people, he had moved to
Katmandu to work in tourism; it was his only chance of a future.
I had been put in touch with him through a mutual friend at an
NGO and he'd agreed to liaise between myself and the village
elders. I was to wait for his arrival in Pokhara where he said he'd
find me easily enough.

Killing time in Nepal proved to be no hardship. I was quickly
bowled over by the warmth and kindness of the place, its gentle
pace and natural beauty. Despite the continuing civil war, life
remained quite uneventful where I was, a stark contrast to the
bloody skirmishes taking place in the highlands. I took long swims
in the icy lake, practised yoga on the roof of my boarding house,
and hiked up to the Buddhist stupa which gleamed from the peak
of a nearby hill.

I soon befriended a local café owner, a young Nepali in his early
twenties, who strongly impressed me with both his environmental views and his high-altitude coffee from a nearby farm. David
was the first of his family to learn to read and write, and had

single-handedly started the AM/PM café in order to help pay for
the education of his brother and sister. He had a shy face, outsized
ears, and a great capacity for wonder. In a society currently coming
apart at the seams, he took great delight in small things: the quality of his arabica beans, the books he read, the ripeness of his
papayas and avocados. Waiting for Chitra to arrive, we spent many
hours in discussion. I told him about my travels and my life back
home; he told me about what was happening in Nepal, and what
the outlook was for his troubled country.

We were chatting one morning when a hugely fat man in a
leather jacket roared up on a motorcycle. He looked like an ageing
Hell's Angel with a penchant for fast food.

'Derek,' said David quickly. 'A Scottish man who was one of
the first Westerners to move here. He married a Nepalese girl.' He
lowered his voice. 'She is beautiful. I don't think a man like that
could get such a girl in his own country.'

Derek turned out to be quintessentially Scottish. He spoke in
strident tones, smoked ferociously, and took occasional nips from
his hip flask. He had vast pink jowls which gave him the appearance of a rather truculent turkey.

While David brewed him some coffee, the Scotsman
commenced the rolling of a titanic joint. The room steamed with
the fragrance of coffee grounds and the sweet, skunk-like smell
of marijuana.

'Stuff grows like a weed here,' he said. 'M'garden's a bloody
jungle of it.'

I asked him how long he'd been here. He had the slightly troubled aloofness of the long-time expat.

'Twenty fockin' yers,' he sighed, licking the paper with a vast wet tongue. 'Course, it wes all defferent back then. When I arrived it was like fockkin' paradise. India without the anarchy. Cheap as cheps. Little outside enfluence. Now look at it. Place is a fockkin' warzone. Not safe any more.'

'Is it really that bad?' I asked. 'I know there are some troubled areas but Pokhara seems safe enough.'

He glared at me. 'You don't know the half of it, man. No one does. Not even the BBC guy in Katmandu – he doesn' know shit. I tell you there's stuff going on here righ' noo that makes Pol Pot look like a fockkin' Sunday school picnic. We hear rumours. Whispers.' He pulled his chair closer. 'Whole villages decapitated. Torture. And no one knows who's responsible. The lines aren't clear any more.'

I didn't know quite what to say. 'But isn't it the Maoists?'

He shrugged. 'Could just as easily be the soldiers. The government have handled this badly from the start. At first, the Maoists attracted student radicals – folks like that. They marched some yers ago outside the university in Katmandu – s'pposed to be peaceful. So what did the government do? They ordered soldiers to open fire on the demonstration. Fockkin' massacre. The Maoists probably doubled their support that night.'

David handed him his coffee to which he added four spoonfuls of sugar.

Derek continued, puffing on his joint like a steam train increasing speed, 'But the people in high places want somethin' done. So what does the government doo? They send their soldiers out into the hills, into Maoist country. 'S'like sending a pussy cat after a fockkin' tiger. Ten-day patrols! No proper food or tents. No warm clothes. Only way these fellas ken keep goin' is to chew fockkin' amphetamines like Tic-tacs.' He gave a hysterical laugh. 'So you've got a load of young guys, armed to the fockkin' teeth, walking through some of the most difficult terrain in the world, expecting to be attacked at any moment by a bunch of ravin' psychos, and they're all jacked up on speed. Probably haven' slept for days. A fockkin' squirrel farts out there and one of them's going to open fire. And hey, a whole village gets wiped out – so what! Blame the Maoists. Shit happens.'

I quickly made my excuses and left. Derek had the wild-eyed look of a man on edge. And whether or not he was telling the truth, it seemed like he had been out here too long.

CHAPTER FOURTEEN

WHILE I WAITED for Chitra, I read over some of the research I had made about hunting honey. It seemed an almost magical occupation – the culinary equivalent of panning for gold.

Man was not the first creature to raid a bees' nest for its sweetness. Many animals have something of a sweet tooth, as well as a liking for bee brood (young larvae) and even wax in the case of the honeyguide bird, whose digestive tract is well adapted for breaking it down.

As popularised by Winnie the Pooh, bears have a particular fondness for honey. Since man began keeping hives himself, bears have proved a constant aggravation, sometimes destroying a year's harvest within a single night. This is the reason why so many hives across the world are placed in inaccessible locations.

In India the sloth bear hunts the honey of *Apis cerana*, the small forest-bee, as well as that of *Apis dorsata* if it is within reach. South of the Sahara and in parts of the Arabian peninsula, bees are preyed upon by ratels or 'honey badgers', which source the nests by sound. Ratels have also been known to work in conjunction with honeyguide birds who lead them to the nests in exchange for a taste of the honey. In Romania's Carpathian mountains, beekeepers must protect against pine martens, and in central America from a nocturnal racoon-like animal named the *kinkajou*. Other honey-lovers include armadillos in Brazil, tigers in the Ganges Delta, kites in southern India, jackals in Bangladesh.

Primates, with their highly developed brains, are expert honey thieves. In 1969, a man named Deschodt described an incident near Lake Victoria in Africa, in which he saw a group of twenty chimpanzees enjoying the fruits of a honey hunt. The chief male was pulling out honeycombs from a crevice in the cliff and tossing them down to the others, who were jumping up and down and screaming, either from pain at being stung, delight, or possibly a mixture of both.

Two years later, Van Lawick-Goodall observed two adult chimpanzees collaborating to get honey. The male used a short stick to enlarge the opening of an underground nest, while the female reached in to extract the prize.

A number of birds raid bees' nests, especially when winter lessens the availability of insects. Honeyguides – so called because they appear to work in conjunction with other animals which can make the bees' nest accessible to them – enjoy bee larvae, pollen, honey and beeswax. In 1569, Joao dos Santos, a Portuguese missionary working in Ethiopia, noticed honeybirds eating his altar candles.

We do not know exactly how long man has been hunting honey but the presence of bees in rock art can be seen from the Paleolithic period. Honey-hunting itself occurs in rock paintings from the Mesolithic period, perhaps most famously in the La Arana or Spider cave, near Bicorp, Valencia, which is some 7,000 years old. In this painting a man is climbing a ladder up a rock face, surrounded by many swarming bees.

What fascinated me, as I discovered all this, was the similarity of this rock painting to the photographs taken by Eric Valli, the *National Geographic* photographer, only a few years before. Both showed men risking their lives on rudimentary ladders and wielding long sticks to cut away the honey. Could it really be true that nothing had changed in so many thousands of years?

Chitra arrived early the following morning. He was of short stature, flat-nosed and with the pronounced Mongoloid features of the Gurung. His straight, well-groomed moustache and solemn grey eyes would have given him a serious air, had they not been set off by round cheeks and an infectious laugh. I warmed to him at once. Grabbing my pack, I bade farewell to David at the café, and followed Chitra to the bus stop. We would travel now to where the roads petered out. Then the journey proper would begin.

Before we left, however, Chitra made sure that I had no passport on me (I left it with David), nor too much money. The Maoists bear particular grudges against the English and the Americans, because of those countries' influence on the Nepalese government. If we were stopped, I should identify myself as Australian. As to the money, the Maoists had begun to demand payment when they met foreign tourists. They'd ask for a lot but if I showed them a slim wallet, and offered them everything within it, it might suffice. Emergency money I shoved into my sock.

I remember those first steps into the foothills very clearly. A renowned destination for trekkers, parts of Pokhara are well trodden. But we were going by a different route, far off the beaten track, through local villages where few Westerners were seen and an old way of life still continued. Although the path would be very steep, this would shave two days off our journey to the Gurung village.

I was glad of the hills.

We climbed hard and quickly along the course of a river. Flecks of gold and silver minerals sparkled in the gravel beneath my feet. Grey clouds swirled at the peak, making the air close. Chitra moved briskly: these were the playgrounds of his childhood and he was used to their sudden dips and inclines. Although I felt fit and energised, I found the going tough, especially considering the weight of my pack which contained presents for the villagers (some jars of English woodland honey!), my notebook, sleeping bag and binoculars, each of whose weight I would curse separately in the days ahead.

Villagers paused on the terraces as we passed, regarding us with expressions ranging from benevolent smiles to bland disinterest. It was harvest time and the hills thrummed with the sounds of threshing rice, the scything of millet, the grinding of flour between massive stone mills powered by the snow-fed rivers. A Nepalese girl, beautiful as fire, stopped with a basket of tangerines and handed me one. It was tart and refreshing and had green leaves still attached to its stem.

Further on, a group of tiny children too young to help with
the harvest came out to meet us, their smiles full of faith and
wonder at the world in which they lived. Three of them linked
hands across the path, their shrill laughter ringing across the valley,
so that we could not pass. I gave them each a 'school pen' which,
for some unknown reason, have become highly coveted by children here, and they squealed with delight and ran off to show
their mother.

After five hours' hard ascent we paused for a rest. Chitra was
unruffled and barely red in the face. I, on the other hand, was
drenched in sweat, and with calf muscles that twitched unnerv-
ingly beneath my army trousers. I drank a long cool draught of
water from my flask. Chitra sat cross-legged on a flat stone and
looked out across the valley.

'Eagles,' he said suddenly, gesturing with his eyes.

Looking up I saw two white-tailed eagles floating across the
sky. They had dark brown plumage and characteristically white
heads; we could hear their short yelping cries above the wind.

'In Buddhism, we believe the state one should aim for in meditation is that of eagles in flight,' said Chitra quietly. 'These birds
flap their wings briefly and then glide for great distances. The mind
should be able to provide the short burst of energy which then
sustains mental flight.'

By late afternoon the landscape had begun to change. With altitude, we entered a forest of birch, mountain oak, maple and also
the giant rhododendron which is endemic here and flowers so
majestically in spring. It was less than a day's journey from Pokhara
but already I felt as if we were in a different realm. We were

entering Maoist country now: a high, lawless kingdom where a desperate group were using any means within their power to make themselves heard.

A recent Amnesty International article highlighted growing incidents of Maoists abducting children for 're-education', another policy which invites comparisons with the Shining Path. And the police, understaffed, underpaid and deeply corrupt, were drawing international attention for their use of torture as a means of interrogation. Their methods included rape, electric shock treatment, *belana* (rolling a heavy-weighted stick along the thigh muscles), *falanga* (beatings on the soles of the feet), random beatings and mock executions. Despite Nepal's ratification of the UN Convention against Torture in 1991, torture is still not a criminal offence here.

That night we slept in a simple village hut. Chitra knew many people along the route and it was easy enough to find someone with sufficient floor space for us to doss down on. Gurung houses are built of wood, then covered with dung and thatched with grass. Their doors are unusually low – a folk protection against evil spirits. The Gurung still retain a certain number of shamanistic beliefs, one of which is that evil cannot bend its head.

Inside, the houses are dark and full of smoke from the cooking fire. At first I could see nothing at all within, but as my eyes became accustomed to the gloom I made out battered pots and pans hanging from nails, cooking utensils, storage jars for grain, water and *raksi*, a potent liquor made from millet. It was difficult not to cough with all the smoke.

Cross-legged around the fire, we ate *dhal bat*, the traditional dish of spiced red lentils served with rice and a chutney made from radishes. Chitra conversed with his friends in the Gurung dialect, while I was happy simply to take in my surroundings, feeling the heat from the fire and tasting the earthiness of the food. We ate with our hands, washing them before and afterwards. As is the custom in Nepal, the family waited until we had finished before eating anything themselves.

When the moment was right, Chitra asked the family about the Maoists. Soldiers had been here a few days before, we were told. We would see their posters the following day stuck to tree trunks and houses.

'Be a little careful,' said the Gurung mother, clearing my plate and scrubbing it with ash from the fire. 'They do not like foreigners.'

The next morning we were up and off at first light. Chitra hoped to make the village of the honey-hunters by nightfall but it was quite a journey. And we were taking the long way round to avoid a pass where we knew the Maoists had made camp.

I saw one of their posters that morning, handwritten in Nepalese. Chitra translated their demands for me:

Notice published by the United District People's Government

(1) All NGOs to leave Nepal immediately.
(2) Interest rates to be lowered.
(3) Price lists to be displayed in all shops.
(4) Introduction of minimum fare in public transport.
(5) Public justice should be meted out quickly.
(6) Education and health sector investigated for corruption.

(7) All army and police must leave jobs.

(8) Innocent people have been called terrorists and forced to leave their villages: they should be acquitted and allowed to return.

(9) No drinking or gambling in villages.

(10) Public land and forest must be systematised and distributed to people.

(11) Actual news must be printed and displayed in public places.

(12) People's rules should be put in suggestion boxes everywhere.

It was salutary to stand in the open air and read this sign, the visible proof of a movement I had read so much about in official foreign documents. All too used to reading about such things from afar, I had now to realise that I was in the midst of things, possibly a mere mile or two away from the rebels themselves.

As we climbed, the flora turned to cloud forest with mosses and lichen, tree ferns and orchids hosted by the hardier trees. Natural windows in the woods opened out on to thrilling panoramas towards the knife-sharp peaks. I was struck by a succession of feelings: exultation at being in the Himalayas, but also the thought that perhaps it was irresponsible of me to be here at all, fulfilling my own rarefied dreams while others fought a bloody war.

I reassured myself with the knowledge that the Nepalese, more than half of whom live below the internationally recognised poverty line, need all the outside money they can get. The dollars which I left for my food and lodging could make a tangible difference to these people's lives.

On and upwards through small mountain villages where life continues as it has for millennia. Archaeological evidence suggests, in

fact, that humans lived in these Himalayan foothills as far back as
2 million years ago. Was it possible that those early hominids were
hunting honey too, as we would shortly be doing?

Smells of buffalo dung and cooking fires, the cockadoodle-do
of a proud Himalayan rooster. Grain spread out to dry on mats
in the sun. A line of baby chicks, like small moving pom-poms,
making their first forays into the bewildering world. Cobalt
six-petalled flowers between stones. Village women, gold hoops
in their ears and nostrils, bent double under seventy-five-kilo
baskets of firewood. A lot of chattering and laughter as we passed.
People seemed excited.

'They are talking about the hunt,' said Chitra as we left one particularly animated village. 'Everyone knows about it. They are very
happy. No one has hunted honey for some three or four years now.'

This was news to me. I asked why.

Chitra looked troubled. 'Well, village life is changing very fast.
Young people are moving to Pokhara or Katmandu to look for
work. Very few are remaining here and following the old ways.'
He rested a hand on my shoulder and together we looked out
across the valley, green rice paddies cut from the hillsides. 'Hunting
honey has to be done at specific times of year,' he explained. 'And
this time of year is also the peak harvesting time. If the villagers
don't get the grain in quickly they may not have enough to survive
the winter. So to let people hunt honey is simply not possible –
they need all the manpower they can get.'

I began to understand.

'It's not just the ten men needed for the hunt,' continued Chitra.
'It takes time and effort to weave the ladders and the baskets. At
least three men working for ten days. Then there's the three days

for the hunt, special food to be made. Back in the old days, the villages were full enough and there were people for the fields *and* to take the honey from the cliffs. Now, as you will notice, these villages have more old people than young. They are poor and tired and often hungry. So that the news that there is a honey hunt happening, even so many hours away, travels like the wind. If the quantity is great, we must set aside honey for all of them. It will bring much joy.'

We said little after this conversation. Chitra picked up the pace still more and it was all I could do to keep up with him. Gaps in the white clouds which intimated the coming of winter provided scant glimpses of the high passes above. It was late November now, the final days of summer. The light had a strange paleness to it – I remember that very clearly. It bestowed a feeling of insularity: an eeriness which dogged my every step as we trudged up through the fading afternoon, through the dank wet forests.

At dusk, we had many miles still to go. A mist was rising up from the woods which wisped spookily around our feet, fogged the way, cast a cold chill across our skin.

Chitra was some distance ahead now, showing no sign of slowing down. I was exhausted and my breath came in ragged gasps. More difficult even than the ascents were the descents which followed. My toes jammed painfully against the front of my boots, and my knees protested against the continuous jars. We had been walking for ten hours already and, unlike Chitra, I was carrying a full pack. My whole torso ached, my head throbbed, my tongue had swollen from dehydration. But I was too proud to ask Chitra to slow down.

Most alarmingly, the light was going. Shadows began to elongate, the contours of the hillside to soften and smudge. I willed my eyes to remain sharp – the last thing I need now was to trip and break an ankle.

As the sun set, we left the forest behind. Now we were on mountain paths, narrow ribbons worn smooth by generations of stocky Gurung feet. Many of these hugged the cliff on one side and dropped sheerly on the other. I could hear the baritone growl of the river below, as it sucked and popped through gullies. Seeing a sizeable switch lying on the ground, I picked it up. From now on I would use it as a blind man's cane, probing the way ahead as it became too dark to see, and most importantly keeping a clear gauge of how far away the cliff edge lay. One slip here might be my last.

Memory has rendered those last few hours formless. Like a marathon runner driven past all limits, I entered a zone in which all my senses shut down. Smell, taste and sound became irrelevant. All my attention focused on placing one foot after the other, on staying away from the edge, on disallowing my legs the satisfaction of collapse.

Inwardly, I became angry with Chitra. Was it really necessary to push so hard? To risk so much by travelling at night? And what would the Maoists think if they saw two shadowy figures coming towards them in the dark? Would they shoot first, ask questions later?

Afterwards I would realise that to him, we simply *weren't* pushing hard. Himalayan children think little of a five-hour walk merely to get to school each day. I saw villagers carrying two or sometimes three fifty-kilo sacks of grain up steep hillsides *in one load,* their faces a mask of furious intent. The Gurung lead impossibly arduous lives: I would have to keep up as best I could.

It was nine-thirty by the time I saw the lights of the village twinkling in the distance. I was in a place where time did not exist, only gradations of grey and the rhythm of the moment. The lights' gentle glow made my eyes water. My level of awareness changed as it occurred to me that, perhaps, we might conceivably have arrived. Was it possible?

'We are here,' said Chitra cheerfully from ahead. His face was a dark outline against the sky.

'About bloody time,' I muttered under my breath.

CHAPTER FIFTEEN

THE GURUNG VILLAGE was little more than a haphazard collection of buildings perched on a ridge. Most of the houses might have sprung from the Middle Ages, though some had roofs of corrugated tin instead of the traditional slate. Mostly the main doors and the windows of the upper storey faced east. Lightning rods, in the shape of tridents, were evident on most houses to protect them from thunderbolts.

I was quickly shown to a room sometimes used to house trekkers, a simple metal-framed bed between mud walls. With the setting of the sun, the temperature had dropped very quickly. I was utterly spent, shivering with cold, and fending off dizzy spells at regular intervals. I would have given my right arm to climb into my sleeping bag then and there. But the day was not over yet.

By the fire in a nearby house, Chitra and I ate ravenously. Lentils and rice, curd, sweet *massala* tea. Pungent strips of buffalo flesh hung from the ceiling, several of which Chitra incorporated into his meal. The food restored me a little, and the fire drove some of the chill from my bones. The excitement of our arrival was palpable too, and the room quickly filled with important figures from the village council: wiry, deeply wrinkled men for the most part, wearing the traditional Gurung *bhangra*, a cloth bag over each shoulder. I shook many hands and stared into many proud eyes.

Spirits were high that night. The *raksi* was flowing. My arrival meant several things for the villagers. Firstly, it meant that the hunt was actually happening. It meant that the men could continue a tradition which had been occurring in these mountains for thousands of years. In a culture being rapidly eroded by Western values, this was important.

Secondly, it meant that a large injection of cash would be swelling the village coffers. Chitra had cautioned me from the start that these men would not go ahead with the hunt unless a suitable payment could be agreed upon. If there were to be fewer men available for the harvest, they would need compensation. On top of that there were the enormous risks to take into account, life-threatening risks, and the fact that tourism had brought them very little money since the Maoists appeared.

While I ate, Chitra outlined the order of events. After supper, we would reconvene in the chambers of the village council. There, among all the important men from the village, we would come to some agreement. Privately, I told Chitra the maximum sum I would pay. I recognised, of course, the degree to which some dollars could help this village and I was happy to help. But I was also aware that I might easily be regarded as a Westerner with limitless pockets, and hence asked for an unrealistic amount. I hoped we could come to some suitable compromise.

It was eleven o clock by the time the meeting began. In Nepalese villages the working day still moves in accordance with the daylight and, though all but the most remote now have electricity, it remains customary to go to bed soon after sundown. That most of the villagers were still up and awake gave some indication of what a big event this was for them. The atmosphere was like that of a festival or feast-day.

The council chamber was a long wooden hut, resembling a schoolroom, with a narrow desk down each side that could seat ten men. Every seat was full. Lesser members of the village were squashed into corners and in the doorway. The ceiling was low, the room filled with smoke. Most of the villagers seemed to smoke as if there was no tomorrow: the cheapest tobacco imaginable that became a yellow fog when burnt.

Chitra and I sat in the middle seats, scrutinised from all sides. I felt nervous and a little unwell and frustrated, too, at having to rely solely on Chitra for the translation. Gurung dialect is a variant of Chinese and Tibetan and quite difficult even for Nepalese to understand. Honey, for example, is *maha* in Nepali but *kwhe khudu* in Gurung.

In the absence of language, I observed the postures and expressions of the men around the room. The village headman with his high cheekbones and knotted brow. The respected carpenter, squat and stocky, a pulse beating on his temple and with a faintly troubled air. The Brahmin with his gravel voice and a wool cap. Only one man remained quiet and watchful.

'That's the chief honey-hunter,' whispered Chitra. 'His father was honey-hunter before him. This is a very important day for him. If he leads a successful hunt he will become enormously respected in the community again. His status has fallen somewhat since they have not been hunting so often.'

There was a sharp rap on the table. The headman was calling the meeting to order. 'I invite Nakkal Bahadur Gurung to speak,' he boomed. The room fell hush.

'Bahadur means "the brave",' explained Chitra.

The honey-hunter got to his feet. He was a short, lean man, without an ounce of fat on him. He had ochre-yellow eyes, a curved moustache, a face whose slant seemed tempered by sadness.

'I have counted twenty-four nests on the cliff,' he began. 'Many of them look very full. And since it is so soon after the full moon, I think that now is a fine time for the hunt – when it is dark the bees eat more honey, when the moon is bright they eat less.' He paused and swept his eyes around the room, clearly enjoying the chance to hold court. 'But since I am talking there is a point to be made. After the last hunt, the ropes, ladders and baskets were abandoned. Left to rot! I have been spending many days making new ones and this has cost me time and money. I suggest that the honey-hunter should be given responsibility to look after these things so that they can be kept safe.'

There was an immediate chorus of shouting from around the room. Others clearly resented the thought that Nakkal should be given this responsibility. The headman held up his hand. 'Very well,' he said. 'To prevent further damage to honey-hunting equipment, I decree that you may look after the ladders in future.'

Nakkal nodded.

'But the main purpose of this meeting is to decide on a price,' said the chief. 'How much do you think we should ask for?'

Nakkal looked at me with what, I felt, was a good deal more benevolence than some of the others. 'I do not think we should be greedy,' he said simply. 'If we set a reasonable price, we may get others coming to our village. We should think about the future.'

The room erupted into shouting.

'Who are you,' burst out one man, 'to deny the village money? I suggest the sum of twelve hundred American dollars. That is what was paid to another village by a film company some time ago. This man wants to see our hunt, then he should pay for it!'

'Yes,' chorused other voices. 'The Englishman should give us the same amount! The same amount!'

Chitra's voice wavered as he translated all this for me. He knew I would never pay so much. And besides, the tone had degenerated almost at once. We could hardly hear ourselves think amidst all the shouting.

'What do you mean, who am I?' shouted Nakkal, white with rage. 'I am the chief honey-hunter. You are nothing but a carpenter. Do I tell you how to build your houses? Are you going to be the one climbing that cliff? Why is it always the poor men who take the risks while the rich remain comfortably on the ground?' Nakkal had his jaw drawn tight, and his voice was pitched high as a violin.

The headman stepped in. 'Enough!' he shouted. 'Let the Englishman speak. He may have an idea of how much he wants to give us.'

There was a sudden, absolute calm. I got to my feet. As concisely as possible, and with Chitra translating, I tried to explain that I was not merely here for my own enjoyment, but to try to record something of their traditions. I wanted people to know how unique were the Gurung honey-hunters. Perhaps my book might bring more people to their area, so that honey-hunting could be an annual occurrence again.

'I am happy to give you all that I have,' I concluded, 'but that is only five hundred dollars. Unless we can agree on that sum, I will have to leave in the morning. But it will be with much sadness that I go.'

Once again the room erupted into bedlam. Several men leapt to their feet.

'Five hundred dollars!' shouted a stick-thin fellow, thrusting his finger in my face. 'Out of the question! How *dare* you!'

'Be reasonable,' shouted another. 'Five hundred is better than nothing.'

'Shut up, you old fool,' shouted a third. 'No one asked your opinion.'

'And there is also the question of what the money is to be used for,' said Nakkal, re-entering the fray. 'Am I to recoup my costs? What of the time I have spent weaving? If there is no hunt, I will lose a lot of money. Always the poor men are the ones to suffer!'

The oldest man in the room, as shrivelled as a raisin but with piercing jade eyes, raised a spindly hand. Much respect is given by the Gurung to the elderly and the arguing ceased. When he spoke, his voice was a hoary whisper. 'The money should be used for trees,' he said softly. 'There are not so many trees any more, and that is why there are not so many bees. Every year there are fewer nests on the cliff. Soon there will be none. So we should plant trees which the bees like in order to keep the honey-hunting alive for future generations.'

'A fine idea,' said the headman, puffing on his cigarette. 'That is a fine idea.'

And so the debate continued. More *raksi* was drunk, more cigarettes smoked. Tempers became frayed. Fists were raised and dropped. Tea was brought in, then cleared away. The pages of my notebook filled. Poor Chitra translated for everyone until his voice became hoarse. At last, in the early hours of the morning, the sum of $700 was agreed upon. For them it was a king's ransom. For me, it was a lot more than I had and it would mean living extremely frugally in the months to come. I had already taken out bank loans to get this far. But I was damned if I was to come this far and turn back now. And besides, anyone could see how much they needed the money. In the coming months, even rice would be a luxury up here. Millet, which they didn't especially like, would become their staple winter diet.

When the deal was struck, and the amount agreed on, the atmosphere became jubilant. Whatever happened now, there *would* be a hunt. Everyone began to shake my hand and slap me on the back. Toasts were made. Laughter echoed. I was so tired by this stage that I could barely stand. Somehow, I found my way to bed where I collapsed, fully clothed, and slept like the living dead.

I had slept barely a few hours, it seemed, when I was woken. Six a.m. and I was the last person in the village to get up. I dressed quickly, putting on every layer I had, and splashed water on my face. The water felt as if it had been part of a glacier only minutes before. I was very excited.

As I stepped out of my door I saw something which will remain with me to my dying day: a line of snow-capped peaks licked by tongues of pure orange flame. The dawn was cracking like an egg yolk over Annapurna. I had not realised how high we had climbed the previous day.

For a time I simply stood there, humbled and awestruck. The idea of running for my notebook or camera didn't even occur to me: there are some things which the act of description can only neutralise. No adjective under the sun could have touched on this. No picture could have captured such energy: what the Indians call *prana*, the elemental life-force which runs through all things.

So I just stood there, physically shocked, moved to my very core by this angle on the roof of the world.

Half an hour later, I found Chitra sitting on his own, cradling some *chai*.

'I saw this every day as a child,' he said as I approached, nodding towards the sunrise. 'In Katmandu I see only buildings and smoke.'

I asked where everyone was.

'Already down at the cliff lighting fires beneath the nests,' he said. 'The bees remain in the nest at night. So the fires have to be lit before dawn or many of them will have started to leave. If that happens, they may return to find us stealing their honey and sting us very badly.'

It made sense. A small boy brought me some *chai*, which I accepted gratefully. Every bone in my body ached. It was so cold that my eyes stung.

No sooner had we finished our tea than it was time to leave. Chitra led the way surefootedly through the small cluster of village dwellings and down on to the path below. The village was exactly as I had imagined it: like something viewed from a time machine, all lit up by white Himalayan light. Shaggy goats tied to stakes foraged outside the houses. Elsewhere there were bullocks, mastiffs or leggy chickens. Several huts had what looked like the stumps of old trees hanging from their porch lintels: these were rudimentary beehives made from hollowed-out logs. Fascinating in their own right but not what I was here for.

Below the ridge on which the village was built there was a path so steep that, were it covered in snow, no skier in the world would attempt it. We were entering a precipitous valley at whose base a river hurtled towards Pokhara. Above the rapids was the famous cliff where the *Apis laboriosa* or rock bees made their nests.

The way was dangerously steep – steeper than anything we'd attempted the day before. It took more than an hour to descend, at which point we branched across the rice terraces to where about ten of the men from the village were gathered outside a small hut. One of them had a goat tethered on a rope. 'For luck,' someone told me.

I was spellbound by this place. The crisp air. The serene terraces recently plucked of their rice. Multitudes of butterflies. Pushed against the sky, the mountains enclosing every horizon. And such green: it was as if the whole world was suffused with chlorophyll.

The men outside the hut were working hard to put the finishing touches to the ladders and ropes. Others were preparing food. Nakkal, the honey-hunter, seemed especially happy, barking orders like a general before a big offensive. The headman looked subdued, however, and he quickly came over to talk to us.

'The Maoists are nearby,' Chitra translated. 'They were here earlier.'

I asked what problems they might cause.

The headman shrugged. 'The Maoists like to claim a portion of all monies made in these mountains. Above the snowline there is a wild herb called *yarsagumba* which fetches a very big price in China. The Maoists tax the locals on everything they find – it makes them a lot of money. What's to say they wouldn't do the same here?'

I took the opportunity to ask the headman about the history of the honey-hunting. Part of his responsibility was to be a repository for the stories of the Gurung. The idea seemed to pleased him. He stretched his legs out in front of him, lit a cigarette, and began. Later I would learn that I was the first Westerner they had ever told this story too – a great privilege for me.

Many years ago, back in the clouds of time, there was a man named Garable who lived in our village. He was married and he had nine sons and he was a great honey-hunter – this was his cliff. After his wife died, however, Garable decided to take a new wife. She was young and extremely beautiful. The sons became very jealous of their father. 'She is too young for him,' they said. 'An old man cannot satisfy such a beauty.'

Together the sons plotted to kill their father in order to get the woman for themselves.

Soon it was the time for honey-hunting. Garable ordered his sons to go and fetch him some honey but they refused. Garable went to the cliff himself, and began to cut the combs away from the rock. But when he was almost finished, the sons came to the top and cut the rope! Then they left and went back to the village, thinking they had killed him.

But Garable was not dead. He had fallen some distance and hurt himself badly, but he had landed on a tiny outcrop of the cliff. He lived on this tiny outcrop for some days, keeping himself alive by eating the honey.

Back in the village, the sons began a competition to see who would have their father's wife. It was an archery competition and the aim was to shoot an arrow through a tiny hole in a tree trunk. Some days passed, but none of the sons could shoot the arrow through the hole.

On the cliff Garable had finished all the honey. He became so hungry that he had to eat his own skin. One day two vultures found him there, a skeleton, and offered to help him. But Garable did not trust the vultures because he thought he was too big for them to carry. 'I'll only trust you,' he said, 'if you can carry four times your weight in stones from the river.' The vultures agreed and carried four big stones in their talons to where Garable was perched.

'Where shall we take you?' said the vultures.

'If you take me to my house, my sons will surely kill me,' said Garable. 'Take me instead to the temple by the waterfall where my wife goes to collect water.' So the vultures did as they were asked and took Garable to the temple.

Next day, Garable's wife went to the temple as usual to collect water. There was no wind that day and so there were no ripples. But from his hiding place, Garable disturbed the water with his hand. When the wife looked to where the ripples came from she saw a ring gleaming from the water. It was Garable's ring and she knew at once that he was alive.

When she found her husband, he was almost dead. He had no more skin, only bones. She carried him home in secret and hid him in the storage area of the house, on the second floor, so that he could recover. In the first days Garable was so thin he could eat only one grain of rice. Soon, he could eat one handful of rice. He began to practise drawing his bow.

Outside the sons were still competing to see who would take possession of their father's wife. Waiting until no one was looking, Garable took aim from his hiding place and his arrow went directly through the hole.

Immediately, all the sons claimed that it had been their arrow which had won. A huge fight broke out. The youngest son, however, knew that there was only one man who could shoot with such accuracy: their father.

'Our father is alive,' he told the other sons at once.

At this point, Garable came out of the house. He was no longer of this world. He had become a god.

'I will tell you what happens after you die,' he said to his sons. 'Some of you will become wind. Some of you will become water. Some earth. You, my youngest son who recognised my arrow, will become fire. Fire is the strongest of all elements, it can consume anything, it is wise. From this day on, place some food in the fire before eating as a sacrifice. Think of me and that I have forgiven you.'

Garable absolved his sons for what they had done to him. He wept.

From then on he wore robes of gold, and the sticks with which he hunted honey were made from silver. He became the protector of his cliff and of all honey-hunters for ever.

The headman pinched out his cigarette between thumb and forefinger. Red sparks drifted to the ground. 'The lamas in our village tell that story whenever someone dies,' he said. 'It is a story of forgiveness. It is a story of love.'

The headman led the way towards the honey-hunting cliff. Several of the villagers, including the Brahmin, followed us to the point where the path ended and the cliff began. I caught my first glimpse of the nests, impossibly large and dangerous, great crescents of honey hanging from the rock face like yellow moons, with black swathes of insects around each one. The cliff had a slight overhang. At its base a river whipped past, a torrent of fury and foam.

'See those four stones?' shouted the headman above the noise of the river. 'Halfway up the cliff, on that small ledge. Four giant rocks of a completely different stone to the cliff itself. How did they get there? The vultures put them there during Garable's test.'

I saw that he was right. There *were* four boulders resting on a tiny ledge. And they were of an obviously different mineral to the cliff itself. It was remarkable.

One of the villagers took some firewood from his *bhangra* and kindled a flame. Another took out an iron skillet. Another rolled some chapattis from rice flour and water.

'Are we eating?' I asked.

Chitra shook his head. 'We are making a sacrifice,' he said, 'to the gods of the cliff. And to the gods and goddesses of the jungle. This will ensure there will be no accidents.'

I watched as a number of chapattis were fried and laid on seven banana leaves on the ground. Some rice was added to each, then a knob of butter. The villagers were grave. Now the headman tore a prayer flag into seven strips and laid these on top of the food. He looked about him. A small plant grew thereabouts and he picked seven of them.

'A sacred plant,' said Chitra. 'We call this *pati*. The headman will stick each plant in the ground before each leaf. Each represents a different god.'

The Brahmin began chanting in a low voice. His eyes were closed and his hands laid out flat before him.

'He is praying to each of our ancestors in turn,' whispered Chitra. 'Their names are Siddha, Ramsan, Garable, Abgar, Dhanrash, Harilal, Jangbir and Chandrasingh. Our village has been hunting honey on this cliff for more than two thousand years. We pray to them to ask their blessing on today's hunt and that they ensure the bees do not attack us. We hope there will be no deaths.'

Finally each flag, made flammable by the oil from the butter, was lit. The ceremony now over, we walked away, seven flags smoking at our backs, the smoke carried gently away by the morning wind.

Back at the hut the ladders were finished and rolled up into giant coils ready for use. Another bonfire had been started while we were away, and men were now busy collecting wood to keep it going. It crackled and flared with the oil-rich herbs from the mountainside.

A dull scraping noise caught my attention. The village carpenter was sharpening his *kukri*,* the traditional curved machete carried by most Nepalese, on a flat stone. The lucky goat, which I had forgotten about, grew skittish.

What happened next occurred so quickly that it was over before I knew what was going on. All of a sudden the carpenter had the goat by the horns and was wrestling it to the ground. It bucked and writhed. Another man laid a stout branch across its neck and, with one quick fluid motion, the *kukri* came down like a hammer. There was a loud popping noise, like the bursting of a balloon, and the goat's head came free from its body. The carpenter held the head up in his free hand — I could see the tendons and arteries hanging from its neck — and sprinted across the pasture.

I was so shocked I almost fell off the rock I was sitting on.

With blood still spurting everywhere, the carpenter ran towards

---

*The common tool (and sometimes weapon) of most Nepali men. Nepali boys are supposed to be able to handle their *kukri* by the age of five. It can be used for building, clearing, chopping firewood, digging, cutting meat and vegetables, skinning and nowadays also opening tins. The *kukri* design is centuries old with the blades typically between twelve and fifteen inches long. There are, however, smaller knives with six- to eight-inch blades and ceremonial versions ranging from twenty-four to twenty-eight inches. *Kukri* sheaths normally hold two small knives called the *karda* and the *chakmak*. The *chakmak* is for sharpening the blade and starting fires with flint and the *karda* is for skinning. All *kukri* knives have a notch at the base of the blade near the handle, which is called the *cho* or *kaudi*. The sheath or scabbard is usually made of wood with a leather covering and a brass cap at the end.

the ladders and dripped the scarlet liquid all over them. Then he moved on to the ropes. The pressure of the spurting blood was incredible, like a garden hose with a thumb constricting the flow. The job done, the carpenter walked rather more sedately back toward us, the goat's eyes staring fixedly from the severed head. Back at the rock, the body still twitched.

'So *that's* what they meant by the lucky goat,' I said to Chitra, my stomach churning.

'They put the blood on the ladders and ropes so that the gods will be appeased,' he said. 'It is a kind of protection for the hunters.'

I saw the logic. And in truth it had been a quick and painless death. It was merely the unexpectedness of it which had shocked me, the brightness of the viscera which even now stained the paddy straw.

More blood was applied to the rock upon which the knife had been sharpened.

'A god lives beneath that rock,' said Chitra. 'He is called "Bhimsen", the strong. We must keep him happy, too.'

There was one more ceremony to undergo. The headman used his own *kukri* to slit open the belly of the goat. Innards flopped into a waiting bowl. Then he plunged his hand into the wound and removed the liver. It was grisly stuff. When he held it up into the air it resembled a sort of smooth white fish steaming faintly in his hand.

Everyone fell silent. The headman leant forward so that his face was almost touching the liver. His eyes narrowed in concentration. The atmosphere grew pregnant with expectation. Then he looked up and smiled. 'Excellent,' he pronounced.

'If the liver is dirty,' said Chitra, 'it means a bad hunt. But the outlook is good. It is clean!'*

Now the cooking began. The body of the goat was thrown on to the fire in order to burn off its hide. Rice stalks and brush-wood were added so that the flames soared. The air filled with the sweet stench of burning flesh. At intervals, the goat was turned over, its hide rubbed with a stick to remove the last of the hair. Finally, it was removed from the heat, its skin stripped off, and the flesh chopped into suitable chunks for cooking.

Everyone was laughing and joking. Tea was brewed and drunk. Vegetables were produced from bags and sliced: peppery moun-tain spinach, radishes, earth-clodded potatoes, garlic. Water boiled. Bones simmered. The tongue and liver were fried in herbs and eaten as a kind of starter, steeped in the rich blood. Pails of basmati rice the size of small baths were loaded on to the fire. Huge slabs of meat were grilled.

'These men will eat meat very rarely,' said Chitra. 'You can see that they are enjoying this very much.'

I watched the chief honey-hunter sitting quietly to one side, drawing on a handrolled cigarette. His eyes flicked watchfully across the mountainside, taking in the position of the sun and the moving clouds. There was an existential mood upon him today, like a mountaineer preparing for some great ascent.

Hepatoscopy or hepatomancy (divination by examining the liver of sacrificed animals). In Babylon this practice was very popular, so much so that they had a specialised priest called a *bara* to perform the service. The Babylonians thought the liver was a 'vehicle' by which the gods revealed their intentions.

Nakkal accepted a plateful of the liver with a smile and began to eat. A young man of about twenty sat down beside him. Both of them seemed marked by the same taciturnity, the same digni- fied reserve.

'That is his son,' said Chitra. 'Mangal Bahadur Gurung. Nakkal is training him to follow in his footsteps. But he is also a Gurung Lama, a priest.'

'Will the son hunt today?'

'Yes. He will also be on the ladder with his father.'

The headman approached us.

'Lower your head,' said Chitra.

The headman pressed some grains of rice on to my forehead, moistened with some holy water. Then he did the same to Chitra and to all the other men in turn. It was the final nod to the deities.

Now that the ceremonies were over, we began to eat. Unlike in the Middle East where my vegetarianism had caused offence, here the villagers seemed unperturbed by it. Instead they simply loaded my bowl with extra dhal, minced spinach, fresh roti breads made from rice flour, a bright yellow omelette. I couldn't help noticing that the hand that offered me my bowl was stained red from the blood of the goat. Nor that the goat's head, whose final location I had wondered about, turned out to be propped on a wooden shelf within the hut, its yellow eyes watching me.

We ate as if there was no tomorrow. No sooner had I taken a mouthful than more was added to my bowl. Each of the villagers ate between half and one kilo of rice. I couldn't fathom how such small men could put away so much. As for the likelihood of them being able to climb ladders with any agility after such a feast, it didn't bear thinking about. The truth is their lives demand too much of their bodies. They work too hard, and have to eat fantastic amounts to provide themselves with the energy they need. The landscape and the life they lead make great demands of them. Their lives are hard and fierce and they die young – at sixty on average.

It was now around eleven o'clock. The hunt was about to begin.

CHAPTER SIXTEEN

THERE WERE TEN of us. Two men carried the bamboo ladders strapped to their backs, so cumbersome they seemed like human snails beneath their load. The thought that they would shortly be walking along a cliff edge like that beggared belief. I had tried to lift one of the ladders back at the hut and estimated it at 100 kilos. Not for the first time did I consider that this hunt was at my instigation. If someone died today, part of the responsibility would lie with me. Others carried the honey baskets (*kutlu*), Nakkal's sticks (*whengo*), the ropes (*pechhu*), several hooks (*kwili*) and a rudimentary funnel (*chhora*).

It took half an hour's steep climb towards the village before we reached a point where we could jump across on to the cliff top. Nakkal leapt first, hopping spryly over the gap. I went next, trying hard not to look down. From here on in we would face thick jungle, with to the right, a drop of many hundred feet to the rapids and sharp rocks.

Leading the way, Nakkal chopped at vines and briars with his machete. Following closely, I kept my eyes glued to his every step. All the honey-hunters were in bare feet. I, on the other hand, was wearing hiking boots – about as useful on such slippery ground as snowshoes.

Monkeys flipped through the trees above us, taunting us earth-bound humans constrained by the pull of gravity. Razor-sharp thorns snagged at our feet, easily piercing my trousers. Ferns growing to chest height were slashed away by Nakkal's blade, though some pinged back to whip me in the face. Thick vines draped from the trees and I soon learnt to search for these. If my footing went, there would be only one chance to find a handhold.

Honey-hunters had died on this cliff before. Earlier I'd heard the story of a Brahmin hunter who slipped and fell because of a loose rope. Famed for his enormous strength, he'd managed to reach the far side of the river after his fall. By the time his friends had arrived he was vomiting blood. He died shortly afterwards. That was eighty years ago, Nakkal had told me. He had left behind a four-month-old son, now an old man still living near by.

After an hour of sluggish progress along the cliff top, I decided to let some of the other hunters overtake me. With the path becoming more dangerous with every step, I knew that Nakkal needed men he could communicate with around him. Equally, I felt that I needed to be near Chitra so that I could understand what was asked of me. I found my guide eight men back in the line, pale with fear.

'We must be insane,' I said, trying to make light of it.

'I have not done this before either,' he admitted. 'They are used to it, I think.'

I grinned nervously. 'Nakkal's moving so fast you'd have thought there was some sort of race on. I decided to let him and the others go at their own pace.'

'Go with care, Mr Piers,' said Chitra. 'It will not be good for my guiding business if you fall off this cliff.'

Chitra and I brought up the rear somewhat more cautiously than the rest. But none the less, my feet slipped twice on the slick undergrowth. Both times I managed to find a nearby branch to grab on to but, if the truth be known, I was beginning to lose my cool. These men seemed to have a natural agility and a lack of fear that enabled them to move up here with confidence. Much as I was feeling the thrill of it, my rational side told me that to go on was sheer madness.

But I *had* to see how they worked. It was why I was here. It was what I had dreamt of from the moment this bizarre quest sprang into my mind. Choosing every step with meticulous care, I picked my way along the cliff edge. Soon we came to the place where Nakkal and his team had stopped. I found a strong sapling to grasp hold of and sat back to watch. Correct preparations from the cliff top were all-important if the hunt was to take place without injury.

First, each hunter cleared the area around him with his *kukri*. The ground was a mass of green foliage, which could easily snare a man's ankle. For some minutes the scene was a chaos of slashing. The debris was tossed over the cliff edge where it floated gently down, its graceful descent only highlighting the enormous distance to the ground.

It was intriguing to watch the hunters working as a team. A nod here, a grunt there. Each knew what was required of him, and they worked efficiently with one another, mutually recognising that their very lives depended on a calm and methodical pace. Nakkal had taken it upon himself to clear the brush on the edge of the cliff. From where I stood he appeared to be hanging off a sheer precipice, holding on with one hand.

At times I could barely watch. The margin for error was simply too small. Every man here had his life in the balance, and yet the seeming levity with which they worked made it seem as if they didn't care. It brought my own small encounter with mortality into the sharpest focus. Did these men fear death so little because of its constant proximity in their lives? And why do we, in the developed world, fear death so much? It also highlighted, as clearly as anything could, just how far man will go for the sensation of sweetness on his tongue. Quite simply, they were prepared to risk their lives for it.

It was time to attach the ladders. Each was constructed out of individual strands of bamboo, pleated many times over. At various intervals, strong slats of wood were incorporated into the weave. The overall effect was rudimentary but for their purposes ideal: it had enormous strength combined with the natural flexibility of the bamboo.

At this point I slipped one too many times. With a creak the sapling I was holding gave way and I took a dangerous lurch towards the cliff edge. Several of the honey-hunters darted towards me with a cry but I had already stabilised myself by grabbing a handful of ferns growing from the slope. None the less, my cool finally went. I resolved to return to the cliff path and watch the hunt from below. This would, in any case, provide a better perspective.

An hour later I was back on the mountain path, ecstatic with relief. Not since San Francisco, so long ago now, had I seen my life flash before my eyes like that. I weaved my way down, crossed the bridge over the rapids and began to trek across to where I could see the cliff face. For the first time that day I could relax. The sun blazed, the waters foamed past. Purple-coned flowers rustled in the breeze.

Reaching the terraces which bordered the river, I found three small Nepalese children lying on their backs against a bale of hay, watching the honey-hunting with great excitement. They laughed when they saw me, danced round in circles, and begged to see the binoculars hanging around my neck. They had the most ingenuous faces in the world.

I showed them how the lenses worked. One of them almost keeled over with shock when he saw the cliff coming so close. He took them off quickly, as if they were some strange Western magic, then thought better and steeled himself for another look.

With some difficulty I retrieved the field-glasses and examined the situation on the cliff. I had arrived at the perfect moment. Nakkal was slowly descending the ladder for the first time. His two long sticks were attached to his *bhangra* with cords. Nakkal's son was already positioned on the cliff face, perched on a small ledge at a halfway point so that he could prevent the ladder from swinging out.

A third man waited at the top of the cliff on the first few rungs of the ladder. It was his job to convey messages from Nakkal to the others. From what I could see, he had also forgone the precaution of a safety line. I could see the tension with which he held himself, his shoulder bones sharp with strain.

Finally, there were two men at the bottom of the cliff. They had made a perilous climb above the rapids to a small ridge. It was from this point that they had lit the early-morning fires so that a general drift of smoke would prevent the bees from flying. Their position was useful for another purpose, too. Now that the ladder had been lowered, they could grasp the bottom end to help position Nakkal.

Nakkal had counted twenty-four nests. They were set all over the cliff, some of them huge, others much smaller and unlikely to yield much. Interestingly, the cliff itself was a landscape rich in Gurung history. Noticing me sketching it earlier, the headman had named many of the clefts in the rocks with the familiarity that a farmer might name his meadows or brooks. He pointed out the 'chicken' cave, the 'witches'' cave, and a particularly inaccessible one: the 'vagina' cave.

Nakkal worked quickly, descending towards a medium-sized nest. Beside it he was dwarfed, a man against a million poisoned spears. Behind the noise of the river, we heard him shout to the men above and there was a pause while a thick bundle of greenery was lit. I could see it giving off a dense white fog, occasionally licked by flames. Lowering it was something to be cautious about. Clearly, any open flames near the ladder would be dangerous.

When it was level with the nest, Nakkal used one of his sticks to push the smoking bundle closer. I watched apprehensively through the binoculars. The nest began to ripple like a rock-pool into which someone was throwing stones. The air around the tiny

Gurung grew thick with bees. They were on his legs and arms, maddened by the smoke. How was it possible that he was not being stung to death?

When the bees had quietened, another signal and the burning leaves were pulled away. Nakkal wound his leg around the ladder for safety and began the painstaking task of cutting around the comb with a knife attached to the end of his stick. I was fascinated to watch his economy of movement. There was not a trace of fear in his work. I imagined the noise up there – it would be like a lion's roar.

From what he had told me earlier, the design of the nests was very specific to this type of bee. The lower crescent of yellow was what beekeepers call the brood, the incubation site for the thousands of larvae waiting to be born. Although all parts are used eagerly by the Gurung, the upper part is the treasure, the honeycomb itself.

When he had cut round it, at another signal a large hook was lowered from the top. Again using his sticks, he positioned the hook into the centre of the wax and gave a shrill call: 'Chhuii, chhuii – pull up, pull up.' Two men at the top hauled gently and suddenly the entire piece of wax came free of the cliff. I could hear their shouts of jubilation from the cliff top. Later the wax would be pressed into bricks and used for waterproofing clothes and ropes.

Now for the final stage, the honey gathering. A special basket called a *kutlu*, made of woven bamboo and lined with animal pelts, was lowered. Still covered in bees, Nakkal cut away the honeycomb. I could see the golden sugars dripping and glinting in the sun. Gobbets of honeycomb missed the basket and fell on to the

ladder and towards the men below. I could see one of them catching it and licking his fingers in delight.

The Nepalese children squealed with joy. '*Kwhe khudu*,' they
shouted. '*Kwhe khudu*.'

There would, indeed, be honey for tea.

As the sun rose higher in the sky, Nakkal moved from nest to
nest. The *Apis laboriosa* can generate more honey than any other
bee species and even one or two well-stocked nests can make a
honey hunt worthwhile. One large nest, hunted at the peak time,
can yield up to seventy kilos of honey.

The three most promising-looking nests were clustered together
in the middle of the cliff. Although they were separate colonies,
they were close enough to look like one from a distance. Nakkal
was nervous about reaching these – he had mentioned as much
earlier – because of the high possibility of attack.

The ladder was swung across, the honey basket emptied, and
the smoke bundle fanned back into life. I was sitting cross-legged
on the grassy bank beside the river, craning upwards to watch the
action. Several Nepalese children, for whom this was the biggest
event in quite some time, had sat down next to me.

Nakkal began to cut away the first of the giant honeycombs.
All seemed fine. But after a few minutes we heard shouts from
across the water. The two men holding the ladder at the bottom
were shouting and flapping their arms. Something was wrong.

'*Chhib, chhib*,' they were shouting. 'Bite, bite.'

Peering through the binoculars, I saw an angry stream of bees
pouring from the nests like a dark liquid. Up on the cliff, Nakkal
had swung the ladder away and was beckoning wildly for the smoke

bundle to be relowered. His worst fears had come to pass. The colonies were attacking.

To his credit, Nakkal never panicked. A seasoned professional, he merely climbed away and began to calm them with the smoke. But for the bees that had already left the nest, this was too late. They wanted something to sting and they sure as hell meant to find it.

Suddenly, the small boy on my right began to scream and flap his arms. Then another joined him. Before I knew what was happening, the air had grown thick with wild black dots and I was being stung on the arms, the neck, the cheeks, the head! We were under attack.

The bucolic scene became one of absolute chaos. Screaming with pain, the children and I turned on our heels and ran across the terraces. Bees followed us, stuck in our hair, crawling into our ears. The air was filled with shrill yelps from the children, and a variety of some of the most obscene swearwords imaginable from me.

We ran and ran, terrified, pausing every few seconds while I picked a bee from one of their ears or they pulled one from my hair. Despite having no language in common, we knew instinctively how to help one another.

It was not until we were about half a kilometre from the nests that the last bee turned back. Many of the children had five or six stings, but as the largest target I had taken more – about ten on my head alone. Charged with bee venom, my scalp began to throb, as if someone had hit me with a baseball bat.

But we were alive. The tough little Nepalese children even managed a few laughs. We picked the remaining barbs from our skin, brushed the dead bees to the ground, and checked every fold of clothing for survivors. I hoped the men on the cliff were all right.

It had been a close shave – in fact we had escaped lightly. A stocky Nepalese man with no front teeth came out from his hut to see what all the commotion was about. When the children explained, he cackled with laughter. Afterwards he invited us to sit on his stone wall, where he served me *chai* and patted me reassuringly on the back. I was shaking with fear.

The hunt continued smoothly. From the wall, I watched Nakkal on the cliff, like a spider swaying on a silken thread. Despite the throbbing of my head, I couldn't help smiling. I was watching honey-hunting in Nepal, beneath a blue-domed sky, and that felt momentous, like the completion of some grand cycle begun long ago.

When the sun lost its ire and dropped a little in the sky, I bade the farmer farewell and began the hard trek back up the cliff. Now that the hunt was coming to an end, I had decided that it would be madness not to go and see what was happening on the cliff top. I wanted to know what they did with the honey, what it looked like when it came up in the basket. Casting aside my earlier reservations about the cliff edge, I leapt the ravine on my own and found my way back along the path.

When I arrived the men let out a cheer. Everyone was smiling and joking – they came forward to pat me on the back and shake my hand. I looked for Nakkal. He had just ascended the ladder and was standing sedately amidst the brimming baskets of honey, with all the quiet pride of an artist beside his magnum opus. There was tiredness in his face but also a sense that all was right in the world again. He had been raised by his father to hunt honey and that was what he loved to do. The last five years had been difficult for him, Chitra told me, faced with a falling standing in the village, a lowered income and all the other myriad troubles of a Third World farmer, eking crops at high altitude in the midst of a war. But now, for a moment at least, the world was perfect.

I took pictures of the hunters standing in a sticky sea of honey, clutching honeycombs the size of mariachi hats. Chitra took my camera and insisted on photographing me too, holding one of the combs like a trophy and smiling. It was a moment of triumph and one I will never forget.

Two hours later, the sky was filling with flourishes of light. It had been one of the longest days I could remember and I was deeply tired. But the fun was about to begin.

Back in the hut, the honey was dripped through bamboo sieves and then into five-litre jerry cans. I was a little dismayed to see that even the filtered honey was thick with the corpses of bees, now black sticky balls. I wondered at the state of the jerry cans, too, which had 'gasoline' printed, in fading type, on their side.

Most importantly, Nakkal had tried the honey and pronounced it excellent. There was a very good reason why we had waited before tasting the honey. The wild Himalayan bees are renown for producing, in the right conditions, a honey so toxic it can have a man vomiting his guts out or even falling unconscious.[*] Centuries of hunting have taught the men that it is therefore prudent to wait for the safety of solid ground before imbibing their hoard.

It is the rhododendron flowers that poison the honey. In fact, the spring honey is very rarely edible because of the carpets of blue rhododendrons which bloom in these high places. But in autumn, there is much less toxic pollen. And as a result the honey is usually edible. 'With only a slight trace of the poison,' Chitra told me with a grin.

So this was the wondrous toxic honey of which Xenephon wrote. I had never thought I would be lucky enough to try it.

'What do you mean a *slight* trace?' I muttered, having just downed the equivalent of about half a glass of this very watery honey.[†] It was the most delicious thing I had ever tasted, hardly recognisable as honey in fact, more like some indescribable nectar. The old men around me had drunk twice as much.

'Well, a little is *good*,' said Chitra. 'Here we call this "butterfly honey". Wait a few minutes and you will see what I mean.'

---

[*]The nectar from rhododendrons contains the poison *grayonotoxin*. Acute cases of honey poisoning indicate severe cardiovascular problems with very low blood pressure and slow pulse rate. Rhododendron honey, however, remains toxic for only a very short period. Honey that is stored in the comb will have lost its toxicity before the first extraction.

In Nepal, likely sources of toxic pollen include *Rhododendron anthopogon, R. cinnabarinum* and *R. ponticum, bikh (Aconitum spp), pangra (Entada spp), pieris (Pieris formosa)*. Intoxicating honey is reddish in colour and has very high medicinal value and relaxing properties. It is sold for a high price to the Korean market. Honey hunters can easily detect intoxicating honey by putting a drop of fresh honey on their skin and then observing its colour.

[†]Honey from the Nepalese rock bee has a much higher moisture content than other honey and hence is extremely thin in consistency, almost like water. It also, however, boasts much higher levels of enzymes, amino acids and mineral content than *Apis cerana* and *A. mellifera* honey.

No sooner had he said this than I began to feel the effects. It resembled drunkenness at first, but then became visual, like a magic mushroom trip I remembered from university. Painted dots were dripping across my irises like technicolor rain. My body felt light and tingly, filled with warm rushes and heat-bursts. It was wild and strangely wonderful.

I looked over at Chitra, who was grinning broadly, and then at Nakkal, who was helping himself to another great mugful of the honey. Everywhere the atmosphere was jubilant, and soon the men began to dance and grin and make riotous jokes which brought the tears to their eyes or gave rise to great heaving laughs.

The sun was almost extinguished now, faint as the embers of a long abandoned fire, and the mountains were peering out again in the gloom. Looking back into that hut, I remember an exultation that I had not felt for a long time. I had regained a sense of control over the course of things and that had led me here, to this remote mountain top, where I had seen something fundamental not just to this tribe but to the human race. 'The pursuit of the perfect,' Matthew Arnold once said, 'is the pursuit of sweetness and light.'

SRI LANKA

CHAPTER SEVENTEEN

ROBERT KNOX, A sailor with the East India Company, was the first to bring news of the Veddhas to the outside world. In 1658, after a bout of stormy weather along the Coromandel Coast and the Bay of Bengal, he was captured, along with a number of his shipmates, by Rajasinghe II, King of Kandy. It would take him nineteen years to escape and return to England.

In 1681, safely back in London, he published *An Historical Relation of the Island of Ceylon in the East Indies* in which he describes his life on the island. 'For as in these woods there are Wild *Beasts* so Wild *Men* also . . . they call them *Veddahs*,* he wrote. Going on to describe their habits, Knox records: 'They are very expert with their Bows. They have a little ax, which

---

*The term Veddha, by which their Sinhalese neighbours denote them, comes from the Sanskrit *vyadha*, meaning a hunter with a bow and arrow.

they stick by their sides, to cut hony out of hollow trees.'

As Knox's book progresses, he makes several more references to the Veddhas, many of which allude to their love of honey. Honey is used to preserve meat in the trunks of hollow trees, usually dried venison or the flesh of the monitor lizard. It forms an unusually high proportion of their diet and Knox notes that Wild Men possess an enormous skill in the raiding of wild bee nests.

Three hundred and fifty years later, only a few pure Veddhas remain. Intermarriage with the Sinhalese, linguistic assimilation and the sheer hardship of maintaining a hunter-gatherer lifestyle in the modern world has reduced the numbers to a few hundred at most. Their language, once a pure and unique tongue, is now an amalgam of modern Sinhala, old Sinhala and their original non-Aryan dialect. And despite the efforts of a few concerned individuals and NGOs, their simple request, to be allowed to pursue their traditional lifestyle within their own ancestral lands, has been largely ignored.

None the less, a Veddha population does still exist in Sri Lanka, and the more I read about them, the more determined I was to seek them out. Calling themselves Wanniya-laeoto (Those of the Forest) the Veddhas' way of life displays an ecological harmony all but lost in the twenty-first century. A tiny enclave of remaining pure Veddhas preserves a line of descent which stretches back to the island's original Neolithic community, dating from at least 14,000 BC and potentially far earlier.

I wondered how I would find them, and whether, today, the Wild Men still enter the jungle in search of wild honey.

Colombo derives from the Sinhalese name *Kola-amba-thota*, meaning 'mango harbour'. The city is white-walled, red-roofed, lush with frangipani and giant baobabs. But it is also tired and smog-baked, stacked with yellow high-rise blocks, thick with the stench of refuse quietly fermenting in the sun. From the wrong angle, all litter and car-horns; from the right, a port city of spices and lively gossip, the flickering of kites pulling high above Galle Face Green.

I took a *tuk tuk* (a Sri Lankan rickshaw) and then an ancient train. As I sped through the countryside, sitting in the open door-way of the train so that my feet rested on the running board, I saw rice paddies, lush jungle, coral reefs pounded by white water. Wild elephants slurped from an inland lake, monkeys chittered on crumbling walls. When the Greeks discovered this island, they named it 'Serendip': literally, beauty discovered by chance.

A friend once described Sri Lanka to me as 'India without the mayhem'. There's a lot of truth in that. After a week of travel through the heart of India I felt drained, that I'd seen enough humanity for a lifetime, its full and bloody spectrum. Sri Lanka, on the other hand, has an almost Caribbean feel to it, the sleepy nonchalance of islands.

Of course, I was well aware of the other side to the coin. Since the late 1940s, the Sinhala-speaking Buddhists have been engaged in a bloody war with the largely Hindu Tamil commu-nity. Initial disputes stemmed from the Sinhalese belief that the Tamils received preferential treatment under British rule. Since then, different resistance groups have further exacerbated the conflict, the most famous of which, the Liberation Tigers of Tamil Eelam (Tamil Tigers), waged a guerrilla-style war against the government, demanding the formation of a separate Tamil nation.

Since 2002, an uneasy peace has reigned. At Norway's instigation, a mediation between the two sides was formalized in a Memorandum of Understanding. Yet even if the peace remains (a prospect that looks shaky at the time of writing), an entire generation in Sri Lanka has been irrevocably scarred by what has occurred.

While I waited for my contact with the Veddhas, I went to stay in a place I had heard much about from fellow environmentalists in London, a self-sustaining organic village in the centre of the island. It would be an ideal place to gain a feel for the country, for the rhythms of its traditional life and its landscapes.

It was a week of utter tranquillity. To be still, after so many months of movement, gave me a chance to reflect on things. From my simple adobe hut, open on all sides, I watched giant lizards crawling past me in the night like miniature dinosaurs: four feet of scales and forked tongue. There were dung beetles, black-armoured, solemnly rolling their sticky creations through the dirt. Birds such as I had never seen: the red-faced *malkoha*, the grey hornbill, the pompadour green-pigeon. One night, I watched a mongoose, reddish-brown with a black stripe on either side of its head, slinking through the dusk like a thief.

Pablo Neruda lived on the island for a time and wrote many of his dark pieces from *Residence on Earth* here. The poems evoke the country with a vigour no one else has matched: a land governed by a crowded surrealism, full of vegetable oppressiveness.

> I am securely and eternally surrounded by
> this great respiratory and entangled forest

with huge flowers like mouths and teeth
and black roots shaped like fingernails and shoes*

One of the oldest inhabitants of the village was a man named
Tennekoon, a spindly, sage-like figure, with pendulous earlobes
and penetrating eyes. He was a man of great intelligence, who
favoured brown home-spun robes which lent him the appearance
of a Buddhist monk. We took to talking in the mornings, sharing a fresh *gotu-kola* tea in a jungle clearing while he reminisced
about his life. He had been heavily active during the Sri Lankan
war, and had done prison time back in the 1960s for his political
affiliations.

'So you want to meet Veddhas?' he said to me one morning in
his gentle singsong voice. 'The people of the forest. They are a
wise people. I have had some dealings with them over the years.'

I mentioned the name of my contact at the NGO.

'Ah yes, he's a good boy,' said Tennekoon. 'He understands the
land. And he speaks Veddha – he will be a fine person to help
you.' The old man watched me intently. There was a quality of
great expressiveness in the fine bones of his face.

'Is it true that they still wear loincloths,' I asked, 'and hunt with
poisoned arrows?'

Tennekoon gave one of his inscrutable shrugs. 'The position
of the Veddhas is a difficult one. If they did not adapt, they would
not have survived. Some of them, today, wear Sinhalese clothes:
trousers and shirts. Others, it is true, still wear the loincloth, but

---

*From 'Single Gentleman', *Residence on Earth*, translated by Donald D.
Walsh, New Directions, 1973.

do they do this because they want to or because it makes them
more money with the tourists? Who can say?'

'And the poisoned arrows?'

'The government has largely stopped them hunting at all,' said
Tennekoon with disgust. 'This is why they are reduced to playing
some stupid circus role. Before, the jungle gave them everything
they needed. Food, shelter, clothes. And now the modern world has
made its trouble. They find themselves susceptible to new diseases.
There are squabbles over money. You will see for yourself.'

A week later I was on my way to see just that. My guide, arranged
through a pro-Veddha NGO called 'The Living Heritage
Network', was a man named Aruna, a mono-browed, shock-
bearded man in his mid-thirties. He had the characteristic
demeanour of outdoorsmen everywhere: composed and soft-
spoken but with an evident inner toughness. He drove our jeep
with a great physicality, wrenching the wheel from side to side as
if it were the reins of some unruly horse. It felt good to spin
along muddy jungle tracks, the wind in our faces, stopping at roadside stalls for green coconut juice or sweet string hoppers, a Sri
Lankan speciality made from a ricemeal dough, filled with crunchy
shards of jaggery.*

'So you want to ask the Veddhas about honey?' Aruna shouted
above the roar of the engine. 'Well, the Veddhas like nothing more.
They risk their lives for it. They sell it for other goods. They store

---

*Jaggery is a natural sweetener made by the slow evaporation of sugar-
cane juice. It has the reputation of being a medicinal sugar and is
prescribed for use in certain Ayurvedic remedies.

their meat in it. They will be able to tell you many things. I have
tasted their honey many times, but actually never seen them hunt
it. They do not often show such things to outsiders.'

'Do you think we could persuade them?' I said.

He drew air through his teeth. 'Difficult. Let me think about it.'

'Where are we going?' I asked.

'Maduru Oya – the National Park where the remaining Veddhas
live. Before, it was their traditional hunting grounds. Now they
have been "allocated" 1,500 acres of it. Only 1,500 acres of an
almost 60,000-hectare park! Their struggle is that of all tribal
peoples, I think.'

I asked Aruna how he got so involved in Veddha culture.

He grinned. 'Believe it or not, I used to wear a suit. Worked in
an office. But I wasn't happy. Something just didn't feel right to
me. Anyway, one day I went with Tennekoon to see the Veddhas.
I felt something very strange. Something powerful. These people
have been treated badly, and yet they have this way about them –
a sense of peace. It changed everything for me.'

He wrenched the wheel to the side once more so that the whole
jeep lurched round the corner. 'Of course my wife thinks I've
gone crazy,' he said. 'Now I have my hair long. And I spend a lot
of time in the jungle with them, sleeping on the ground and so
on.' He beamed. 'I think she will find that I will be doing this
more and more in the years to come. I am planning to build my
own mud hut!' He roared with laughter. 'She will not like that.'

Some time later we stopped at a roadside stall. A wily-looking
Tamil, his beard stained with nicotine, was trimming fresh brown
tobacco leaves with his machete.

'I'll tell you a secret,' said Aruna, 'which may be of great use.

The Veddhas *love* betel nut. They all chew it – even the women and children. If they could afford it, they would chew it day and night. So I suggest we buy them some as a present. It will make them more receptive to your arrival.'

Betel (or in India *paan*) is another term for the palm nut of the *Areca catechu* tree and its consumption is a favourite pastime in much of Asia. Often, the nut is chewed in conjunction with the betel leaf, which is peppery in taste, or with tobacco. Many also add lime powder, an alkaline residue made from cooking coral over an intense bonfire for several days.

The world's most popular drug, betel contains arecoline, a mild stimulant of the central nervous system. More memorably, it leaves the chewer's teeth and gums a lurid purple and increases saliva production, resulting in the user's constant need to spit. One of its most famous advocates was Queen Noorjehan, mother of Shaahjehan who built the Taj Mahal.

Well, if it was betel that the Veddhas wanted, betel we would give them. Aruna began to bargain with the stallholder, whose own beetroot-shaded lips broadened into a wide smile when he realised the size of our order. We began to put together individual parcels, each containing a wad of sticky tobacco leaves, several fistfuls of betel nuts, a pouch of white lime dust and even a packet of cardamom which some of the Veddhas liked to include for flavour.

When we had settled up, the stallholder insisted on showing me how the betel is prepared. First the nut is cracked with a special tool, then finely chopped and laid on a green betel leaf. After being moistened with a pinch of lime powder and sprinkled with spice, the whole thing is tightly rolled into a kind of parcel. I put one into my mouth and began to chew. It had a kind of astringency which seemed to flood the mouth with saliva. I nodded my head appreciatively, while my taste-buds threatened to burst. Certainly, an acquired taste.

The stallholder wheezed with enjoyment, clapped me warmly on the shoulder and went back to trimming his leaves.

Back on the road, we headed up over the Knuckles massif, a ninety-square-mile block of central highlands rising to more than 3000 feet. The air grew foggy and cool, and the roads tapered and glistened with the characteristic reddish-yellow mud of the area. In the jungle around us I saw toque monkeys, giant squirrels, butterflies the size of birds. The Sinhalese call this region 'Dumbara', meaning 'the mist-laden mountains', and it was easy to see why. It was faintly ghostly as we sped through the foliage twisted with orchids, mosses and ferns.

Dusk was falling when we reached the Maduru Oya reserve. We were sticky after the long drive, and Aruna pulled the jeep off the road and stopped beside a huge *wewa* or artificial lake where we could swim. Many of these lakes were built over a thousand years ago by the ancient Sri Lankan kings. Today they look no different from a naturally occurring waterhole, awash with wildlife pausing in the gloaming to drink.

Throwing off our clothes, we dived into the muddy brown water. Perched on rocks in the middle were an array of herons, cormorants and darters. Hornbills squawked from the trees in their strident metallic voices. Opening my eyes beneath the surface, I saw the flickering of fishtails among the weeds.

'Any crocodiles in these lakes?' I said to Aruna.

'Many,' he said casually. 'But they won't come near us.'

'How reassuring,' I muttered, suddenly finding the swim some-what less refreshing than it had been a moment before.

After a while, though, I got over my inhibitions and returned to my appreciation of where I was. The lake was surrounded on all sides by jungle. The sky was a dull monotone, freckled with smudges of vapour. The water was deliciously cool and the lakebed soft and yielding under my feet. I lay on my back and floated, at peace.

That night we slept in a mud hut on the edge of the reservation. Our host, Sulliya, was a Veddha who had chosen to assimilate himself, to a degree, into the modern Sinhalese way of life. He wore Western-style clothes, rode a bicycle to work, and spoke fluent Sinhala. Yet in appearance he was clearly Veddha, with a rich brownish-black skin tone, deeply set eyes and prominent cheek-bones. His nose, too, was markedly broader than either the Tamils' or Sinhalese's.

Another aspect of his ancestral culture which Sulliya had chosen to retain was that of protecting his wife from contact with strangers. She peered at us from the gloom of their hut, surrounded by four shyly smiling infants and a wizened grandmother.

As the night thickened, Aruna and I sat at a rickety table outside the hut drinking wood-apple juice. Sulliya brought us a fiery vegetable curry, rich with coconut milk, spices and ground almonds. Afterwards we lay back contentedly, fireflies shimmering in the night sky.

The following morning we set out early along the Mahiyangana–Batticaloa road, turning left at Dambana. It was going to be a scorching day – one could already see the heat-lines rising from the mud. For the first time I saw Veddhas in their traditional dress, essentially a white cloth tied round the waist. They walked leisurely along the edge of the jungle, joking with one another and eyeing our jeep curiously as we passed. All the men carried the traditional axe (*asirikatuwa*) so that the blade hung backwards over their left shoulder. Despite a keen sense of ownership (historically, this related to land, especially certain valuable honey-hunting cliffs), Veddhas have very little concept of personal property. The only items they are likely to own are an axe, bow and arrows, a betel bag, and perhaps a dog.

As we passed, Aruna hailed many of them with a friendly wave or a few words. He was clearly a regular visitor around here and I could see from the Veddhas' reactions how much he was liked and trusted by them. Given the enormous hardships imposed upon their community by the outside world in the last century, I took this as a great tribute to Aruna's character. He was utterly genuine and without affectation.

'We are coming to the chief's hut,' Aruna explained. 'Just do as I do, watch the way I greet them, and sit quietly. If there are any particular questions, I can translate them for you. But first make sure you have the betel bags – that will be a good start.'

We trudged up a narrow track through the jungle, potted with chocolate-brown puddles. Feral chickens clucked around our feet. Up ahead I made out a large mud hut, open on three sides and roofed with straw. Several shaggy goats watched us from their tethers. It was immediately evident who the chief was: he sat flanked by younger men and had a proud and commanding expression.

A great shout went up as we arrived. The chief came out,

beaming, and clasped Aruna warmly. The Veddhas have a particular salutation which involves the grasping of both forearms simultaneously. I followed suit, maintaining direct eye contact as Aruna had done.* It was a solemn and quite personal greeting, implying a mutual respect.

All the Veddhas present wore loincloths and had long dark beards, elongated faces and wavy black hair. Their feet were bare. None of them showed any particular reaction to the arrival of a white man, merely regarding me with a reticent, though not unfriendly, gaze.

'Offer them the betel,' said Aruna.

I gave one of the bags first to the chief and then to the other men in turn.

'Give a second to the chief,' instructed Aruna, 'and I will tell him it is for his wife.'

There were broad smiles now and the hut was suddenly noisy with rustling as the Veddhas delved into their hoards. I watched with interest while they brought out betel cutters from their pouches and expertly prepared the small parcels in the way they liked. One of them even gave some to a small boy, no more than ten, who stuffed it into his mouth with glee and began to chomp with all the aplomb of a Texan tobacco farmer.

When everyone was masticating contentedly, we began to listen. Chief Wanniyala Aththo started to tell me about the Veddhas.

'In the past, the Veddhas were a happy people who lived in perfect harmony with nature. In the time of my great-grandfather there

---

*This is known as *ingiya* – the language of the eyes.

were both wild and village Veddhas. They feathered their arrows with feathers from hawk and peacock and shot only what they needed. They never used traps. There were strict rules among us about what could be hunted. For example, we would never shoot a pregnant animal, or an animal in the act of drinking. We had our own ways – ways which respected the land. We believed we were the guardians of the jungle.

'Things have been difficult for us these last years. In 1983, the government of Sri Lanka turned the last of our forest territory into a National Park. Overnight we were transformed from hunters into poachers. Our traditional way of life became a criminal offence. Our people have been on this land for perhaps as much as 500,000 years. It is a land shared by our ancestors, by gods, goddesses and the forest spirits. It has been taken from us.'

I brought up the subject of honey. The chief nodded enthusiastically, and pointed to a row of sticky jars on his shelf.

'For the *Waniya letto*, honey is one of our most important foods. In June and July we take honey from the *Bambara* – a special bee which makes much honey. Also there is a type of bee with no sting who sometimes produces good honey. We eat as much of it as we can and always feel more healthy when the honey is plentiful.'

'Is there much honey at the moment?' I asked.

He nodded. 'A little. When there is a small amount, we give it first to children. It increases their growing, and also their thinking power. For adults it is very good for getting rid of phlegm.' He demonstrated noisily. 'Sometimes we use it for medicine. But the best honey for this is the old honey. If you have a honey which is one hundred years old, this is the best medicine in the world.'

This was riveting. I asked him whether there were as many bees now as there had always been.

He shook his head vigorously. 'Today there are many fewer bees than before. I do not think there are enough flowers any more. I am very worried for the future.' He paused, clasped his hands together, and looked me straight in the eyes. 'When I was small we lived in thick jungle. There were nice jungle monkeys and birds and bright flowers. Now, as you can see, we live in open areas. People are clearing the jungle for' – he laughed – 'what they call "human development". Soon, perhaps, the honey will be finished and we will have nothing left to hunt.'

Aruna cut in now and for some time they conversed between themselves. I sat in silence for some half an hour, listening intently. At last the chief turned to me – I thought I even detected a fleeting smile.

'Aruna tells me you are our friend,' he said gravely. 'And that you write things which may bring some attention to our cause. In return I shall help you. Expect us tomorrow morning while it is still dark. We will come to your hut.'

Bambara, I later discerned, is the Veddha name for the *Apis indica* or Indian honeybee. For the Veddhas, as in many developing countries, honey is more than a source of food, a medicine and a tonic. It is also an important source of revenue. In countries like Bangladesh and Thailand, the money involved has prompted the government forestry departments to start charging for the issue of a collecting permit.

For the Veddhas, however, the sweetness of the forest, if little else, is available to them as it has always been. Writing in 1886, the anthropologist Hugh Nevill recorded:

Honey forms a great part of their diet. It is eaten fresh in large
quantities, wax and all; combs with young bees in them being
considered especially wholesome. It was also the practice
formerly to store strips of dried meat in honey, filling in a
cavity of some tree with it, the cavity being first lined with clay.

To procure honey they rapidly cut open hollow trees, even
of the hardest wood; and to take the hives of the large black
bambara bee, they make long ladders of cane, called 'rang
kendiya' by which they descend precipices, and cut off combs
adhering to their sides.

They do this at night, generally, as the bees are not so
savage then; and smoke them with a sort of resin. The hives
are often cut off with a sort of wooden sword, made for
the occasion. These frail ladders swing fearfully, and the task
is so dangerous, only the boldest and most athletic attempt
it. While engaged on the task they sing lustily, songs especially made, which appease the spirit of the rock, and prevent
him from dashing the hunter off the ladder. They also go
about their songs, so as to get up a certain degree of excitement, necessary to carry them through the task. A song is
chanted, and a little honey sprinkled for the spirits, before
the combs are cut off the rock.

I was particularly interested in this notion of appeasing the 'spirit'
of the rock. The Veddhas call such spirits *yaka* and they form an
important part of tribal religion. Traditionally, the Veddhas had a
shamanic figure among them, whom they called *kapurale* or
dugganawa. It was this man's job to commune with the *yaka* and to
ensure a propitious relationship.

I couldn't help making the comparison between the Veddhas' spiritual beliefs and those of the Nepalese Gurung. Not only were both groups deeply rooted in a particular patch of land, both were of the opinion that the spirits of their ancestors resided there. Both religions might be termed *shamanic* – that is, a range of traditional beliefs relating to a special relationship with spirits. In *The Spell of the Sensuous*, David Abraham's masterpiece of eco-philosophy, he writes eloquently about exactly this.

> The traditional magician, I came to discern, commonly acts as an intermediary between the human collective and the larger ecological field, ensuring that there is an appropriate flow of nourishment, not just from the landscape to the human inhabitants but from the human community back to the local earth. By their rituals, trances, ecstasies, and 'journeys' magicians ensure that the relation between human society and the larger society of beings is balanced and reciprocal and that the village never takes more from the living land than it returns to it – not just materially, but with prayers, propitiations and praise . . . To some extent every adult in the community is engaged in this process of listening and attuning to the other presences that surround and influence daily life.

Without an understanding of this view of the world, it is impossible to really comprehend what the Veddhas lost when their tribal lands were taken from them. For the timber corporation grounded in a Western monotheistic outlook, the acquisition of Sri Lankan forest land is little more than another business deal, translating into so many planks or sheaves of paper. For the Veddhas, however, it meant the lost of history, the loss of a world teeming with numinous powers, the loss of things we can only guess at. For where would the *yakas* roam when the trees were gone?

That night I went to bed early, but I couldn't sleep. On the other side of the room Aruna snored so loudly, it sounded as if a helicopter were circling overhead. Mosquitoes whined. Night birds made chuck-chucking noises from the jungle.

Our room was simplicity itself, a mud hut with an oval-shaped door and window open to the air. Lying on my bed, I watched the enormous rose-grey moon hovering over the trees. The night was so laden with stars that I could see the texture of the sky.

CHAPTER EIGHTEEN

A T 3.30 A.M. I splashed my face with ice-cold water from the well. I felt as though I had barely slept; my entire body protested at the break with its natural rhythms. Disregarding the ache, I pulled up another bucket from the depths and tipped it over my head. For what was to come, I would need to be in full possession of my wits.

Returning to the hut, I made out three figures in the gloom. The Veddhas had arrived silently, like wraiths from the mist. I recognised the chief's son, a young man of about thirty, lightly muscled and with attentive grey eyes. The other two were new to me, both wearing axes over their shoulder-blades and bows and quivers of arrows across their backs. They nodded mutely.

Without ceremony, we set out. For a mile or more, we padded down a mud track, the jungle pressing in on us from the sides, patches of moonlight sifting through the canopy. The air felt wet and heavy with moisture. Every step seemed loud as a tree falling, although the Veddhas managed to move without disturbing so much as a twig. Barefooted, and perfectly at home here, they were as noiseless as clouds.

The pace was swift. We quickly left one path and moved to another. I was fully alert now, scanning the ground for obstacles and the jungle for the briars which reached out like claws in the darkness.

For a time my attention narrowed. As in Nepal, it took every ounce of focus to hold my ground. I lost myself in the rhythm of the moment, the steady clomp of my feet over the soft earth.

Suddenly, the chief's son stopped dead. What had they heard? On tiptoe, I strained to make out what they were doing. They were signalling to each other, and cocking their heads to tune in on some jungle sound.

Very slowly, Aruna took several steps back to stand beside me. 'Elephant,' he whispered. 'Very close. It is a mother with child. Dangerous for us.'

I knew only too well the dangers of wild elephants. During my long train journey in India, an old man had regaled me with the story of how his best friend had been gored to death, right before his eyes, after they had got too close to a jungle elephant. Fifty years after the event, the old man's eyes had filled with tears.

I remember the light very clearly. It was that peculiar moment of the day when the moon is still out and the first morning light penetrates the clouds. There was something magical about it, the light taking on a blue-green opalescence. My eyes, sharpened by adjustment to the dark, could see the world in intimate detail. The

Veddhas had found a pile of dung which they were examining like detectives. Motionless, their senses reached out into the land around us, alert to the smallest sounds of danger.

No one moved for some five minutes. At last, we moved on. But the Veddhas seemed to maintain their poise. These were very different men from the characters who had greeted us in the chief's hut the day before. As Tennekoon had pointed out, in public they are forced to play a role, that of 'professional wild men'. But here they were on their own terms, utterly in tune with their landscape. What for me was a maze, a deeply inhospitable place of leopards, elephants, and more poisonous snakes per square foot than anywhere else on earth, was for them a natural habitat, home.

After several miles, the path ended. To all intents and purposes we were hacking through untouched jungle. The Veddhas used their axes when necessary but, for the most part, merely ducked and jumped, hardly slowing their pace. Even more bizarrely, their bare feet seemed unaffected by the inch-long thorns, sharp rocks and spiny plants which matted the jungle floor. I was more than grateful, on this occasion, for my thick-soled hiking boots.

Dawn had broken now and with it all Sri Lanka's wildlife seemed to be waking up. I slapped constantly at the back of my neck where any number of buzzing creatures were queuing up for a meal.

'This is the time when the bees wake up,' explained Aruna. 'The Veddhas will watch them and then try to follow them back to their nest. Because the jungle is still quiet, now is the best time to do this.'

It seemed an unlikely possibility but I was intrigued none the less. While the chief's son remained with us, the other two stepped into the jungle and quickly disappeared.

Nothing happened for a few minutes. I strained to follow the son's line of sight. Could he really make out individual bees and follow them to their honey?

Standing there, holding my breath in the first minutes of dawn, I wondered for a moment if I had leapt back in time. For how many thousand years have Veddhas entered the forest in just such a manner as this? And in how many other cultures have indigenous peoples done likewise, their tongues lured by the promise of sugars hidden within the trunks of trees? Most salutary of all was the ever-present question of the future. After so many millennia of human history, for how many more years will Veddhas still roam?

I was astonished to hear a great booming call some distance away. It sounded like an ape, the noise that Tarzan caricatured so badly by beating on his breast.

On the far edge of the clearing the chief's son nodded, then mimicked the same resonant sound. All became clear: it was a means of Veddha communication in the jungle, a way of gauging their distance from one another. I was fascinated by it, by its proximity to the noise of a wild animal, by the precise timbre of it, by its harmony with the natural sounds of the jungle. It struck me how easy it might be to judge a man on the basis of such a sound, to imagine him 'primitive' or any number of terms suggesting some closer proximity to the animal kingdom. The truth of the matter is that the sound represents a deep intuitive understanding of the jungle environment. It is a testament to the profound sense of place which the Veddhas feel for the jungles of Sri Lanka.

With that we were off again, running and weaving through the undergrowth. In a blur, I saw monstrous flowers sprouting from the trunks of trees, contorted fungi glistening like sculptures.

Pinpointed between two plant stems, a spider tended to its swollen sac of eggs. Scabrous trees with sun-bleached leaves, their trunks grey with stringy lichen. Enormous cactuses, bloated and obscene with their immense needle-like spines.

For the next hour we ran fiercely, then stopped, then ran again. I had long since lost sight of what was going on. To me, we seemed to be moving without reason; I was tired and scratched and bitten. My heart was pumping like an ironworks, and I had a stitch in my side so painful it felt as though one of the Veddhas had attacked me with their axe.

But the Veddhas knew what they were doing. At last, one of them turned to me and flashed a rare grin.

'They've found one!' said Aruna excitedly. 'This is very fortunate. Sometimes it can take a whole day or more to find one nest.'

Beaded with sweat, I stopped and followed the line which stretched from the Veddha's finger. It ended in the branches of a vast tree some distance away. At first I could see nothing. But with persistence, I made out a tiny fissure in the tree trunk. And from that fissure, subtle as a thread of smoke, came a stream of tiny bees.

We stood at the base of the tree for some time. I judged it to be about eight o' clock now, and the sun was beating steadily down through the foliage. The Veddhas considered their options. It was not an easy tree to climb, by any standards. The first fifteen feet were almost completely smooth, without a single branch or foothold. After that the branches grew sporadically from the trunk, but whether they could support the weight of a man was dubious.

Eventually, one of the Veddhas decided that too much waiting around wasn't getting us anywhere. He peeled some long strings of bark from a nearby sapling and tucked them into his belt. Then he chose an extremely frail-looking tree which grew parallel to the one housing the bees, and flew up it with a quite extraordinary agility. It was a brilliant manoeuvre. At the top, he simply leant forward so that the whole tree bent, as if blown by a gale. Using the bark from his belt, he bound it to the larger trunk and tied a firm knot. The whole operation had taken no more than a few minutes.

One of the other Veddhas soon followed up this makeshift ladder, this time handing his friend an axe and a large hollowed-out gourd which they would use to collect the honey in. In tandem, they moved up the larger trunk until they were both at the level of the nest.

Clustered together in the clearing, the remaining Veddha, Aruna and I watched nervously. They were at least fifty feet up now, and preparing to begin.

'Why is there no smoke?' I asked Aruna. He spoke with the Veddha still on the ground and turned back to me.

'He says that if we show no fear, then they will not see us as enemies. We do not need smoke for a nest like this. But even when we are stung, since we do not consider it poison, then we do not consider it pain.'

Up on the tree, the rhythmic thunk of the axe rang out across the forest. Aruna explained that the bees seek out hollow spaces within trees, and sometimes build their nests fairly deep inside. Before the honey can be taken it is first necessary to cut away all the surrounding wood. But, unsurprisingly, a nest of bees takes none too kindly to a man attacking them with an axe. Bees began to pour from the opening, as if a valve of thick smoke had suddenly been opened.

No one panicked. On my own, I almost certainly would have, the memory of my severe Nepalese stinging still sharply in mind. But the Veddhas' confidence gave me self-assurance. They just continued methodically, chopping away at the wood. It was slow progress, not least because with one hand needed to grasp on to the tree, there was only one available for chopping. After a while they swapped, and soon a large gash had formed. We took care to avoid the falling chunks of timber.

Using my binoculars, I peered upwards. A gleam of gold was appearing from the cleft, and a sticky liquid trickled down the branch.

The chief's son handed the axe to his friend, adjusted his position on the tree, and thrust his hand into the trunk. That took real courage. To thrust one's hand into a narrow, enclosed space which might contain 100,000 or more stinging insects seemed close to insane. Bees, in any case, were matted across his torso, but he appeared calm.

He withdrew his hand. Clutched in his fist was a fist-sized piece of wax. But it was old and brittle and he tossed it down. He searched again, his arm vanishing almost up to the shoulder, and this time we heard a grunt of approval. He had reached the honey.

The Veddhas shouted excitedly to one another now, and the gourd was held out expectantly. Slowly, and after more chopping with the axe, the gourd filled. But the quantities were tiny. Compared to the giant honeycombs of the Nepalese rock bee, this was a paltry harvest indeed.

When there was nothing left to take, the Veddhas descended. It was fairly unimpressive: some crumpled, almost black fragments of comb, much of it filled with unhatched larvae. There were also dead bees, live bees, some grubs, pollen, propolis, and a good deal of dirt.

Aruna spoke with them. 'The Veddhas say that this is nothing,' he said. 'They took it because they wanted to show you. But usually they would have left it and come back in a few months when there is more honey. We will continue looking for a better one. But first, they would like you to try the honey.'

I accepted a piece and bit into it. The Veddhas watched me expectantly. It was extraordinary. The predominant taste was pollen, a bitter, mineral-rich flavour. On top of that was a vague medicinal sweetness. It was like no honey I had ever eaten.

'Fantastic,' I pronounced. There was much smiling.

One of the Veddhas reached into the gourd now and took out a piece of broodcomb – a piece of comb filled with tiny unhatched bees. For many cultures, this part is even more valuable than the honey, being made up of almost pure protein. showing off under my nose, wearing the expression of a proud baker showing off a *millefeuille*, the chief's son squeezed it so that tiny worm-like larvae oozed out. Needless to say, I would sooner have faced *samne* again than eat it.

'I would like him to have it,' I muttered to Aruna, who was grinning widely. 'I would be honoured.'

Aruna translated and the chief's son nodded gratefully, broke the piece in three and then shared it with his friends. Inwardly, I breathed a sigh of relief.

Back into the jungle. This time we crossed a broad stream where we all gratefully bent to drink. Above us, grey monkeys leapt shrieking from bough to bough. A magical bird with a long azure tail paused on a palm frond to watch me with its kohl-rimmed eyes.

We followed the course of the stream for a while, the water surprisingly cold beneath my feet, and then branched out into the dense green. Glancing behind me, I noticed that two of the Veddhas had vanished again, silent as ghosts when they chose to be.

For two more hours we searched. It was a hot and exhausting process, full of sweat and mounting tiredness. From time to time the Veddhas communicated with one another through their strange simian calls. It was impossible to tell whether they were on the trail of a particular nest, or merely making contact.

Just when exhaustion was setting in, we heard a triumphant shout. They had found another nest, Aruna said. It was bigger.

Up close, I could tell this at once, because even from ground level the noise of it was palpable. Using much the same techniques as before, they scaled the tree, chopped away the dead wood, and this time gained access to a large and delicious honeycomb.

'They say that you have brought them luck,' Aruna translated. 'Two nests in one morning is a fine thing at this time of year.'

The gourd even proved too small. It was filled and lowered down to us, where we emptied the contents on to some large banana-like leaves. This time the honey was amber-red in colour, and thankfully there were far fewer larvae to contend with.

A second nest successfully raided, the Veddhas relaxed a little. They led Aruna and me through the jungle, chatting merrily with one another. In twenty minutes we came to a natural clearing, a patch of flat slate-like rocks upon which no plants grew. Geologically speaking, I had no clue why such a place should occur in the midst of thick jungle. To all intents and purposes it was like an island, a respite from the dark and claustrophobic greenery which grew with such exuberance for miles around. For the Veddhas, it appeared to be a familiar resting place. I saw the marks of old fires on the rock, and even the sun-bleached skeleton of an animal – perhaps a small deer.

While Aruna and I collected wood, the Veddhas busied themselves selecting a large flat stone. The piece they chose was massive and two of them staggered across the clearing with it. Then they laid it across two smaller rocks so that it formed a convenient table-like surface.

Under that flat surface, they now made a fire, which was itself a fascinating procedure to watch. The chief's son withdrew a pinch of something from his waist pouch.

'Cotton sprinkled with charcoal,' explained Aruna.

From the same pouch the Veddha took two flints and with a deft movement conjured a flurry of sparks on to the cotton. A wisp of smoke, then a small flame. The chief's son smiled, then added dry grass and brittle twigs, all the while cupping the flame with his small hands. In no time a fire was crackling cheerfully.

'They are making us breakfast,' said Aruna. 'Good! All this honey-hunting has given me quite an appetite.'

One of the Veddhas unrolled another pouch, this time revealing a large ball of chapatti dough. I was amazed that I hadn't noticed all these pouches – they had been packed tightly around the Veddhas' waists the whole time. He kneaded the dough quickly, then separated it into small balls. From these he stretched and pinched out some flatbreads, which he tossed on to the now sizzling piece of slate. It was a perfect natural cooking surface.

When the flatbreads were cooked we spread them thickly with honeycomb and ate them piping hot. The honey was exquisite, as bold and animated as the jungle itself. It had a maple-like smokiness and, smeared on the soft, charred breads, it was about the best thing I had ever eaten.

Honey on toast, Veddha-style, eaten with aching limbs in a jungle clearing. I could not imagine a better breakfast on this planet.

INDIA

CHAPTER NINETEEN

BACK IN INDIA, I waited at Trivundrum for the Chennai Express. Like most stations in India, Trivandrum central is a miniature universe. Whole families exist in its confines, as well as particular rules of etiquette, certain hierarchies and currencies. It was early morning, the city still asleep. But here night had shrunk to a few meagre hours, abbreviated by the constant hum of migration.

Two porters, saffron turbans tied loosely round their heads, yawned greetings at me. Coolies carrying oversized trunks dashed up and down the staircases of the pedestrian bridge. An old man wearing a *khaddar* shawl brushed his teeth meticulously in the public drinking fountain. His chin, covered in white bristles, suggested that he had been travelling for some time. He wore a pair of narrow almond-shaped glasses on the bridge of his nose which slipped, while he bent to drink, landing in the water with a gentle splash.

Sitting on my bag, I was eating some dhal and rice from a paper plate when a man approached me. He was smartly dressed, wearing municipal pin-stripe, a bow-tie and finely polished shoes. A thin moustache hovered on his top lip. I took him for a travelling businessman of sorts.

'Hello, sir. You were giving *what* to that girl?' His voice was abrupt, even rude.

I stared at him. He referred, I assumed, to the banana which I had given to a beggar girl a few minutes before.

'What business is it of yours?' I retorted.

'I am an Indian, sir, and what you do in my country is of import.'

I almost choked on my dhal. 'I gave her some fruit,' I said. 'A banana.'

He tutted. 'Oh no, sir, this is a *very* bad idea. These childrens are *beggars*! They are pilfering things. They do not deserve bananas.'

'Well, I felt guilty,' I said. 'I'm sitting here eating; she clearly hasn't had a good meal in days. What's one banana?'

The anger left his face. He sighed. 'Oh sir, you will never understand India. These peoples must be left to their own devices. A firm hand is needed, sir. Oh yes, most firm.'

'Well, I'm sorry if it upset you,' I muttered. 'But I'm afraid I won't change. The problem, anyway, is one of population, don't you think? There's just too many people.'

His eyes lit. 'Sir, you have hit, as we say, the nail firmly on the head. There are two problems to take into account.'

I nodded.

'The first is one of religion. In India we believe that children are a gift from God. So how can it be wrong to have many?' He lowered his voice now and drew towards me with a conspiratorial air. 'But the second issue, my friend, is the more serious. These people are bored. They do not have video players, as you do. They do not have laptop computers. Oh no! You see, sir, without these things they are in need of *diversion*. And so they are using sexual relations as a form of evening entertainment!'

Once again I almost choked on my dhal. But there was no time for a retort.

'I'm glad we had this little chat,' said my new friend, shaking me by the hand. 'You will know in future. Leave these people to their own devices! Cheerio then.'

I boarded the Chennai Express and searched out my seat: Wagon D4, Seat 21. As we chugged away under the heavy iron girders of the railway bridge, I shut my eyes. I was headed for Madras, a twenty-four-hour journey across India, where I had reserved a place on a meditation course, due to start the following evening.

Meditation. How many times over the previous years had I considered it? Yoga had been a daily habit of mine for some time, but at my level that was more a physical practice than anything. The natural stiffness of my body prevented me from accessing any heightened or prolonged sense of peace. Of course I touched on it, on a particular day or if the mood was right, but the stillness I felt was gone before I could identify it. And since the hit and run, that stillness had seemed even further from me, clouded by the fear and turmoil which so addled me.

Over the previous year I'd heard much about a particular style of meditation, Vipassana, based on the principles of a man named S. N. Goenka. Goenka came from a conservative Hindu family of Burmese merchants and had grown up steeped in privilege. At the age of thirty-one, he began to experience severe migraines and, when both Eastern and Western medicine failed him, he was persuaded to go on a meditation course. During that meditation course, based on the core teachings of Buddhism, Goenka found a new path in life: a meditation style that was free of any ritual, any clergy or hierarchy, and which seeks no conversion from its practitioners. Within a few years he had abandoned his business interests in favour of teaching this technique full-time.

Today there are Goenka Vipassana centres all over the world. Many travellers attend the courses – largely, perhaps, because it is easier to offer a ten-day commitment when one has no fixed schedule. But travellers, too, are seekers by their very nature, hoping for a clearer view of things on the mental as much as the geographical plane.

In Nepal I had met a Greek couple in David's AM/PM café, both in their late fifties, who'd asked, frankly, where I got my scars from. I didn't mind such forthrightness at all, actually – one of the gifts of meeting people on the road is the fact that etiquette can be dispensed with. And besides, I could see that they meant it kindly: they had the berry-brown, open faces of free spirits.

While I explained about the accident, I spoke briefly about my honey quest and my search for a sense of peace. They seemed to understand unequivocally, as few people had. The Greek man, an architect with a passion for making olive oil, had referred then to what he called 'the best present I could ever give myself'.

We talked on. But when he mentioned 'ten days of silence' I recoiled. How could I ever endure such a thing? I didn't have it in me.

'You don't think about it, my friend,' he said. 'You don't plan ahead for weeks and weeks and get nervous. Don't give it any thought. Just turn up on that first day and tell yourself that no matter what happens, you will not leave until it is finished. It is simple.' He laughed. 'But in its simplicity, it is sometimes very hard. You will see.'

Here I was then, moving slowly across India on my way to do just that. In Sri Lanka I had gone to Polonaruwa to see the giant rock sculptures of the Buddha, smiling out at the world with half-closed eyes. That expression of beatitude, so perfectly realised by the sculptors, was the diametric opposite of what the accident had brought me. All the days since then had included alienation, self-absorption, grief. Perhaps this meditation, at last, would give me some peace of mind: an acceptance of the past, and the strength to face the future.

It was the morning of 20 December when I disembarked. Madras was humid, a chaos of bumper-to-bumper traffic, greasy fumes, the ugly glare of modern advertising. Dazed from lack of sleep, I chose a friendly rickshaw wallah and asked him to take me to his favourite place to eat.

'I take you to shopping mall, sir. Very nice McDonald's they are having.'

'No, no. Local food. *Your* favourite place.'

He grinned sheepishly. 'Ah, you are liking Indian food. In which case, you have come to the right fellow.'

We sped through the city, through a catacomb of dingy streets and into an older part of town, where bony cattle clopped across the roads, and sellers of fruit and *paan* and lotto tickets watched us from tiny roadside huts. I remember the smells, the sweet sugar-cane being cut in the sun, the clove-tinged smoke of bidi cigarettes.

We came to an untidy restaurant, thick with the smoke of frying dosas, the classic south Indian pancakes made from fermented rice. I sat down at a plastic table and ordered an onion variety, inhaling the smells of sizzling ghee, and drinking *massala chai* while I waited. My fingers drummed the table restlessly.

When the dosa came it was hot and golden, smeared with a fresh coconut chutney and served on a fresh green banana leaf. Utterly delicious. While I ate, I leafed through my notebooks, mulling over the past months and trying to compose my state of mind. After lunch I would ask the rickshaw wallah to drive me to the meditation course, and then it would all begin. My Greek friend had warned me not to think too hard about what to expect, or I might never go through with the whole thing. Sound advice, no doubt, but it was very hard not to envisage the next days. Would I stay the distance? Would I come out stronger or fall apart?

I came across a quote from Saul Bellow on a tea-stained page.

Death is the dark backing a mirror needs if we are to see anything.

I had written that long ago now, when the black dog of depression had been at my door. It had made powerful sense then – even more so now. The accident had altered the course of my life, as a gust of wind tilts a weathervane. At first there had been the fall, what I saw now as a kind of breakdown, and then flight – those far-off travels to seek out honey in old jars and boxes.

All of those travels had been a kind of escapism, I saw that now. Some attempt to break the patterns of self-absorption, to shatter that mirror against which the dark backing had so painfully adhered itself.

Now was the time finally to come to terms with the whole damn thing. Since that ill-fated morning it was as if I had been in limbo – what Buddhists refer to as the *bardo* – a state of intermediate existence between two lives on earth. In Sanskrit there is a similar term: *antarabhava*. In both cases, a state of *bardo* is linked with a period of degeneration and sometimes terrifying hallucinations, both of which I had experienced.

More positively, it is also believed that the *bardo* state allows a great opportunity for liberation. Having seen reality in its clearest light, the individual has the opportunity to learn from it and therefore directly influence their next rebirth.

With these thoughts very much in my mind, I paid for my lunch and made my way to the Vipassana centre. It was far from the centre of town, a forty-minute drive, and it would have been cheaper and faster to take a taxi. But I love rickshaws, their perspective on the world, and the amiable banter their drivers encourage. Besides, it would be my last view of the outside world for ten days – I didn't want to miss a thing.

CHAPTER TWENTY

THE MEDITATION BEGAN at 4 a.m. the following day. The slow tolling of a bell broke the night, raucous as an elephant trampling soft grass. I crawled out of bed, splashed water on my face, dressed in loose-fitting clothing and made my way to the meditation hall. From now on I would not utter a sound for ten days. I did the maths in my head: That was 240 hours, 14,400 minutes, 864,000 seconds.

It was a large room lit by candles. Perhaps thirty cushions were laid out on one side of the room, and another thirty on the other. Men and women are separated during Vipassana to avoid any possible distractions. Between us, at the front of the hall, sat the teacher, a fat-cheeked old man who wore an equanimous smile.

There were a few minutes of instruction, then we began. Seated on a square cushion, our legs crossed or in lotus, we began to concentrate on the breath, the sounds of inhalation and exhalation, to feel the two streams of air passing beneath the nostrils.

At first I was filled with distractions. The man to my right had a coughing problem and continually hawked his throat. Someone else behind me couldn't get comfortable, constantly shifting their legs from one side to another, first crossing them, then uncrossing, then stretching.

My brain whirred in the gloom. My legs hurt. My stomach rumbled. A minute became ten and the problems multiplied. My mind was a nest of red ants: a still mound of earth on the outside, yet seething within: a million variable currents.

After two hours we finished and trudged our way in silent procession through the dawn to the breakfast hall. Noiseless gardeners tended to the flowers and lawns which encased the centre in its tranquil shell. Not even a bird call broke the calm.

The food was simple but good. Steamed rice cakes called *idli* with a simple dhal. Hot *chai*. A sign on the wall cautioned us to take only what we could eat. Fill your bowl as many times as you want, it said, but do not waste. Cultivate *mindfulness*.

We ate, in silence of course, against whitewashed walls. I tried to stay in the moment, to be aware of the tastes and textures of the food but nothing beyond that, no memories or projections of the future. Afterwards each person washed and dried their own plate, then filed out for a few minutes to himself before the sitting began again.

An hour and a half's meditation. A five-minute break. Then another hour. Concentrate only on the breath, we were told again. Everything else will happen in its own time. Just breathe.

The concentrating of attention on the breath is an ancient

technique. It is not so easy to begin with to simply *not think*, so a focus is directed towards breath in order to allow the mind something to grasp upon. And in this grasping, much extraneous thought falls away. We stop worrying about the past or fearing for the future. By living with the breath, we are existing only in the moment. This in itself is the ultimate goal.

But so much gets in the way of this. To start with, the demands of a body unused to sitting still for hours at a stretch, let alone motionlessly with crossed legs. My knees throbbed. My calf muscles ached. My hamstrings burned. I had to move – I was going to go insane! The more I tried to disregard the physical, the more my physical self demanded my attention. It was as if I were in a balloon, desperately tossing out sand in order to gain altitude, while hundreds of ropes coiled upwards from the ground to keep me anchored.

'Forget the body,' came the teacher's gentle voice in my ear. 'It is not important. Those physical sensations are not real. They will pass away. Don't react. Just observe. Just *observe.*'

Well, they felt pretty damn real to me, but I understood what he meant. Every physical sensation, pain or pleasure, must first be projected by the mind. Conquer the mind and you conquer the sensation.

That first day, and for the next nine after it, we meditated for eleven hours. Just as a marathon runner faces new and heightened challenges with every passing mile, it became progressively more difficult. When I went to bed at the end of the first day I wondered if I was going to faint before I got there. In bed, my knees twitched involuntarily as if in the aftermath of some electric shock. My sleep was filled with bitter dreams.

I began to place stricter demands on myself. For the next twenty minutes you will not move a muscle, I decided, no matter how great the pain, no matter how strong the desire to move.

My knees burned as if branded with hot irons. My whole torso filled with pins and needles; my eyes pulsed with a white heat. But just occasionally, as an oasis is glimpsed by a desert traveller, I thought I saw something pure and clean and full of peace.

Of course it was gone again a moment later. Buried so far beneath discomfort than I wondered if I had seen it at all – if it had been a mirage, the conjurations of a troubled mind.

But then it rose again on the horizon. Nothing tangible – barely a hint – but enough to keep me sitting. Enough to stop me from climbing to my feet and getting the hell out. Several people did leave, in fact, some with a look of nonchalance, as if they had seen the error of their ways and were leaving us fools behind to waste our time, others with a look of disappointment, as if they had failed themselves. And though I wanted to follow them, time and time again, a still voice kept whispering in my ear.

Don't react. Just observe. Just observe.

Sitting meditation is often compared to muddy water in a bucket. When we move the bucket around, the water moves too. But if we let the bucket sit, the water becomes still, the mud settles and the water becomes transparent. This is the goal.

Easier said than done, of course. Because the mind does not like to be still. In the modern world, bombarded as we are by a million unceasing stimuli, it is almost impossible. Merely to open one's eyes in the morning is to receive some signal, some consumer product it is absolutely necessary to buy, some pop song, car horn, fire engine, tyre screeching, plane passing overhead.

In that meditation hall in Madras I began to catch sight of a type of silence I had never known existed. A total mental silence. The cessation of all the buzzing annoyances that had become such a part of my daily life and which magnified in the aftermath of the hit and run so that I felt as if I were going mad.

As I battled with my own physical limits, and with the restless nature of my own psyche, I understood, for the first time, just what the Buddha was really smiling about in all those statues. He was smiling about nothing at all.

By the fifth day, which happened to be Christmas, I was achieving a measure of emptiness for several minutes at a time. As had been explained in the evening lectures, this was the equivalent of a deep surgical cut being inflicted on the psyche – a wound through which impurities could float to the surface.

Such a thing was, indeed, occurring; I could feel it. But as these so-called *sankhara* or deep-seated impurities began to bob to the surface, I felt an intense agitation. Sitting there, surrounded by forty or more meditators, I felt a wave of the most profound sorrow rising up my gullet. It threatened to engulf me.

Even now, looking back on that event with the benefit of hindsight, I shudder at the power of that feeling. My eyes filled with tears in a second. But while the tears dripped, pouring from my closed eyes down my chest and on to the wooden boards of the hall, the utter inadequacy of that as a means of expressing what I was feeling stopped their flow.

All I could do was to sit there and struggle to observe the breath as we had been shown. I didn't have the strength to run, but neither did I have the courage to stay. In the end it was pure exhaustion that kept me in my seat. For a moment I pictured my family, eating turkey around the dining-room table on a cold island so many miles away, and then that image, too, faded. I was utterly alone.

The days passed. I had not spoken a word to anyone else within the hall and yet it was impossible not to form opinions about those around me. A young traveller with a shaved head caught my attention: he was always the first into the hall after the breaks and could maintain full lotus position for hours on end. My own ego immediately cultivated a dislike for this keen fellow – he was an American, I supposed: full of himself, super-cilious or condescending.

When it was all over I would discover he was German, soft-spoken and intensely humble. But at the time, the ego is so inflamed with one's attempts to subdue it that thoughts like this arise whether we like it or not. It's all part of the same battle. The vacillations of the mind.

Everyone has a day, we are told, that is particularly difficult. For some it is the third, for some the fifth. For me it was the seventh. A trial which seemed to stretch out like Groundhog Day, an endlessly repeating spool.

The accident, its unfolding and aftermath, was bound to come up at some stage. It was, after all, one of the principal reasons why I was here. And yet when it arose in my mind, I had not dreamed it could be so vivid, the tastes and scents of that still morning so exact that it was as if I was there again, careening down that same steep hill without a care in the world.

Where is my breathing? Where does it begin? Where does it end?

Perfect memories like bubbles from a fish's mouth. Images in a crystal ball cupped between two hands. The homeless man who pulled me off the street. What happened to him? Where is he now? I remember the rough texture of his clothes and the musty street smell of his hands.

Or do I? How can I know what is real or what is my imagination?

Sitting there with my knees burning on the cushion, my mouth filled with the nauseating taste of metal, which is my strongest sensory recollection of that day. The taste of the street as I sped down it like a rag-doll caught under a truck's wheel. My teeth ached with it.

And then the teacher's voice. Like a hand reaching in to pull me back. He had come up behind me, noticing the tears running down my face. I felt a gentle touch on my shoulder, and then a voice in my ear, a whisper that only I could hear.

The nature of all sensations is that as they arise, so they pass away.

So I started breathing again. Returned my attention to the breath. The heart slowed. A calm came over me. The image faded, the mind still once again as I sat, waging my own internal war against the world, which is nothing but my own imagination.

On the evening of the final day, the vow of silence was lifted. Vipassana, sensibly, does not believe in releasing you back into the world directly from absolute silence. On the final evening you begin to talk again, getting to know your fellow meditators for the first time, sharing your experiences, preparing the psyche for the return to the world that tomorrow will bring.

Once the Noble Silence was lifted, everyone began chatting merrily. It reminded me of leaving exams back at school – the sudden buzz of chatter. How was it for you? What about this question? How much do you think you scored?

But for some reason, I didn't have it in me to speak just then. So I turned and walked gently to my room where I lay on the bed and looked up at the ceiling and tried to pull myself together. It had been the most difficult trial of my life. To return to the analogy of the bucket, I had stirred up something very deep over the last ten days. I had taken a stick and plunged it right to the bottom and then swirled it round so vigorously that I'd been lucky not to tip the whole thing over.

And now it was up to me to let it settle. It was up to me to keep that bucket still not just for today or next week but continually, so that I could keep on with my life and build on the foundations I had laid here. That would take time and much effort. But it was the only choice I had.

AFTERWORD

'The world is tolerable because of the empty places in it – millions of people all crowded together, fighting and struggling, but behind them, somewhere, enormous empty places. I tell you what I think,' he said, 'when the world's filled up, we'll have to get hold of a star. Any star. Venus or Mars. Get hold of it and leave it empty. Man needs an empty space somewhere for his spirit to rest in.'

Doris Lessing, *Going Home*

SINCE THE BEGINNING of the journey, two seemingly separate threads have run through my notebooks. Both influenced the writing of *Honey and Dust*.

On the one hand, a personal battle with depression – what Virginia Woolf called 'a painful wave swelling about the heart'. Its symptoms pulled down the scaffolding upon which my life was built. Left at base level, I had to redefine my place in the order of things. To do that I looked to nature, and to the sweetness at its heart.

As I travelled, a second thread spooled out. A sense that our physical environment is falling apart at the seams. Intensified by my research into hunter-gatherer lifestyles, and the holistic world-views espoused by the honey-hunters of the past, I felt, and continue to feel, a sense of disappointment at the world my generation has inherited – a house with cracked windowpanes.

Untouched landscapes are few and far between in this day and age, and the bees humming too quietly for us to conclude any positive outlook for wild nature.

The psychologist Kirby Farrell, in his book *Post-traumatic Culture*, writes that

> terror afflicts the body, but it also demands to be reinter-preted and, if possible, integrated into character. In an effort to master danger the victim may symbolically transform it, compulsively re-experience it, or deny it.

I hope that this book reflects a choice of symbolic transforma-tion rather than the other options. If I have tried to 'master' the danger, it has been by channelling my ennui into travel, by taking long walks in the mountains, and by focusing my attention on the notion of sweetness, and the men and women who spend their lives in its pursuit.

If I have raised the inevitable question of 'where did we go wrong?', it has not been with the intent of sermonising, so much as in the spirit of personal enquiry. In questioning the sources of my own decline, I could not help but apportion some of the blame to a world in which the boundaries between man and nature have become so fixed. I do not propose a return to pre-industrial life, so much as a re-establishing of links that were severed too quickly in the twentieth century, and without proper forethought about the quality of life here once they were gone.

With that 're-establishing' may come a recalibration of priori-ties. This is already happening with such organisations as the Slow

Food Movement, a group of foodies championing recipes that demand patience, attention to detail, discernment – and long, slow, convivial eating – and through that land stewardship, local history and family values. It is happening in the resurgence of farmers' markets and organic agriculture; it is happening in the anti-globalisation movement, a grassroots revolution if ever there was one, which stands for anti-consumerism and a redefinition of the very concepts of 'growth' and 'development'.

As for honey, I will continue to seek out and taste its variants in every place I go. I'll continue to look for the stories within each jar, the histories, geography, legends and healing medicines connected to that golden substance. If I'm in the right locale, and circumstance and inclination allow, I'll look for butterfly honey, and let my mind float up to the limits of its own atmosphere as I did on that Himalayan pasture.

Perhaps one day I'll revisit the friends I made: the mayor of Ham with his terracotta bee-jars; Habib pollinating his own high-altitude marijuana and making some fine honey in the process; in Syria, Naguib with the clay cylinders, a true gentleman if ever I've met one; Nakkal the Nepalese honey-hunter; Aruna and the people of the forest.

Perhaps, some day not too far from now, I'll find a place with enough space to put a few hives of my own. I'll make a garden filled with flowers specifically planted for bees. Purple asters, bergamot, borage, goldenrod, lavender. I'll jar my own honey and give it to friends and I think I will find a satisfaction there, something akin to what Gunter feels as he peers into his old hives on that patch of Tuscan hillside, studded with those great trees he planted with his own hands.

BIBLIOGRAPHY

Abram, David, *The Spell of the Sensuous, Perception and Language in a More-Than-Human World*, Vintage, 1997.

Adam, Brother, *In Search of the Best Strains of Bees*. Northern Bee Books, 1983.

Bate, Jonathan, *The Song of the Earth*. Picador, 2000.

Bellow, Saul, *The Dean's December*. Penguin, 1998.

Crane, Eva, *A Book of Honey*. Oxford Paperbacks, 1980.

————— *Honey: A Comprehensive Survey*. Heinemann, 1975.

————— *The Archaeology of Beekeeping*. Duckworth, 1983.

————— *The World History of Beekeeping and Honey Hunting*. Duckworth, 1999.

Cronin, Vincent, *The Golden Honeycomb*. E. P. Dutton and Co, New York, 1954.

Dalrymple, William, *From the Holy Mountain*. Harper Collins, 1997.

Edwardes, Tickner, *The Lore of the Honey Bee*. Methuen and Co, 1908.

Farrell, Kirby, *Post Traumatic Culture: Injury and Interpretation in the Nineties*. Johns Hopkins University Press, Baltimore and London, 1998.

Fedden, Robin, *Syria and Lebanon*. John Murray, 1946.

Gibran, Kahlil, *A Tear and a Smile*. Knopf, 1950.

Gould J., Gould C., *The Honey Bee*. Scientific American Library, New York, 1995.

Kimbrell Andrew (ed.), *Fatal Harvest: The Tragedy of Industrial Agriculture*. Island Press, 2002.

Knox, Robert, *An Historical Relation of the Island of Ceylon in the East Indies Together with an Account of the Detaining in Captivity the Author and Divers other Englishmen Now Living There, and of the Author's Miraculous Escape*. Navrang Booksellers and Publishers, 3rd facsimile reprint (ed.) edition, 1995.

Lane, John, *Timeless Simplicity: Creative Living in a Consumer Society*. Green Books, 2001.

Lessing, Doris, *Going Home*. Harper Perennial, 1996.

Pollan, Michael, *The Botany of Desire: A Plant's Eye View of the World*. Bloomsbury, 2002.

Neruda, Pablo, *Memoirs*. Translated by Hardie St Martin, Penguin, 1968.

Neruda, Pablo, *Residence on Earth*. Translated by Donald D. Walsh, New Directions, 1973.

Ransome, Hilda M., *The Sacred Bee: In Ancient Times and Folklore*. Bee Books New and Old, 1937.

Rilke, Rainer Maria, *Ahead of all Parting: Selected Poetry and Prose of Rainer Maria Rilke* (95 Edition). Translated by Stephen Mitchell, Modern Library, 1995.

Solomon, Andrew, *The Noonday Demon: An Anatomy of Depression*. Chatto and Windus, 2001.

Singh, Khushwant, *Nature Watch*. Harper Collins India, 2003.

Teale, Edwin Way, *The Golden Throng: A Book about Bees*. Museum Press Ltd, 1943.

Thapa, Deepak, *Understanding the Maoist Movement of Nepal*. Martin Chautari, Centre for Social Research and Development, Kathmandu, 2003.

Thubron, Colin, *The Hills of Adonis: A Journey into Lebanon*. Penguin, 1968.

Tolstoy, Leo, *War and Peace*. Penguin Books, Reissue Edition, 1982.

Tonsley, Cecil, *Honey for Health*. Tandem Books, 1969.

Valli, Eric, Summers, Diane. *Honey Hunters of Nepal*. Harry N. Abrams, 1998.

Virgil, L. P. Wilkinson (editor), *The Georgics*. Penguin, 2004.

Wedmore, E. B., *A Manual of Beekeeping*. Edwin Arnold and Co, 1932.

White, E. B., *Here Is New York*. Little Bookroom, New York, 2004.

Whynott, Douglas, *Following the Bloom: Across America with Migratory Beekeepers*. Tarcher, 2004.

ACKNOWLEDGEMENTS

A great deal of kindness, sound advice and hard work helped this book upon its way: Thank you to The Authors Foundation for a life-saving grant, to Peter Straus and Rowan Routh at RCW, and to Rosemary Davidson and Mary Davis at Bloomsbury. To Roger White in Cyprus and Mary Taylor Simeti in Sicily. In Lebanon, special thanks to Carroll Ferghali and Kamal Mouzawak and Nabil and Ghassan Naaman. In New York, David Graves was a patient and considerate host. In Nepal, David of the AmPm café and Chitra Gurung kept me away from Maoists and much more. In Sri Lanka thanks to Tania, Pikka, Aruna, and Patrick Harrigan of Living Heritage.

On the home front, George Festing deserves a particular mention for friendship above and beyond the call of duty. Early readers Ladonna Hall and Alan Sharpington made invaluable comments. Thanks to Brendan, Sean and Miguel in San Francisco. To my sisters Minna and Lettice Moore Ede. To my father for the evocative illustrations. And to both parents for absolutely everything.